# THE AUTHOR

John Marshall is a British diplomat whose overseas postings have included Japan, Malaysia and Ethiopia, where he served as Deputy Head of Mission from 2007-2011, also working in Djibouti and Somaliland. From 2011-2015 he was British Ambassador to Senegal, and non-resident Ambassador to Guinea-Bissau and Cabo Verde. From 2016-21 he served as British Ambassador to the Grand Duchy of Luxembourg.

# A BRUTISH COLONY

## THE BRITISH PRESENCE IN PRE-INDEPENDENCE SENEGAL

JOHN MARSHALL

Copyright © 2021 John Marshall

The moral right of the author has been asserted.

Apart from any fair dealing for the purposes of research or private study, or criticism or review, as permitted under the Copyright, Designs and Patents Act 1988, this publication may only be reproduced,stored or transmitted, in any form or by any means, with the prior permission in writing of the publishers, or in the case of reprographic reproduction in accordance with the terms of licences issued by the Copyright Licensing Agency. Enquiries concerning reproduction outside those terms should be sent to the publishers.

Matador
9 Priory Business Park,
Wistow Road, Kibworth Beauchamp,
Leicestershire. LE8 0RX
Tel: 0116 279 2299
Email: books@troubador.co.uk
Web: www.troubador.co.uk/matador
Twitter: @matadorbooks

ISBN 978 1800464 100

British Library Cataloguing in Publication Data.
A catalogue record for this book is available from the British Library.

Printed and bound in Great Britain by 4edge Limited
Typeset in 12pt Minion Pro by Troubador Publishing Ltd, Leicester, UK

Matador is an imprint of Troubador Publishing Ltd

For Marie
Alex, Hannah and Madeleine
with all my love

# CONTENTS

| | | |
|---|---|---|
| Introduction | | ix |
| Chapter One | In the Beginning | 1 |
| Chapter Two | A First Foothold on Gorée | 16 |
| Chapter Three | A Senegalese in England | 29 |
| Chapter Four | Evicting the French | 39 |
| Chapter Five | Rule by Committee | 59 |
| Chapter Six | Governor O'Hara and the Province of Senegambia | 71 |
| Chapter Seven | The Province of Senegambia: Descent into Infamy | 92 |
| Chapter Eight | In Search of the Niger | 117 |
| Chapter Nine | Ending the Slave Trade | 135 |
| Chapter Ten | The Recovery of Saint-Louis | 149 |
| Chapter Eleven | Lowering the Flag | 162 |
| Chapter Twelve | The Smile on the Face of Africa | 176 |
| Chapter Thirteen | Diplomatic Representation | 204 |
| Chapter Fourteen | Operation Menace | 215 |
| Postscript | | 241 |
| References | | 245 |
| Index | | 249 |

# INTRODUCTION

I am not a historian and this is not a history. I am a diplomat, acutely conscious of the importance of history in the conduct of modern diplomacy, but aware too that a lot of history lies buried, accidentally or deliberately, under time.

I have not attempted to write an exhaustive chronological account of all the interactions between Britain and Senegal between the mid-1450s and the present day. Instead I have tried to be more selective, choosing those moments in our shared history that seem to me the most interesting or intriguing and which deserve to be better known. The book draws on countless, endlessly fascinating hours of research at the National Archives in Kew and other institutions in the UK, at the National Archives of Senegal in Dakar and from a surprisingly rich source of books and online material in English and French.

Discovering just how much British history there is in Senegal was one of the rewarding surprises of the four years I lived in Dakar. I'd been interested in Africa from quite a young age, my uncle having worked in East Africa for the United Nations. As a child, I associated different countries on the continent primarily with their former colonial powers. As I grew older, and spent time either living on the continent or following developments there, I understood better the complexities of Europe's involvement in Africa, and began to learn something of Africa's own history. I still associated Senegal's colonial past with France. However, as I prepared to take up my job as British Ambassador to Senegal I began to realise both how much Britain was involved in Senegal's history and how little this was generally known, especially in the UK.

I decided to write a book. Inevitably the more I researched the more I learnt about the historical encounters between Britain and Senegal. Visits to the island of Gorée, to Saint-Louis and Podor, fascinating places in themselves, were further enriched by the history I had read about and the associations I now felt. Some connections I only discovered on my return to the UK, having failed to pick up the clues when I was in Senegal. For example, on a couple of occasions, I had stopped off in the sleepy river port of Elinkine on the Casamance River, from where you can get a pirogue to the old French settlement of Karabane. I did not realise it at the time but Elinkine comes from the name given by English traders to the settlement they established there – Lincoln.

A daily reminder of the links between Britain and Senegal, and of the historical rivalry between France and England, was a painting that hung over the fireplace of the British Ambassador's Residence in Dakar. *The British Attack on Gorée, 29 November 1758*[1] by the marine painter Richard Paton shows the British fleet commanded by Admiral Keppel lying off Gorée shortly before the attack on the French garrison that led to Britain's first long-term occupation of the island. This view of Gorée was not so different – bar the absence of eighteenth-century warships – from the one I enjoyed every morning from my balcony. It was a view of which I never tired and one I will never forget.

One of the great joys of researching this book was reading letters and other documents from the seventeenth to nineteenth centuries, often the originals, written in the most beautiful and evocative language. I found it fascinating to read the accounts of early voyagers

---

1   In fact the painting is incorrectly titled as the attack took place on 29 December 1758.

and their reflections on local customs, behaviours and practices: on wrestling, baobabs, shea butter, gris-gris, marabouts or the brightly coloured head wraps worn by Senegalese women, which still attract the attention of the visitor today. For this reason, I have often let the authors of the time do the talking, quoting passages in full where I thought I could not hope to match the colour, rhythm or impact of their words.

While it gave me immense satisfaction to discover the extent of the ties between Senegal and Britain, our shared history is complex. The early English traders were mainly interested in gold, and the importance of Saint-Louis to Britain was primarily about gum. But English traders shipped thousands of slaves across the Atlantic from Gorée and Saint-Louis when these ports were under British occupation. A street in Liverpool, England's main slave trading port, still bears the name of Gorée as did huge dockside warehouses, since demolished. Notwithstanding Britain's role in the abolition of the slave trade, our part in the history of slavery remains a shameful one.

Nor is it possible to take any pride in British administration of these territories. Instructions from London to governors invariably showed good intentions as regards safeguarding the security, rights and property of the inhabitants of Gorée and Saint-Louis. Some governors genuinely tried their best, particularly during the final British occupation of 1800-1817, which coincided with Britain's abolition of the slave trade. But others – most famously Joseph Wall – gained deserved reputations for violence, brutality and corruption. Their abhorrent behaviour set a poor example for their troops, often former convicts, who were frequently drunk and often mutinous. The title of this book is not chosen lightly; British rule was often brutish and cruel.

The story of Britain's administration of Gorée and Saint-Louis is little known, especially in the UK, and yet the Province of Senegambia, administered by a Governor in Saint-Louis, was to become the first Crown colony in Africa, even before the British settlements in Sierra Leone, the Gold Coast (present-day Ghana) or what today is Nigeria.

In this book I explain why Senegal was for a moment in history Britain's main foothold in Africa and why it didn't last.

The Gambia, a British colony until 1965 is, for that reason, better known to British historians and holiday-makers than its larger neighbour. As this book is primarily about the British in Senegal, I do not discuss the British colonial presence in the Gambia in any detail. But I do explain how the cartographic oddity that is The Gambia might never have come to be had it not been for our rivalry with the French, and the push, in the second half of the nineteenth century, to bring the interior of Africa under European control. It is futile to speculate what the political map of Africa might have looked like had it been shaped not by Europeans but by centuries of inter-tribal wars, as Europe's has been. Yet I can't help wondering how different things might have been had the nineteenth century negotiations to exchange Gambia for French settlements in Côte d'Ivoire or Gabon been successful. It was only in researching this book that I discovered how advanced those negotiations had been.

More recently, the British were responsible, with General de Gaulle, for the bombardment of Dakar in September 1940. Casualty figures vary but it seems likely that in addition to French and British losses seventy-four Africans were killed, the vast majority civilians, and over two hundred injured. Such figures might seem a drop in the ocean of a global war in which sixty million died. But for the people of Dakar it must have been a terrifying three days.

Knowing the story of Operation Menace, an embarrassing failure for both Churchill and de Gaulle, helped bring to life the many defensive fortifications still visible around Dakar, on Gorée and on the nearby Îles de la Madeleine. One of my favourite things to do in Dakar was to walk along the coast from my house to Cap Manuel and to stand on the old gun placements and bunkers looking over the sheer cliffs onto the crashing waves below. Sometimes there would be an osprey there – perhaps a migratory visitor from the UK – and looking out to sea I would imagine what it might have been like, had the weather in September 1940 been better, to see offshore a fleet of thirty British warships and merchant ships, including the great battleships HMS *Barham* and HMS *Resolution*. An impressive sight no doubt, but with awe turning to consternation, confusion and terror as British shells overshot the French warships in Dakar port and fell on the populous African quarter beyond.

For better or worse our history, the history of Britain and Senegal, is a shared one which, through this book, I hope will become better known.

CHAPTER ONE

# IN THE BEGINNING

EARLY HISTORY TO THE SEVENTEENTH CENTURY

The British were relative latecomers to West Africa. For the coastal populations of Senegambia and Guinea (a term used for centuries to define the forested stretch of coast from near modern-day Guinea south to the Equator) the first Europeans they met were the Portuguese in the fifteenth century.

Before the Portuguese, it is said, the Carthaginian Hanno, and the Persian Sataspes, sailed down the West African coast, others too for all we know. But for nearly two thousand years, until the arrival of the Portuguese, there is almost no record of any other expeditionary travel down this coast.[2]

Portugal was the great naval power of the fifteenth century and Portuguese captains were regularly sailing down the African coast by the 1450s. Prior to this, sailors had been too scared to venture too far. All sorts of spine-tingling myths existed for what would happen if you sailed past Cape Bojador (in present day Western Sahara); sea monsters were said to inhabit the fiery waters of the ocean beyond the Cape and sailors feared they would turn black.

---

2   There are suggestions that a Chinese fleet reached Cape Verde and left an inscribed stone at Santo Antão (Janela) in 1421.

So while the Genoese Lancelotto Malocello had set foot in the Canary Islands as early as 1320, giving his name to the island of Lanzarote, it was not until 1434 that a Portuguese sailor by the name of Gil Eannes ventured, presumably with some trepidation, past Cape Bojador. His claim to fame is the simple fact that he passed the Cape, rather than to any great discovery he made when he did so (though the historians tell us he brought back a sprig of rosemary on his first voyage). In sailing past Cape Bojador and down to what we now know as Senegal he destroyed the myth of certain doom for all who should so dare and opened a door through which others, with increasing confidence, would follow.[3]

At a time when England and other potential rivals were distracted by wars, Portugal was in expansionist mode, looking for opportunities far beyond its shores. In 1415 the Portuguese seized Ceuta, then held by the Sultanate of Morocco, hoping to control the end point of the caravan routes that brought gold, slaves and other commodities from the interior. As a maritime nation, close to Africa, with skilful shipbuilders, and fishermen that were used to travelling down the Moroccan coast, it was natural that the Portuguese should be the first of the European nations to push further down the African coast.[4]

The visionary, driving force for Portuguese exploration of the West African coast and the Atlantic islands was Prince Henry the Navigator. He seized the uninhabited islands of Madeira and the Azores and financed expeditions down the coast, hoping to find the source lands for the gold that was traded across the Sahara. In 1442, in a triumph for Portuguese diplomacy,[5] Prince Henry persuaded Pope Eugenius IV to give the Portuguese exclusive trading rights over the West African coast, rights that were renewed and enhanced under Eugenius's successors Nicolas V and Calistus III. Two years later, the Portuguese explorer Dinis Dias was the first European to discover the Senegal River and the peninsular of Cap Vert on which Senegal's capital, Dakar, is situated.

---

3   Thomas, The Slave Trade, pp. 49-50.
4   Ibid, pp. 51-52.
5   Ibid, p. 66.

In 1455, Alvise Cadamosto, a Venetian in Prince Henry's employ, and the Genoese Antoniotto Usodimare sailed four miles up the Gambia River before turning back when confronted by hostile locals in canoes. The following year they returned, sailing sixty miles up the river. In 1458, Diogo Gomes penetrated even further up the Gambia reaching Cantor (probably the modern-day town of Kuntaur in the Central River Division of The Gambia) before turning back.[6]

It was gold that first lured Portuguese traders to the West African coast. Gold from West Africa had long been known to Europeans who traded in North Africa and early Portuguese sailors also brought back gold dust from their West African voyages, as well as salt, ostrich eggs and malagueta pepper. But it did not take long before their primary interest turned to the trade in slaves. As early as the 1440s slaves were sold at Lisbon slave markets or taken to the Portuguese Atlantic islands (initially to Madeira and the Azores and later to the islands of Cape Verde). Sugar cane had been planted on Madeira in 1452 and by 1500 the island was the largest exporter of sugar in the world, with a high requirement for slave labour. African slaves sold in Lisbon were used for many purposes, mainly where heavy labour was required. In Lisbon and other cities they worked as stevedores and builders. They were also employed in agriculture, draining marshes and working in the sugar plantations in the Algarve. In some households, having an African slave at hand was seen as a mark of distinction. Other slaves were used as musicians and entertainers.[7]

By 1460, the Portuguese had ventured further round the coast, reaching Sierra Leone in 1462 and later what became known as the Gold Coast (Ghana today). Here, at Elmina, in 1481 they built a fort, thought to have been the first solid building constructed by Europeans in West Africa. From Elmina they sought to protect their trade on the coast, particularly from "interlopers", ships of other nations that sought to trade on the coast of Guinea in defiance of the papal orders that gave exclusive trading rights on the coast to Portugal.

---

6   Ibid, Chapter 4.
7   Ibid, p. 64.

But the Portuguese had competition. There was significant demand for slaves in Spain too, with the Spanish buying directly from the market in Lisbon. In 1462 a Portuguese merchant was given permission by the King of Portugal to sell slaves from Lisbon in Seville. The Spanish supplemented this supply with slaves they captured themselves from the coast directly opposite the Canary Islands which they had held since 1402. But when war broke out between Portugal and Spain in the 1470s ships regularly left Seville, bound for Guinea, to meet a demand for slaves in Madrid that could no longer be met via Lisbon.

Spain's forays down the west coast of Africa only increased tension between the two countries. This eased in 1480, when Spain recognised the Portuguese monopoly in Africa in return for Portugal renouncing all claims to the Spanish throne and leaving to Spain the coast opposite the Canaries. This stretch of coast was to become the Spanish colony of Rio Oro, now known as the Western Sahara, a territory disputed by Morocco and the indigenous Saharawi people led by the Polisario Front.

As Portugal's horizons continued to expand, with Portuguese sailors rounding the tip of Africa and sailing onto India, Spain also began to look for power and wealth beyond the Iberian peninsular. Queen Isabella of Castille and her husband King Ferdinand of Aragon approved the plans of Columbus to sail west in order to find a new route to "the Indies". Columbus's arrival in the Caribbean in 1492 led to the Treaty of Tordesillas, signed between Portugal and Spain on 7 June 1494, which effectively divided the world beyond Europe between the two Iberian nations, and gave rise to the Spanish colonisation of the Americas. One of the first places the Spanish settled, attracted and enticed by the lure of gold, was the island of Hispaniola. The Spanish enslaved local Indians to work in the mines but with the Indian population rapidly decimated by disease, overwork and trauma, the colonisers soon faced a major labour shortage. From 1510 Spain started shipping slaves to Hispaniola to work in the mines. And with that, the transatlantic slave trade was born.[8]

---

8   Although the very first slaves to be shipped in numbers across the Atlantic were South American Indians to Europe and Africa.

While Spain continued mainly to rely on Portuguese captains to deliver slaves to their new American possessions Spanish ships were also increasingly involved. An estimated 40,000 slaves were sent to the Americas in the first quarter of the sixteenth century, though until 1550 more slaves were imported to Europe, to Portuguese possessions in the North Atlantic and to São Tomé and Principe than to the Americas. São Tomé had by this time succeeded Madeira as the world's largest sugar producer and was the main slave station for the early transatlantic slave trade. It was a profitable business. Slaves bought in Europe or Africa could be sold at twice the price in the Americas.[9]

To the further irritation of the Portuguese, other countries started to take a keen interest in the opportunities for trade along the coast of West Africa, notably the French. The French king, Francis I, had been riled by the Treaty of Tordesillas, which sought to divide the New World between Portugal and Spain, as he had imperial ambitions of his own. By the 1530s French captains, with the approval of their king, and notwithstanding the papal bulls that remained in force, were regularly plundering Portuguese shipping and had begun to establish themselves around the Senegal and Gambia Rivers. They even contemplated seizing the island of São Tomé from the Portuguese.

At this point, the English enter the scene. After defeat to the French in the Hundred Year's War, which ended in 1453, England had dissolved into anarchy and geopolitical insignificance during the War of the Roses (1455-1487). As such they presented no threat to the expansionist ambitions of the Portuguese and Spanish during the early and middle part of the fifteenth century. The situation in England began to stabilise with the arrival on the throne of Henry VII in 1485. Henry brought order at home, replenished the Exchequer and created an environment in which individual entrepreneurs and adventurers could prosper. His son, Henry VIII, significantly expanded the Tudor navy. England began again to look far beyond its shores. After Henry VIII's split with the Catholic Church in 1534 and the Church of

---

9   Thomas, Chapter 6.

England embracing the Protestant Reformation the papal bulls that gave Portugal a monopoly on the Guinea coast ceased to have any relevance in England.

The first Englishman known to have visited the coast of West Africa was William Hawkins, of Tavistock in Devon, who first sailed to the Guinea Coast in 1536. He was to make two further voyages in 1553 and 1554. William Hawkins was an adventurous trader, interested principally in acquiring dyewoods for printing calico and other cloths.[10] Several other English ships ventured down the coast in the 1550s, in search of gold. Captain Thomas Wyndham set off in three ships in 1553, venturing as far as present-day Nigeria. He lingered too long, and he and the majority of his crew died of disease. The rest of the crew struggled home in two ships with a profitable cargo of gold and pepper. Another expedition, under the command of Captain John Lok, returned in the same year with its own money-making cargo of 400lbs of gold, thirty-six butts of chillies (malagueta pepper) and 250 elephant tusks. With investors excited by the potential profit to be made from trade in Africa – and at this stage there is no evidence that this involved slaves – further voyages followed, including by Captain William Towerson in 1555, 1556 and 1557.

John Lok's observations are among the earliest by an Englishman on West Africa. He remarked on the difference between the Moors, of Arab-Berber origin, to the north of the Senegal River and the African tribes to the south. On one side of the river "the inhabitants are of high stature and black, and on the other side of brown or tawnie colour and low stature" and he noted that the river marked the boundary between "the dry, bare waste of northern desert, the home of wandering tribes of brown-skinned men, and the fixed dwelling places, the towns and cornfields of the negroes who dwell upon its southern bank".[11]

Along with his cargo of gold and ivory Captain Lok also took four or five Africans back with him to England. These men were not intended as slaves, though I suspect they did not travel voluntarily,

---
10   National Archives online exhibition Black Presence.
11   Quoted in Lucas, A Historical Geography of West Africa, 1899.

but were brought back to England for their curiosity value and they were later sent home.

It was not long before England also became involved in the slave trade. Although it has been shown that English merchants based out of Andalusia were involved generations earlier, the beginning of ships sailing from England to participate in the slave trade is usually dated to 1562 when John Hawkins, son of William Hawkins, set sail from Plymouth with three ships. He visited the Cacheu and Sierra Leone Rivers seizing 300 Africans, mostly from Portuguese ships, before sailing for the island of Hispaniola in the Caribbean.[12] Having made a good profit on his human cargo he repeated the journey with even greater financial success in 1564. A third trip, in 1568, ended in disaster however as his fleet was intercepted by the Spanish on the return journey. Hawkins lost three of his five ships and any hope of profit in the ensuing battle. Thereafter English ships were not to be involved in the slave trade in any significant way for another hundred years.[13] Nevertheless English ships continued to explore the West African coast, including the region of Senegambia. The first evidence of the English entering the Gambia River, which in time they were to control, dates back to 1587, when a Portuguese refugee piloted two English ships which returned with a cargo of hides and ivory.[14]

Sending ships to the coast of West Africa for the purpose of trade was an expensive and risky business. The risk and cost was shared by merchants and others of means clubbing together in partnerships (an early example of the share-based capitalism that drives our economy today). This model was used by English merchants and adventurers seeking new trading opportunities around the world, and paved the way for the British Empire's global expansion.

Queen Elizabeth I bought into one of the first partnerships planning to trade down the African coast in 1561, perhaps earlier. She provided four ships and undertook to refit them at a cost of about £500. Merchants supplied £5,000 of goods (generally at that time

---

12   Thomas, The Slave Trade, Chapter 9.
13   Olusoga, Black and British, pp. 51-52.
14   Gray, A History of The Gambia, p. 18.

linen and woollen goods, iron and copper work and glass beads). The profits anticipated were to be divided by three: one part for Elizabeth and two for the merchants. Out of the gross profit the merchants had to pay wages and other costs including the hire of the ships from Elizabeth. In the early days, before trade in slaves began in earnest, there often wasn't any profit, but merchants were prepared to continue to invest as they believed in the promise of "a golden trade".

Because of the cost and risks involved in international trade it was becoming common practice for English merchants to seek to protect themselves from competition – at least from their fellow nationals – by obtaining a monopoly by royal charter. By 1588 the first monopolistic charter in Africa had been issued to the "Senegal Adventurers", eight merchants from London and Exeter who had previously sent ships to the coastal area between the Senegal and Gambia Rivers. The charter gave these eight merchants the sole right to trade on the two rivers and the coast between them for ten years from 3 May 1588. For a while thereafter English traders were active around the Senegalese coastal villages of Rufisque, Portudal and Joal, encountering considerable hostility from the Portuguese, who had already settled there. Forty Englishmen were killed at Joal and Portudal in 1589.[15] However, it seems that the "Senegal Adventurers" were not sufficiently excited by the prospects of trade in West Africa to seek renewal of their charter and while a second charter was awarded in January 1598, and some evidence exists of continued English trading at Joal, there is little to indicate that the trading opportunities in Senegal – or the Gambia River – were pursued by the English with much vigour.

A further charter for the region was issued on 16 November 1618 incorporating the "Governor and Company of Adventurers of London trading to Gynney and Bynney".[16] About thirty merchants were involved in the original partnership, which did not prosper. Their first ship, the *Catherine*, left England in 1618 under the command of George Thompson. Thompson sailed the *Catherine* as far as Gassan

---

15   Gray, p. 19.
16   Guinea and Benin

(possibly also Kuntaur) on the Gambia River where he and some of his men transferred to a smaller boat. While they were gone the *Catherine* was attacked by the Portuguese and the remaining crew all killed. This disastrous foray into West African trade came at a loss of £1,856.19s.2d, not to mention the lives of many men.

The Adventurers sent another ship, the *St. John*, the following year. It appears most of the crew died of sickness and the adventure returned just £80 on the sale of hides against an original cost of £1,968.6s.0d. At this point, investors must have started to get worried. Nevertheless, encouraged by messages back from Thompson, who remained in the Gambia, they decided to send a further expedition in 1620 with two ships this time, the *Syon* and the same *St. John*. This expedition fared a little better, but not much, returning £1,386.12s.3d on a cargo of hides, wax and ivory from an investment of £1,920.16s.8d.[17] Thompson himself never returned, having been killed upriver by one of his own men, who could stand no more of his autocratic leadership.[18]

Richard Jobson sailed on the 1620 voyage. We know little about Jobson himself, but we know a lot about his voyage thanks to his own detailed account. *The Golden Trade: or a Discovery of the River Gamra, and the Golden Trade of the Aethiopians* was the only work on West Africa written by an Englishman in the seventeenth century (and possibly the earliest detailed account of a visit to any part of sub-Saharan Africa by an Englishman). Jobson tells us about the peoples who lived along the Gambia River, their trades, the system of government, the habits of local kings, of marabouts and griots, of religion and initiation ceremonies, of the seasons and of the "wilde beasts", fish and plants that could be found along the river. He vividly captures the locals' fear of the Bumbo (crocodile) that made these river dwellers afraid to go near the water. And he talks of the "monstrous" and dangerous sea-horse (here referring to the hippopotamus).[19]

---

17  Scott, p. 12.
18  Gray, p. 22.
19  Although intriguingly the meaning of the genus hippocampus to which sea-horses belong comes from the Ancient Greek hippos meaning horse and kampos meaning "sea-monster".

It is clear that for Jobson, at least, the objective of all his travels was gold, not slaves. Although by 1620 slaves had been traded from the coast of West Africa for nearly 200 years, with English participation – though still at a modest level – since the 1560s, it seems Jobson himself strongly disapproved of the trade. He notes that the populations living at the mouth of the Gambia were "very fearefull to speake with any shipping, except they have perfect knowledge of them, in regard they have beene many times , by severall nations, surprized, taken and carried away"[20] adding that "blacke people are bought away by their owne nation, and by them either carried, or solde unto the Spaniard, for him to carry into the West Indies, to remaine as slaves, either in their Mines, or in any other servile uses, they in those countries put them to."[21]

At one point Jobson is brought some women to buy, and claims to have answered that "we were a people who did not deale in any such commodities neither did wee buy or sell one another, or any that had our own shapes". The local trader "seemed to marvell much" at this reply "and told us it was the only marchandize they carried downe into the countrey where they fetch all their salt, and that they were solde there to white men who earnestly desired them, especially young women as hee had brought for us".[22]

Jobson's morals may have been unimpeachable but elsewhere on the West African coast English sailors were increasingly involved in the slave trade. As a result, Englishmen trading in commodities other than slaves started having a harder time, the trust that had sustained their commerce rapidly eroding as their compatriots became involved in the slave trade. On the whole, it seems Jobson's party got a generous reception and he records how survivors of the first Thompson expedition were "lovingly entertained, lodged and fed"[23] and safely shepherded under the protection of local kings from the river up to the peninsular of Cap-Vert from where they were able to return to England.

---

20  Jobson, p. 34.
21  Jobson, pp. 35-36.
22  Jobson, p. 112.
23  Jobson, p. 39.

Thanks to Jobson's account the educated elite in England would have been able to learn a little more about some of the peoples of coastal West Africa. He was particularly impressed by the pastoralist Fulani or "wandering Fulbie"[24] as he calls them. Fulani, or Peul, make up about a quarter of Senegal's population today. Jobson astutely noted that "in some places they have setled Townes, but for the most part they are still wandering… [to] where they find the ground and soyle most fitte for their Cattle. These mens labour and toyle is continuall, for in the day time, they watch and keepe [their cattle] together, from straying, and especially from comming to neare the River, where the Crocodile doth haunt, and in the night time, they bring them home about their howses, and parting them in severall Heards, they make fires around them, and likewise in the middle of them, about which they lie themselves, ready upon any occasion to defend them from their roring enemies, which are the Lyons, Ounces[25] and such devouring beasts, whereof the Country is full".[26]

The Fulani women, who clearly delighted him, brought Jobson and his crew "new milke, sowre milke, and curdes, and two sorts of butter, the one new and white, the other hard and of an excellent colour, which we called refined butter, and is without question, but for a little freshnes, as good as any we have at home". The gourds in which the women brought the butter "would shine with cleanliness", "and if at any time, by any mischance, there had beene a mote, or haire, which you had shewed unto her, she would hav seemed to blush, in defence of her cleanely meaning."[27] Later English authors, such as Francis Moore, also commented on the cleanliness of the Fulani.[28]

Jobson, it has to be said, is less impressed by the Mandinka, the largest ethnic group in The Gambia but representing only 3% of the population in today's Senegal. He had an especially low opinion of the

---

24 Jobson, p. 42
25 It is likely that Jobson is referring here to a leopard.
26 Jobson, pp. 42-43.
27 Jobson, pp. 45-46.
28 Moore, p. 24.

men who "do live a most idle kinde of life, imploying themselves… to no kinde of trade nor exercise, except it be onely some two moneths of the yeare, which is in tilling, and bringing home their country corne, and grain".[29] Mandinka kings, according to Jobson, had a particularly easy life. "The life of the Kings truly, is, that they doe eate, drinke and keepe company with their women, and in this manner consume their time, until Time consumes them."[30]

Jobson describes drinking ceremonies at which "the Kings and all will drinke, until they be starke drunke and fall fast asleep."[31] He thought the average African would sell the shirt off his back (Jobson's image) for a drink, though not the marabouts (Muslim holy men) who "will by no meanes take or touch the drop thereof". He tells the story of a marabout who fell from a boat, was sucked down into a whirlpool and rescued by one of Jobson's men. Revived by the scent of rosa-solis, an alcoholic cordial, the marabout asked whether he had been given any of the liquid to drink while passed out. On being reassured that he hadn't, he said that he would rather have died than have any of the liqueur pass his lips.[32]

Writing four hundred years ago, Jobson's comments on the importance attached to gris-gris (or "Gregories" as he calls them) could be as relevant today: "The Gregories bee things of great esteeme amongst them, for the most part they are made of leather of severall fashions, wounderous neatly, they are hollow and within them is placed, and sowed up close, certaine writings or spels which they receive from their Mary-buckes, whereof they conceive such a religious respect, that they do confidently beleeve no hurt can betide them, whilst these Gregories are about them."[33] Gris-gris are as popular in Senegal today. Often blessed by marabouts they are worn by believers to fend off evil spirits and ill-wishers and to bring good luck, good health and prosperity.

---

29  Jobson, pp. 47-48.
30  Jobson, p. 74.
31  Ibid
32  Jobson, p. 96.
33  Jobson, p. 63.

One tradition horrified Jobson. This was the practice of male circumcision or, as Jobson puts it, "the Cutting of Prickes".[34] In expressing his dismay and opposition to a local cutter he got more than he bargained for. "To our thinking" he relates "it was exceedingly feareful and full of terror, insomuch as I told the doer in a very angry manner he had utterly spoyled him; when he askt wherein, I replyed, in cutting him so deepe: His answere was, it is so much the better for him, and without any curiosity taking up his cloath shewed his owne members."[35] Jobson's interference on behalf of the circumcised boy – who was expected to join other initiates in a kind of purdah – brought a swift rebuke from village elders.

Jobson also appears troubled by the fate of the griots (or Juddies as he calls them), musicians feted while alive but deprived of burial and propped up in a hollow tree after their death. The griots' reputed association with the devil and the low esteem in which they were held persuaded the musicians amongst the crew members to leave their lutes and other instruments in their cases.

Jobson praises the local bananas ("as delicious good and great as any that are in the West Indies")[36] and, surprisingly perhaps for those familiar with the drink, the palm wine ("the tast whereof, doth truly resemble white wine when it comes first into England having the same sweetness of tast, and in colour, if they were together, not to be distinguished").[37] He was presented with six kola nuts (forty-four short of what would be required to buy a wife).[38] Elephants – then in abundance in the Senegambia – were killed by local populations for their flesh, described by Jobson as "good and savoury meate".[39]

Jobson ends his account with an appeal to the Adventurers not to give up (for the third time in a row ships would return with no gold and no profit), and in a final flourish, proclaims how their

---

34  Jobson, p. 139.
35  Jobson, p. 144.
36  Jobson, p. 166.
37  Jobson, p. 167.
38  Jobson, p. 171.
39  Jobson, p. 180.

approach "is allowable by our Lawes, fitting and agreeing with the peacefull time we live in, opposite to no neighbourly love or amity, neither confronting any forraine Prince, by entring, or intermedling within any forbidden terrorities, neither is it done in any warlike, or hostile manner, but by the auncient and free Commerse, that uniteth nations, the course of marchandizing, a commodious exchange answering to either side".[40] Jobson was no slave trader but those that were would probably have argued that these lofty principles applied to their own ghastly but legal trade in which African traders were fully complicit.

—

The English were bit players in the first one hundred and fifty, even two hundred years of European exploration of the West African coast. In the mid-fifteenth century as Portuguese horizons were expanding, and their seafarers were venturing ever further into the unknown, England was retreating from France and was soon to be embroiled in 30 years of civil war. By the time Henry VII restored peace and order to England in 1485 the Portuguese had already established a trading base on the African coast at Elmina, discovered the River Congo and were returning home with shipfuls of slaves, in addition to gold and pepper, for sale at the Lisbon and Seville markets.

The sixteenth century saw the first English ships sail down the West African coast lured at first, as the Portuguese had been, by gold. The promise of a handsome profit attracted investors to finance several voyages but the risks involved in those early years were so great and the rewards so uncertain that the interest was not sustained. Nor, despite John Hawkins' exploits, did the English take much interest at this stage in seizing a greater share of the slave trade. Here, the Portuguese and Spanish remained dominant. Even after Henry VIII established the Royal Navy English priorities remained closer to home – wars in

---

40   Jobson, p. 196

France and Scotland and protecting itself from Spanish invasion. And when England did lift its sights, having defeated the Spanish Armada in 1588, English adventurers, merchants and colonists seemed more captivated by the opportunities in the Americas, rather than the African coast.

## CHAPTER TWO

# A FIRST FOOTHOLD ON GORÉE

### EARLY SEVENTEENTH TO EARLY EIGHTEENTH CENTURY

The island of Gorée lies about two kilometres from the port of Dakar, less from the rocky coastline of Cap Manuel, the southernmost point of the Cap-Vert peninsular on which Dakar stands. It is a small island, around 900 metres in length and only about a third of that at its widest point. Before the arrival of the Europeans it was uninhabited. The Portuguese built a church on the island in the mid-fifteenth century and buried their dead there. In time it would become a major departure point for slaves to be transported across the Atlantic. The island, now a UN World Heritage Site, is a popular destination for tourists and VIP visitors to Senegal alike. Particularly visited is the eighteenth-century Maison des Esclaves, from which slaves would depart directly, through the "Door of No Return", to the ships that would transport them across the Atlantic. In 2013, while I was in Senegal, President Obama and Michelle Obama visited Gorée and were photographed as they stood in "The Door of No Return", looking contemplatively out to sea.

—

By the early seventeenth century the Dutch had replaced the Portuguese as the primary naval power in the Atlantic. By this time the Dutch had been at war with their former Spanish rulers for 30 years, and were keen to disrupt the Atlantic trade of both the Spanish and the Portuguese, who had been in a dynastic union since 1580, as well as to establish their own trading empire. The Dutch-Portuguese war was to last over sixty years (1602-1663) and spread across the globe from Brazil to India and the East Indies. But while the Dutch were in time to seize Portuguese forts in West Africa, they had already weakened the Portuguese influence along the coast by selling cheaper and better goods. They acquired Gorée peacefully from the Portuguese in 1617. By 1648, at the end of the Thirty Years War in central Europe and what ended up being their eighty year war with Spain the Dutch were the dominant world power. Nonetheless it was the French who had displaced the Portuguese in the Senegal and Gambia Rivers, French pirates having harassed Portuguese settlements along the coast for years. Their own colonies were to expand rapidly under Louis XIV, whose long personal reign began in 1661.

As the seventeenth century unfolded the English also began to have more of a presence on the West African coast. In 1632, Charles I granted a new patent for the exclusive right (among English traders) to trade along the coast of Africa between Cape Blanco and the Cape of Good Hope to five men: Sir Richard Younge, Sir Kenelm Digby, Humphrey Slaney, Nicholas Crispe and William Clobery.[41] These investors were principally interested in gold from the Gold Coast, hardwood from Sierra Leone and slaves from wherever they could get them, in order to meet the nascent demand for slave labour in the new English colonies of the Caribbean.

In 1651, towards the end of the English Civil War, a new patent was issued for Ghana and Sierra Leone leaving the rest of the coast open to all-comers. The Navigation Act of the same year banned the import into the Commonwealth of England of all products from

---

41  Thomas, p. 176.

Africa that were not conveyed on English ships manned by English crews. The aim of the Navigation Act was to build up the strength of the English merchant navy, so that both ships and crew would be available in time of war; to undermine the Dutch, England's main rivals at the time, who had been taking an increasing share of the trade between England and its North American and other colonies, and to secure that trade, including in slaves, for English traders; as well as to increase the dependence of their independent-minded colonies on mother England.[42] The Act served to encourage English traders to frequent the west coast of Africa, as they could no longer use Dutch middlemen, and contributed in time to the growth of the Royal Navy and to Britain becoming the global power.

The following year, 1652, the region of Senegambia was to receive its most illustrious "English" visitor to date. Prince Rupert, Prague-born son of the winter King and Queen of Bohemia,[43] nephew of Charles I and cousin of Charles II, was at the time commander of the Royalist fleet. Charles I had been executed in January 1649, England was a de facto Republic under Oliver Cromwell and Charles II was an exile in Europe. Prince Rupert's priority as commander of the Royalist fleet was to seize English ships in the Atlantic to boost Royalist finances. In February 1652, forced by storms and the loss of one of his ships to regroup his fleet he retreated to Cape Blanco in Mauritania. From there, acting on a tip off that there were English ships in the Gambia River, he continued down the coast, stopping on the way at Rufisque. On arrival in the Gambia River he seIzed the three English ships as prizes, before heading home, stopping off at Portudal on the Senegalese coast south of Dakar. There locals took two of his officers captive – including one Major Robert Holmes – with Rupert himself being wounded by an arrow in attempts, ultimately successful, to rescue them.[44] Undaunted by this incident, Prince Rupert's short visit to Gambia convinced him of the potential for trade and led him to play an influential role in the first company of

---

42  Elton, Imperial Commonwealth, p. 61.
43  So-called because their reign only lasted one winter.
44  Ollard, Chapter IV.

Adventurers to be established after the restoration of the monarchy in 1660.

Inspired by Prince Rupert's accounts of his visit to the Gambia a new group of merchants and investors, with close links to the restored Stuart monarchy, formed in 1660 to exploit the opportunities of trade on the coast of West Africa. They were granted a charter under the name of "The Company of the Royal Adventurers into Africa" on 18 December 1660 with the intent of furthering trade in redwood, ivory and hides and to discover the gold mines still reputed to exist up the Gambia River. The trade in slaves was not mentioned in the charter,[45] which granted exclusive rights to trade on the whole of the coast from Cape Blanco to the Cape of Good Hope for the generous duration of a thousand years. It also specified that Charles II would be given two thirds of all the gold mines seized.

Having obtained the charter an expedition was mounted to the Gambia River led by the same Major Robert Holmes who had been captured on the beach at Portudal. The aim was to establish a fort on Elephant Island which was situated over a hundred miles upriver. Holmes had under his command the ships *Kinsale, Henriettta, Amity, Sophia* and the *Griffin*. Undeterred by his previous visit his fleet anchored near Portudal on 2 March 1661, warning French traders there to stop trading as the Royal Adventurers had been granted a monopoly by the English king. On entering the Gambia River, Holmes landed soldiers at Dog Island, renaming it Charles Island in honour of his king, and on 19 March he took possession of St. Andrew's Island, then held by half a dozen Europeans on behalf of the Duke of Courland, and renamed it James Island.[46] The island was garrisoned and factors (commercial agents) appointed. This became England's first permanent settlement in what was much later to become the Crown colony of British Gambia. Although quickly ruling out Elephant Island as a base the Royal Adventurers continued to explore upriver and one of their employees, a Dutchman by the

---
45 Zook, p. 10.
46 The Duchy of Courland, part of Latvia, enjoyed a semi-independent status in the 16th-18th centuries.

name of Vermuyden, claims to have followed the river as far as the tributary of the Nerico (in the Senegalese region of Tambacounda).[47]

English activity in the Gambia River attracted the interest of the Dutch at Gorée. The Dutch, by virtue of an agreement signed in 1659 with the Holland-based agent of the Duke of Courland, believed they too had a claim on what the English now called James Island. Officers from the Dutch West India Company sent the *Black Eagle* from Gorée to recover James Island in December 1661. The English garrison resisted, and the Dutch withdrew. Dutch ships returned in January and June the following year but by the later date the Dutch had already recognised the Duke of Courland's claim and therefore did not seek to seize back James Island for themselves.

The December 1660 charter was renegotiated on 10 January 1663 with the company being renamed the "Company of the Royal Adventurers of England Trading into Africa". The new agreement provided a better basis on which to raise funds and granted explicitly to the Company a monopoly for the trade in slaves.[48] What promised to be a profitable business was almost immediately put at risk by the Company's unplanned seizure of the Dutch fort at Gorée. Concerned by reports of Dutch activity inimical to the Company's interests on the Gold Coast the Company had despatched Holmes to the coast of West Africa in November 1663. His instructions were to protect and promote the interests of the Company with the power "to kill, take, sink or destroy such as shall oppose you". He was also tasked to look out for, and ideally seize and send home, the Dutch ship the *Goulden Lyon,* whose activities had been of particular concern to the Company.

Holmes set sail in HMS *Jersey* bound for the Gambia where he was to enlist the support of the Company's ship *Katherin* in protecting the interests of the Company further along the coast. On route, and just off the Cap-Vert peninsular, Holmes came across a Dutch ship, the *Brill,* which was carrying a cargo of lime, iron and brandy for

---

47   Gray, Chapter VI.
48   Zook

Gorée. Holmes seized the *Brill* though his justification for doing so is unclear. He continued on to the Gambia River where, a few weeks later, he learnt that a ship that sounded like the *Goulden Lion* was at Gorée. He arrived at Gorée on 20 January and sent a messenger onshore to demand the island's surrender. Not receiving satisfaction, he bombarded the island on 21 January with the Dutch returning fire. The exchange lasted nearly six hours with Holmes' ship, the *Jersey*, suffering damage to its mast and rigging. Nevertheless, Holmes took two Dutch ships as prizes and two others were sunk in the bombardment. None of the four was the *Goulden Lyon*, which had not in fact been at Gorée.

The Dutch surrendered the following day and on 23 January 1664 Holmes took formal possession of the fort. He left on the island a garrison of eighteen men under the command of Captain Morgan Facey provisioned for eighteen months.[49] In this way England took possession of Gorée for the first time, the island having been controlled by the Dutch for fifty years. England's first seizure of Gorée may never have happened had it not been for the belligerent Holmes interpreting his instructions rather broadly. The Company had not expected him to attack the Dutch until he reached the Gold Coast. Holmes left Gorée on 10 February, heading first to Sierra Leone and then to the Gold Coast where he seized the Dutch forts at Anta, Cape Coast and Elmina.

Knowing the Dutch would want to retake Gorée quickly, and conscious of the need to strengthen the garrison there, the English sent reinforcements under the command of Sir George Abercrombie. However, these only arrived on the island on 2 October. They discovered little had been done in the meantime to prepare its defences and were certainly not prepared to resist a determined attack nine days later by a thirteen-strong Dutch fleet under the command of Admiral de Ruyter, who three years later was to command the Dutch fleet that inflicted a humiliating defeat on the English in the raid on the Medway in the Second Anglo-Dutch War. The Dutch re-

---

49   Ollard, p. 93.

took the island without a fight. The first English occupation of Gorée had lasted less than ten months.

"The Company of the Royal Adventurers of England Trading into Africa" never recovered financially. For a brief period, they effectively sub-contracted the rights to sole trade along the northern part of West Africa to an organisation called "The Gambia Adventurers". This was for a period of seven years beginning on 1 January 1669. If any records were kept of The Gambia Adventurers' operations none exist and little is known of their business. The Company of the Royal Adventurers of England Trading into Africa re-emerged, in a restructured form, as the Royal African Company. The Royal African Company was awarded a new charter on 27 September 1672 and was to become the longest-surviving and most well-known of the English companies that traded on the west coast of Africa.

Although Dutch naval primacy continued for most of the second half of the seventeenth century, three naval wars against the English and the Franco-Dutch war of 1672-78 sapped their strength. In 1677, the French, who had established their first trading post on the coast of Senegal in 1628 and constructed a fort at Saint-Louis in 1659, seized Gorée for the first time.

Under Louis XIV, the French were determined to expand their overseas possessions. In 1673, a year after the creation of the Royal African Company (RAC), the French formed their own version, the Compagnie du Senegal with the aim of enhancing France's share of the transatlantic slave trade. Having established themselves on the coast of Senegal the French sought both to monopolise control of trade on the coast and to extend their influence into the interior, something other European powers had made little effort to do, with the exception of the Portuguese much further south at Luanda.

By 1687, Louis Moreau de Chambonneau, Director-General of the French Compagnie du Senegal at Saint-Louis, was exploring the upper reaches of the Senegal River and had established a factory at Dramanet, near Galam. For the English this was a little too close to the fabled gold mines of Nettico and also to the slave markets of the interior, where Mandinka merchants bought the slaves who they then sold on to European traders on the Senegal and Gambia Rivers. The Royal African Company were alarmed by French penetration into the interior, rightly concerned that the French would seek to sign treaties with local kings – as they did in Boundou – to discourage slave caravans from heading to English settlements on the Gambia River.

In 1689, in an attempt to stop the French disrupting the trade in slaves down through the Gambia, the RAC sent its employee Cornelius Hodges in search of the gold mines and slave markets of the interior. Hodges' account of his trip – one of the first by an Englishman of travels deeper into the heart of Senegal – survives in a letter he sent back to the Royal African Company from James Island on the Gambia River, dated 16 September 1690.

Hodges had left James Island on 11 March 1689 and sailed to Barrakunda Falls, rapids on the river situated just inside modern-day Senegal which could not be passed by larger vessels. Here Hodges and his party transferred to small boats before eventually leaving the river and striking north. Things seem to have started well enough and with elephants still abundant in West Africa possibilities for trade in ivory were certainly there. "In my travelling through Cumberdoo to Bamboo[50] almost every day Hunters would come and desire me to buy yr Teeth, some Tellg me that they had 4, some 6, some 8, and more buried in the Woods, which had I had convenience of Carriage for them, I could have bought at very small price". In view of what happened subsequently he probably regretted not making the trade and returning sooner to the Gambia.

At first Hodges found the local populations "very Desirous of Traid". But as he headed north they became more threatening, particularly when they realised he wanted to travel to the gold mines. After travelling through what Hodges describes as "ye greatest Wood in all ye Wt[51] parts of Africa" he arrived at a large branch of the Senegal River and from there proceeded to the gold mines of Nettico.

---

50   It is not clear where Hodges meant by Cumberdoo – though he later refers to the Senegal River as the "River Cambardo" but Bamboo is presumably Bambouk.
51   Western.

His description makes Nettico out to be a desolate place, laid waste by famine. Disappointed to find that there was little gold to be had he sent some of his men off to Tarra "the only market for slaves in all those Western parts of Africa".

Historians have failed to pinpoint where present-day Tarra might be. Hodges described how his men helped the ruler of Tarra repel a force of 40,000 horsemen and camels, the ruler later sending a message for Hodges to join him. Hodges recounts numerous difficulties on the way, including an attack by 400 armed men who wanted "my Life for Dairing to attempt a passage through ye country, for it was never known that ever any white man ever did ye like and I should pay dearly for my Bouldness". He never made it to Tarra.

The authenticity of Hodges' account was challenged by some who came after him. But it seems likely he made the journey, even if he could be accused of some embellishment in the telling of it. Hodges is said to have married a woman of mixed Portuguese and African descent and to have had several children by her. According to local stories, when his wife gave birth to a black boy, he accused her of adultery, killed the baby and fed the body to dogs. There is likely also to be some embellishment in this account, possibly encouraged by French competitors anxious to discredit the English.[52]

Seized by France from the Dutch in 1677 to ensure the supply of slaves to their own possessions in the West Indies, Gorée remained in the hands of the French for over eighty years, except for a five-month period in 1693 when the island was grabbed for a second time by the English. France and England, the latter as part of a Grand Alliance against the expansionist Louis XIV, had been at war[53] since 1689 and the English governor of the Gambia, James Booker, had received the go-ahead from the Company to launch attacks on the French. He needed no further encouragement, but his resources were limited so it was not until the end of 1692 that he felt he had the necessary strength to do so.

---

52  Brooks, G.E p. 154 citing Cultru P, Histoire du Senegal du XVieme siècle à 1870, 1910.
53  The Nine Year's war, 1688-97.

Booker seized Saint-Louis, facing no resistance, on 1 January 1693 the first and shortest of three occasions on which the island was to fall into British hands. The French garrison of thirty-odd debauched and ill-disciplined troops at Gorée surprisingly put up a bit more of a fight before surrendering on 4 February. Booker installed a factor by the name of Throgmorton Humphreys at Saint-Louis, along with a surgeon, a carpenter, a sergeant and fifteen soldiers. But having insufficient troops to garrison Gorée he contented himself with destroying its defences before returning to James Island. In June a French force under Captain Bernard retook first Gorée and then Saint-Louis.[54]

In July 1695, the French in turn seized James Island, the British stronghold on the Gambia River. With their own base at Albreda[55], a short distance downstream on the northern bank of the river, the French had no need for James Island so they blew up the fort and left. The Royal African Company made no attempt to take back the island, hoping that peace terms might exclude the French from the Gambia altogether. To their disappointment the Treaty of Ryswick, which brought an end to the Nine Years War, simply provided for a return to the status quo before the outbreak of hostilities.

After the war the rivalry between the Compagnie du Senegal and the Royal Africa Company grew even more intense. The French sought to maintain their trade on the Gambia, primarily at Albreda and Geregia,[56] and the English their ability to trade and to establish a presence on the coast at Portudal and Joal. But even more troublesome to both Companies were the activities of English and Dutch "interlopers", who sought to trade on both the coast and the Gambia River in defiance of the monopolies that had been awarded to the two Companies. After 1698, many of the English interlopers became legal, when the Trade in Africa Act, passed by Parliament the previous year, came into force. The Act responded to pressure

---

54  Gray, p. 114.
55  Which they had held since 1681
56  Situated upstream from Albreda and James Island on a tributary of the Gambia River called Bintang Creek.

from other merchants for a share of the African trade, especially the transatlantic trade in slaves, and sought to protect and strengthen the infrastructure of English forts along the coast of Africa. The Royal African Company was entrusted with the upkeep of the forts, receiving income from a 10% duty payable by non-RAC members on all goods imported from Africa. The newly acquired legality of English privateers under English law was unsurprisingly of no concern to the French who would regularly seize British ships– the *William and Jane* in 1699 being a well-known example – and haul them off to Gorée to discourage others from the trade.

Local rulers resisted French attempts to monopolise commerce on the coast, wanting to be able to trade with all comers. At the turn of the century a local king, Latsukaabe, attacked French forces in response to the French seizing English ships trading on the coast.[57] Local rulers particularly welcomed the presence of private traders, because they bought slaves in large numbers and paid a good price, often double what the Compagnie du Senegal would pay.

Around this time local representatives of the two Companies received instructions from their respective headquarters to work together to reduce the risks, including from privateers, to their businesses; but the discussions that took place were inconclusive, unsurprising perhaps given years of hostility and mutual suspicion between the two companies.

By 1702, France and England were again at war, this time over the Spanish succession. In that year, the French made another attack on James Island, seized whatever was of value and forced the RAC employees present to draw three sets of bills on the Royal African Company for a total of £6,000, backed by their personal bonds, in order to buy it back.[58]

The RAC began to realise that the French base at Gorée presented a constant threat to their operations and secured agreement that two men of war (HMS *Deptford* and HMS *Lowestoft*) which were

---

57   Searing, p. 23.
58   Gray, p. 133.

escorting Company ships to the Gambia, should take the forts of Gorée and Saint-Louis. Two half-cocked and lacklustre attempts to do so in December 1703 and January 1704 ended in dismal failure. James Island was plundered again at the end of 1704 by a French privateer, contrary to the wishes of the Compagnie du Senegal who hoped to make the coast between Cape Blanco and Sierra Leone a neutral zone. Articles of neutrality were duly signed on 8 June 1705. But the agreement appears not to have held for long since in September 1708 James Island was again plundered by a French privateer. Shortly thereafter other French privateers, apparently in league with the Compagnie du Senegal, seized a British ship and its cargo of slaves. By the end of 1709 the RAC had abandoned James Island. But the Compagnie du Senegal was in no position to take advantage. That year it went bankrupt and sold its rights on the coast.

By the end of the seventeenth century the chartered companies of all the European powers were in disastrous financial shape and private merchants were taking an increasing amount of African trade. The trade in slaves was rapidly growing in importance for England given the urgent demand for labour in their Caribbean colonies and in the tobacco planations of the colony in Virginia. Whereas in 1665 trade in slaves accounted for about one quarter of the business of the "Royal Adventuers" (with half being gold and another quarter from ivory, wax, hides, woods and pepper) by the end of the century three-fifths of the RAC's income came from the trade in slaves.[59]

Nevertheless at the end of the seventeeth century England still had only a precarious toe-hold on the West African coast. The main concentration of Englishmen, numbering only a couple of hundred, were based in a handful of forts and trading posts on the Gold Coast, with a much smaller presence to the west on the River Sherbro in Sierra Leone and to the east at Whydah (in today's Benin). Fort James, the Royal African Company's main base in the Senegambia, was especially vulnerable to attack by the French from their base at Gorée.

---

59  Thomas, pp. 199-202.

Twice in the seventeenth century, in 1664 and 1693, England occupied Gorée (and on the second occasion Saint-Louis too), for a total of less than sixteen months. But by the end of the seventeenth century the English knew that the French presence at those two strategic points on the coast would represent a constant threat to their own growing interest in the region. Henceforth, with Dutch influence in Africa and the New World waning, European rivalry in West Africa pitted Britain – as it was to become in 1707 after the union of the Scottish and English Kingdoms – against the French.

CHAPTER THREE

# A SENEGALESE IN ENGLAND

THE EARLY EIGHTEENTH CENTURY

Despite declining global influence, the Portuguese had remained the largest slave traders throughout the sixteenth and seventeenth centuries, holding the *asiento* – the contract for selling slaves to the Spanish colonies – until 1701.

In 1702, the *asiento* was given to France by the French-born King of Spain Philip V. The contract gave the French a ten-year monopoly and imposed a requirement for 4,800 slaves a year to be exported to the Spanish Indies. Wars, illegal trade and deliberate English interference meant the French missed their target by a substantial margin (by their own estimates exporting 10-12,000 slaves over the period of the contract). In 1713, the *asiento* was awarded to Britain in the Treaty of Utrecht that brought an end to the war of Spanish Succession. The Treaty of Utrecht also ceded control of Gibraltar to Britain, further enhancing its maritime strength. The *asiento* granted Britain a thirty-year monopoly with the same requirement previously imposed on France of an annual 4,800 slaves to be exported to the Spanish Indies.

In total, Britain carried an estimated 100,000 slaves across the Atlantic in the period 1721-1730. Between 1723 and 1727 on average fifty-six slave ships a year left London while Bristol sent thirty-four and Liverpool eleven.[60] London was to be supplanted by Bristol as England's main slaving port in the 1730s. This was the decade in which for the first time Britain shipped more slaves across the Atlantic to its own and Spanish colonies than Portugal did to Brazil. It is estimated that British ships carried a total of about 170,000 slaves in the 1730s, including around 40,000 to its colonies in America, 42,000 to Jamaica and 30,000 to Barbados. Jamaica and Barbados, both British colonies, were used both as entrepots for slaves bound for Spanish colonies and also as the final destination for slaves working in the sugar plantations on these islands.

Bristol was in turn overtaken by Liverpool as Britain's main slaving port in the 1750s. The city had a better location for heading out into the Atlantic, avoiding pirates, and was less exposed to France in time of war. Liverpool prospered on the slave trade, as did nearby Manchester, whose production of cotton goods for export was rapidly expanding. Manchester's export trade was only £14,000 in 1739 but by 1779 was over £300,000. Historians estimate a third of this business went to Africa, principally goods that were exchanged for slaves.

Gorée was well-known to British slavers, but as a place to take on stores and water rather than as a source of slaves. The vast majority of slaves carried on British ships came from the Gold Coast, Dahomey and modern-day Angola and those that did come from Senegambia came mostly from the Gambia. Gorée gave its name to huge warehouses built in Liverpool in the 1790s. These were rebuilt after a fire in 1802 but were demolished for good in 1958 having suffered considerable damage during bombardment of the city in the Second World War. A street, Gorée Piazzas, ran alongside the warehouses. Now known simply as Gorée it runs behind Liverpool's famous Cunard building and forms a short stretch of the main road through the city's former docklands.

Although British ships dominated the transatlantic trade in the first half of the eighteenth century the French were not far behind.

---

60   Thomas, p. 244.

They shipped around 85,000 slaves from Africa in the decade 1721-1730 and over 100,000 in the 1730s. One consequence of the English winning the *asiento* in 1713 was the abolition of the monopolistic French companies in Guinea and Senegal. Thereafter trade to Africa was open to all French merchants provided they came from one of five ports: Rouen, La Rochelle, Bordeaux, St. Malo and Nantes.

—

Reading files on the Royal African Company in Gambia in the second half of the seventeenth and early eighteenth centuries it is difficult at times to conceive that its operations on the river and on the coast of Senegal contributed much to the Company's profits or business. For much of the time the fort on James Island seems to have been in a state of disrepair, staffed by ineffective, drunk or criminal employees, poorly supported and supplied from London and in perpetual tension with the French, privateers of various nationalities, pirates and the local populations. In short, the Company lived a precarious existence. The 1730s, however, saw a relative and rare period of stability for the Company's operations in the Gambia, with new factories opened at various points on the Gambia River beyond James Island.

One young factor, posted in the 1730s, spent nearly five years on the Gambia River and his account of his experiences *Travels into the Inland Parts of Africa* is, after Jobson's narrative of 1620, one of the earliest detailed accounts by an Englishman of his experiences in the Senegambia region.

Francis Moore's instructions from the Company stipulated the importance of regular correspondence, accurate accounting and the highest standards of personal behaviour. In particular they forbad Moore to do any trading on his personal account, embezzlement by employees of Company goods for the purposes of private trade having been a serious problem for many years.

Moore's instructions also reflected the fact that slaves at the time were in plentiful supply, specifying that he should not pay more than forty bars[61] a head. Moreover, they continued, "you are to be very careful and circumspect in your choice of slaves, that you on no account purchase any but as shall be merchantable, free from Sickness, Distempers, Ruptures and loss of Limbs."[62] If it were to be found that Moore had bought for the Company any slave deemed to be unsellable he would personally be charged fifty bars for each. Strict audit controls were also in place for recording the deaths of slaves in an attempt to prevent duplicitous factors from falsely recording a slave as dead and then selling the slave on their own account.

According to Moore most of the slaves sold to them by travelling merchants were prisoners taken in wars far in the interior.

"Their Way of bringing them is tying them by the Neck with Leather-Thongs, at about a Yard distance from each other, 30 or 40 in a String, having generally a Bundle of Corn, or an Elephants Tooth upon each of their Heads. In their Way from the Mountains they travel thro' very great Woods, where they cannot for some Days get Water, so they carry in Skin-Bags enough to support them for that Time. I cannot be certain of the Number of Merchants who follow this Trade, but there may perhaps be about an Hundred, who go up into the Inland Country with the Goods which they buy from the White Men, and with them purchasing, in various countries, Gold, Slaves and Elephants Teeth."[63]

Slaves were also bought along the Gambia River from local kings. These were also either prisoners of war or convicted criminals. Moore notes however that the punishment of slavery had been used by local rulers for a far larger number of crimes since the arrival of the slave trade. He recalls how a man who had accidentally killed another when shooting at "a Tyger" was sentenced to be sold into slavery along with his mother and six siblings.[64]

Moore's instructions strenuously encouraged him to secure other items to trade, including gold, ivory, hides and skins, buffalo horns,

---

61 Iron bars were used as an accounting unit for trade in West Africa.
62 Moore, Appendix II p. 9.
63 Moore, p. 29
64 Moore, p. 30.

indigo, pepper and different types of wood. Moore comments on the very high quality of the gold that was on offer and the fact that the merchants who supplied it were unwilling to say much about where it came from other than it was at least twenty days' travel away. As for ivory, the bigger the tusk the better: "One tooth which weights 100 pounds is worth more than three teeth which weight 140 pounds. Many of them are broken-pointed, these are considerably less in their Value; some are white, others are yellow, but the Difference of Colour makes no Difference of Price". Another sought-after commodity was beeswax, sold in cakes of 20-120 pounds in weight, which was used in England to make candles, as a sealant and as a cosmetic.[65]

Moore also tells us something of his daily life.[66] He would rise at dawn to ride in the cool of the morning. He would then breakfast on tea, sweetened with honey if sugar was not available, and local cakes made of rice flour or corn. For lunch, he might eat beef with couscous or boiled with pumpkins and a spinach like vegetable. Chickens were plentiful and cheap and fish easy to obtain. Hunters could procure wild boar, deer, duck, geese and other wild birds to order. The afternoon was the time to trade. After supper he would amuse himself "with writing, reading or visiting my neighbours till bed-time, where I commonly was treated with palm-wine." He added, "Guests I was used to have sometimes in plenty, some being Traders, and others Messengers from Great Men of the neighbouring Kingdoms, who would frequently send me Presents of Cows, Cloths and sometimes a Slave: but this was not very pleasing to me, because I was sensible to that they expected I should return them Presents to more than the Worth of what they sent me." And he had received strict instructions from Company HQ on present giving. He was generally to be very frugal in his expenses and on no account was he to make unnecessary presents. If he judged it necessary to make a gift the type of gift and the reason for giving it were to be clearly

---

65   Moore, p. 31.
66   Moore, p. 169.

noted in the accounts. Moore noted dutifully that all the presents he received "were for the Company's benefit and I accordingly accounted for them."[67]

Moore mentions that he lives alone but elsewhere in his text notes that the girls "are very obliging: for if you will give them a little Coral, or a Silk Handkerchief, you may take what Liberty you please with them". Even those "who pretend to be of the Portuguese religion", though generally more reserved, had no scruples about moving in with a white man "in the nature of a wife, without the ceremony of matrimony."[68] On the whole Moore seems to have got on quite well with the local populations ("the natives, really, are not so disagreeable... as we are apt to imagine.")[69] Like Jobson he had a high regard for the Peuls he met. "They have chiefs of their own, who rule with so much Moderation, that every Act of Government seems rather an Act of the People than of one Man. This form of Government goes on easily, because the people are of a good and quiet disposition, and so well instructed in what is just and right, that a Man who does ill, is the Abomination of all...".[70] Wolofs he describes as blacker and more handsome than the Mandinkas, and naturally strong, fierce and warlike.[71] The Joola he characterises as wild and warlike, unforgiving of any sleight but appreciative of any service rendered.[72] The Mandinkas are invariably portrayed as idle, mendacious, mercurial and drunk, in keeping with Jobson's assessment more than one hundred years earlier.

Moore was to meet, in Gambia, a freed Senegalese slave who captured the imagination of eighteenth century England. Ayuba Sulaiman Diallo (also known in England as Job Ben Solomon) was born in Boundou, a kingdom in eastern Senegal. The son of an imam, he was well-educated and spoke Arabic. In 1730, he was sent

---

67  Moore, p. 170
68  Moore, p. 85.
69  Ibid
70  Moore, p. 21.
71  Ibid
72  Moore, p. 25.

by his father to the Gambia River to sell slaves, trade cattle and to buy paper. On his return journey he was kidnapped by Mandinkas and himself sold into slavery (supposedly to the same man, a Captain Pike, to whom he had wanted to sell his own slaves). He was shipped to Maryland where he worked on a tobacco farm. He escaped, was imprisoned and there met an English lawyer, Thomas Bluett, who recognised that he was an educated man and, with the assistance of James Oglethorpe of the Royal African Company, arranged for him to be sent to England.

On arrival in England Diallo stayed first at Limehouse in London and then at Bluett's house in Cheshunt. Word spread and soon he was being introduced to the great and the good, many of whom clubbed together to buy his freedom (for £59 six shillings and eleven pence). Among those he met was Sir Hans Sloane, Royal Physician and Collector whose bequests to the nation were to form the foundation of the British Museum (Sloane also developed a therapeutic use for quinine and came up with the idea of adding milk to cocoa).

Sloane worked with Diallo on translations of Arabic inscriptions and introduced Diallo to the Royal Family (Queen Caroline, wife of George II, is said to have given him a watch). He also sat for a portrait by William Hoare described by the National Gallery as the earliest known British portrait of a freed slave. Diallo, who apparently needed convincing to sit decided he wanted to be painted in traditional clothing and when told by Hoare that he was unfamiliar with it replied, "If you can't draw a Dress you never saw, why do some of your Painters presume to draw God whom no one ever saw."[73] The picture, hitherto known only from a miniature, was thought lost until 2009, when it came up for auction from a private collection.

Diallo departed England for the Gambia in July 1733. Moore at that point had recently been appointed to be the Company's factor in Joar and received a letter from the Company representatives

---

73   Bluett, Thomas. *Some Memories of the Life of Job, the Son of the Solomon High Priest of Boonda in Africa; Who was a Slave about two Years in Maryland; and afterwards being brought to England, was set free, and sent to his native Land in the Year 1734.* London: Richard Ford, 1734. p.50

downstream at James Island introducing him to Job Ben Solomon "whom you are to use with the greatest Respect and all the Civility you possibly can."[74] Moore reports how travelling together upriver they came across the very same group who had sold Diallo into slavery and how he had to restrain Diallo from launching himself at them. He also records that Diallo's kidnappers had revealed how a gun, which had formed part of the payment they received for Diallo, had killed the Mandinka king because, tied around his neck on a piece of string, the gun had accidentally fired, "the Balls lodging in his throat". According to Moore Diallo took satisfaction from the fact that the king had died "by the very goods for which he sold him unto slavery". He forgave his captors however because had he not been sold into slavery he would never have known "that in the World there is such a Place as England, nor such noble, good and generous people as Queen Caroline." Moreover, according to Moore, Diallo "spoke always very handsomely of the English" to the Fulanis he met "and what he said took away a great deal of the Horror … … for the state of Slavery amongst the English for they [the Fulani] generally imagined that all who were sold as slaves were generally either eaten or murdered since none ever returned"[75]. Diallo's father died before his son's return but not before he had received letters from Diallo in England informing him of his freedom.

Moore was excited by the opportunities he thought Diallo's return home would bring for developing the gum trade. Diallo's home lay on the edge of the gum forests and Moore hoped the anglophile Diallo would encourage his compatriots to sell their gum to the English.[76] Alongside gold and slaves gum arabic had for centuries been one of the most sought-after commodities on the west coast of Africa. It was one of the reasons the Portuguese established a trading post at Arguin (in Mauritania) in 1442, and was to be at the heart of Anglo-French rivalry on the West African coast for much of the eighteenth century.

---

74  Moore, p. 145
75  Moore, pp. 146-148.
76  Moore, p. 149.

Gum arabic is a natural gum made from hardened sap from two species of acacia tree found throughout the Sahel.[77] The Egyptians used it in the third millennium BC to make sticky the bandages they used for mummifying. In the fifteenth and sixteenth centuries its main use was in the textile industry where it was used to fix colours. Over time, it was also used as a lickable adhesive on stamps, envelopes and cigarette papers, in sweets and throat lozenges and as a binder for watercolour painting. Today, also known as E414, it is still used in fizzy drinks as an emulsifier (to stop all the sugar falling to the bottom of the bottle and crystallising), in wine (to take the edge off the tannins) and for thickening yoghurts. A versatile substance it is also used in edible glitter and shoe polish. Locally it is still used in drinks – mixed with fruit juices – and given to women who have just given birth. Senegal was once the second largest producer of gum arabic in the world with most destined for France but trade in gum declined when the French colonial authorities decided to shift towards peanut production. Over the years a number of synthetic substitutes have been produced. Today Sudan dominates the much-reduced market.

It is not clear that Job ever did get involved in the gum trade – he seems to have resumed his involvement in the slave trade instead – but the RAC did continue to attempt to bring the gum trade into the Company's hands, at least for a while.[78] In 1734, the French Government made an official complaint claiming the French Compagnie du Senegal had exclusive rights to this trade, a claim judged to be groundless by the English.[79] The French said they had not complained before because they had believed those vessels trading illegally did not have the sanction of the Government. But they changed their minds when two English warships, HMS *Antelope*

---

77  *Senegalia Senegal* and *Vachellia Seyal*
78  By the mid-1740s the Company was financially on the ropes and in 1750 Parliament stepped in, passing an Act which set up the Company of Merchants Trading into Africa as a successor to the RAC. The Royal African Company however was not formally divested of its charter until 1752.
79  Letter from Earl Waldegrave, dated 5 December 1734, SP 78/205, f. 274.

and *Diamond*, turned up to protect English gum traders and, when the Compagnie du Senegal protested, threatened to sink their ships if they tried to stop them.[80] Anglo-French rivalry over the gum trade was to continue for nearly a hundred years.

---

80  SP 78/205, f. 284.

CHAPTER FOUR

# EVICTING THE FRENCH

1758-1763

Britain and France were at war for much of the eighteenth century. In fact, in the 127 years between the start of the Nine Years War in 1688 (which led, as we have seen, to the English seizing Gorée for the second time in 1693) and the defeat of Napoleon at Waterloo in 1815 Britain and France were at war for sixty of them. In 1758, war between Britain and France returned to Senegal.

The Seven Years War, which played out in Europe, the Americas, the Philippines and the coast of West Africa lasted from 1756-1763. But in reality it started a couple of years earlier, in 1754, in Ohio. Ohio at that time lay between Britain's colonies on the east coast of America and "New France", the French colony to the north and west, which stretched from Newfoundland to the Gulf of Mexico. In an attempt to keep control of the fur trade and to prevent British settlers moving westward the French set out to delineate their eastern border by building a series of forts from the Gulf of St. Lawrence southwards. Initial skirmishes between British and French troops escalated, prompting both governments to despatch sizeable forces across the Atlantic. The British Cabinet, in an emergency session on 22 January 1755, decided to intercept the French fleet and on 10 June Admiral

Boscawen captured two French ships off the coast of Newfoundland. France immediately broke off diplomatic relations with Britain. But it was not until 18 May 1756, once a surprising new set of alliances had formed on the continent of Europe, and which had been put in place to prevent conflict, that war was formally declared between Britain and France. The war saw Prussia and Hanover, traditional rivals, ally with Britain against Austria and France who had been fighting each other for centuries. The war was essentially a conflict between France and Britain played out on a global scale.

The French quickly launched an attack on Minorca, which had been in British hands since 1708 and, alongside Gibraltar, provided a strategic base in the western Mediterranean. Shortly after, Frederick of Prussia – recently allied with Britain – crossed the border of Saxony to pre-empt an invasion of Silesia by the new Austrian-French alliance. By 1757, the forces of Prussia, Austria, Sweden, France and Russia (but not Britain) were all at war on the continent of Europe. Britain meanwhile was suffering a series of defeats at the hands of the French in North America. This led to the ineffectual Duke of Newcastle being replaced as Prime Minister in November 1756.

The turning of the tide in the war in America coincided with the increasing influence exerted by William Pitt the Elder, who forged an unlikely political alliance with Newcastle in July 1757, when Newcastle was again nominally Prime Minister. It was Pitt who gave his agreement to an attack on French possessions on the west coast of Africa.[81] The plan was hatched by an American, Thomas Cumming, a merchant and a Quaker, who persuaded Pitt that the French had secured a monopoly over a profitable trade in gold, slaves, ivory and gum Arabic with a handful of ill-equipped forts.

Of most interest to the British was the opportunity to secure cheap supplies of gum for use in their textile industry. At the time gum from Senegal dominated European markets and French control of the gum trade from their base in Saint-Louis had pushed up the price in Britain. The price of gum was even higher for the British in

---

81  Pitt to Lords of the Admiralty, 10/1/58 CO 267/12.

times of war against the French as they then had to buy it from the Dutch who themselves had bought it from the French.

The strategic value of Saint-Louis to the British was primarily seen in terms of gum rather than slaves. After 1750, Senegambia only accounted for about 5% of the slave trade, with most slaves shipped from the Bight of Benin or further down the Gulf of Guinea in present day Angola. While gum was the main attraction, slaving was to provide a further profitable source of income to both the British and French in Saint-Louis for years to come.

Duke, the biographer of Major-General Richard Worge, the second British Governor of Saint-Louis, has suggested other motivations for Britain's attack on Saint-Louis in 1758.[82] He considered it to be partly a response to provocation by the French further along the coast, where they had captured British ships off the Gulf of Guinea and launched a failed attack on Cape Coast castle (in present day Ghana). Seizing the islands of Gorée and Saint-Louis, he argued, would also make it harder for the French to supply their sugar plantations with slave labour and therefore prevent them underselling the British in foreign markets. Clearly, in the midst of a war, any action that would lessen French influence – but not tie up significant forces that could be deployed elsewhere – was to be welcomed.

Cumming explained to Pitt that he had met some Moors in London in 1749, and had later visited them in their own country in 1754.[83] There he had met the King of Legiboli who had promised to support the English with 7,000 men if they were to come to defeat the French troops who were on the southern boundary of his territory at Saint-Louis. Cumming was later to be entrusted with a letter from King George III to Amir Sultan, King of the Legiboli.[84]

In the letter King George explained to his Moorish counterpart that as proof of his friendship and esteem he had "ordered a Number of Our Great Ships of War to repair to your dominions and to assist such forces as your Majesty shall employ, in reducing the Forts and

---

82  Duke, G. *The Life of Major-General Worge*... p.62.
83  Memorial of Thomas Cumming to Pitt 26 Jan 1756, CO267/12.
84  George III to Amir Sultan, King of Legiboli, 1 February 1757, CO 267/12.

Settlements that have been unjustly erected by our common and perfidious enemy, the French, on the River Senegal." By 10 January 1758, Pitt was writing to the Lords of the Admiralty with orders to "attack, if it shall be judged practicable, any French Fort or Forts, and settlements, on the River Senegal on the Coast of Africa or to annoy the Enemy in any other manner that shall be found most effectual."[85]

On 9 March 1758, a small squadron sailed from Plymouth, under the command of Captain Will Marsh, bound for the west coast of Africa. The squadron consisted of HMS *Nassau* with sixty-four guns, HMS *Harwich* with fifty guns and HMS *Rye* with twenty-four guns. Accompanying them were the *Swan*, a sloop, two "busses", the *Portsmouth* and *London*, and five small armed vessels hired by the Government.[86] On board the ships were 200 marines under the command of Major Mason and a detachment of artillery under Captain Walker.

The squadron stopped at Portendic in present day Mauritania where the English had set up a factory for the gum trade. There they hoped to pick up the extra troops promised by the King of Legiboli though it appears these failed to materialise. Undeterred the squadron continued its journey and arrived off Saint-Louis on 23 April.

Saint-Louis is situated about 25km from the mouth of the River Senegal, entry to which was blocked for larger ships by a treacherous sand bar. The English spent a few days trying to get some of their smaller boats across the bar, encountering considerable difficulty. They lost a couple, including the *Portsmouth* bus, as well as tents, guns, considerable ammunition and other stores in the process. It was only on 28 April that the French sent one brig and six armed sloops down to the mouth of the river to meet the English boats. Battle ensued with the result that the French were forced to retreat upriver.

Major Mason and his troops appear to have met little further resistance in their advance on Saint-Louis. As they approached

---

85   CO 267/12.
86   Beatson, p. 181.

the town, they were met by emissaries from the French fort with proposals for their surrender.[87] These were approved with only minor alteration and on 1 May 1758 an agreement was signed under which the French handed over to the English the forts, storehouses, boats, arms, provisions, and everything else belonging to the Company on the Senegal River, including the up-river factories at Podor and Galam. In return the English agreed to return all the Europeans then in Saint-Louis to France. They were allowed to take their personal effects but no trade goods or "uncoined treasure".[88]

At the time 232 French officers and men were based at Saint-Louis along with around two thousand free locals and their slaves. The agreement also provided that free Africans would be allowed to remain so, their property – including slaves – would be protected, and they would be free to continue their religion unmolested.

The French garrison at Gorée proved to be of sterner stuff than their compatriots in Saint-Louis and the British attempt to take possession of the island on 24 May failed, with the loss of twenty men. But this simply prompted Pitt to send a larger force. While Cumming had had to expend considerable effort to get agreement for the despatch of the initial expedition it is notable how quickly the British Government now decided to appoint a Governor for Saint-Louis and to despatch a strong naval and military force to take Gorée.

On 15 June, Pitt wrote to Mason[89] to inform him that the King had the previous day approved the Commission appointing him Governor of Saint-Louis. He further informed Mason that reinforcements of 400 men were being sent to maintain the forts already in his possession but also to secure Gorée in case the efforts of Captain Marsh to capture it were successful (news that they hadn't been successful hadn't yet reached London).

Mason's instructions, approved by the King, were fourfold:

---

87   Letter from Marsh to Cleveland, 7 May 1758, CO 267/12.
88   Article de Recapitulation, CO 267/12.
89   Letter from Pitt to Major Mason, 15 June 1758, CO 267/12.

- To preserve and defend Fort Lewis (as the English at times called it) and any other places taken from the French, and to "use the most watchful vigilance against any surprise or insurrection of the natives", while doing everything possible to "cultivate and improve their friendship" and to persuade them to live in harmony and trade with the new British administration.
- To discover the nature of the trade "and the sources of the riches" on the Senegal River.
- To assist British nationals coming to trade.
- To send regular reports on developments.

Governor Mason was not however given much chance to prove himself. On 9 September 1758 Major-General Richard Worge was appointed Governor "in the room of John Sutton Mason"[90] and early the following month Pitt wrote to Worge[91] with "Secret Instructions which the King has been pleased to sign for your guidance and direction".

The force sent to capture Gorée was considerably larger than that used to seize Saint-Louis. The squadron was led by the Honourable Augustus Keppel and consisted of five destroyers (HMS *Torbay, Nassau, Fougeaux, Dunkirk* and *Lichfield*), three frigates (HMS *Prince Edward, Experiment* and *Roman Emperor*), a sloop (*Saltash*), two bomb vessels (*Firedrake* and *Furnace*) and two tenders (*Cambridge* and *Lydia*). The squadron carried 700 men, the majority from the 76th Regiment of Foot, under the command of Lieutenant Colonel Newton who was soon to become the first Governor of Gorée.

Keppel's instructions[92] impressed upon him that he should not suffer a moment's delay in proceeding with the squadron to the coast of Africa. But bad weather was to bring delay. The squadron were forced back to Cork soon after setting sail and finally departed only on 11 November 1758. Meanwhile Mason was settling into Fort Lewis as

---

90  Worge's Commission from George III of 9 September 1758, CO 267/12.
91  Letter from Pitt to Worge of 3 October 1758, CO 267/12 (but Worge's secret instructions are missing from the file).
92  Instructions to Keppel dated 6 October 1765, CO 267/6.

best he could. Not surprisingly the climate was presenting challenges. Towards the end of the rainy season Mason was reporting back on the "fluxes and fevers" the garrison had endured and suggesting that it would be good if the King would allow the troops one pint of wine a day as part of their rations. He suggested the troops would pay for another themselves given that just one pint would not by itself be sufficient.[93] Ships were already arriving from Bristol, and other English ports, with supplies of sugar, cheese, butter, beer and cider but these were expensive.

Mason also took steps to take possession of Fort St. Joseph, one of the dependencies of Saint-Louis situated at Galam 800 km up the Senegal River, dispatching troops there in December 1778. It is only towards the end of a letter[94] reporting this and other developments that he mentions that he has learnt, via a letter dropped off by the *Saltash*, that Worge had been appointed to replace him. Although he does not dwell on the development in his letter, his disappointment at being replaced is evident and it is clear that he felt he had been diligent in carrying out his instructions. He notes in his letter that his original instructions had been his only instructions; he had received no other correspondence since his arrival at Saint-Louis. What's more his brief governorship appears to have left him out of pocket. In his final letter, reporting Worge's arrival, he records that the Government owes him £3000.[95]

The bad weather Keppel's fleet endured off Cork was nothing compared to the storms they were to encounter off the Barbary Coast in Morocco. Unaware they were so close to land the HMS *Lichfield*, a fifty-gun vessel, ran aground 400m from the shore. A harrowing account of the shipwreck written by a survivor in a letter dated 1 January, 1759 survives.[96] The ship ran aground shortly before dawn on 29 November.

---

93  Letter from Mason to Pitt of 18 October 1758, CO 267/12.
94  Ibid
95  Letter from Mason to Pitt of 22 January 1759, CO 267/12.
96  Abstract of a letter from an Officer of the Lichfield, dated Morocco 1 January 1759 included in The Naval Chronicle Volume XIV of 1805 and in Beatson pp 184-189

"The sea was going mountains high and was breaking over us at all quarters, and as our broadside was to the land, our masts soon went overboard, and carried several of our men along with them. ... In this situation we remained for some time, our masts and yards hanging alongside, the ship beating violently upon the rocks, and the waves braking over us with such force, that we expected every moment to be our last."

Things temporarily looked up as a large wave righted the ship, but with their smaller boats broken and their provisions on board ruined by water they realised they had no choice but to swim for shore. One man went first and when he reached the shore ninety-five others, including the author of the letter, followed. On shore they were surrounded by the local Moors and stripped of their clothing.

The next day, at low tide, more of the crew managed to swim ashore while others pulled themselves along a rope taken to shore from the boat by one of the swimmers. Many died in the attempt. Later that day the Captain, a non-swimmer, made it to shore, the crew facing up to the Moors to ensure that he too was not robbed of his clothing. The ship broke up and foundered that night with thirty to forty men still on board.

The following day they took stock and found the number saved amounted to "220 in all, having lost 130 men, among whom was our first lieutenant, the captain of marines, his lieutenant, the purser, gunner, carpenter and several midshipmen". The *Somerset*, a transport vessel and *Lydia*, a bomb-tender, were also wrecked but without much loss of life. The combined total of 338 shipwrecked men were brought before the Emperor of Morocco, who gave them accommodation ("so full of dirt and vermin that it cost us several days to make it tolerable"). However, within a few days an order came from the Emperor "for all our men to turn out and work like other slaves". Eventually an Ambassador, Captain (later Admiral) Milbanke was sent by London to secure their release which he achieved on the payment of "170,000 hard dollars". Captain Barton "was tried for the loss of the ship, and most honourably acquitted and immediately appointed to the command of a bigger ship along with the surviving officers and crew of the *Lichfield*".

Having stopped in Tenerife to regroup and for repairs the rest of the squadron reached Gorée on 27 December. If they had hoped the French garrison would capitulate at first sight of this considerable force, they were wrong. The French immediately began preparing their defences. The English attack commenced at nine o'clock on 29 December. The French scored an early hit on HMS *Prince Edward* but soon came under heavy and sustained fire from the powerful HMS *Torbay* and HMS *Fougeaux*. Under the bombardment of the English guns, and with rumours already circulating that the English troops had landed (in reality they were still aboard the transport vessels, awaiting the order to land) Governor St. Jean lowered the French flag. He proposed surrender terms – that the French troops should be allowed to march out with the honours of war – which were unacceptable to Commodore Keppel. The bombardment briefly resumed before the French finally surrendered.

Two reasons were ventured at the time for the ease of the English victory.[97] First, the French were unprepared. While they knew the English would return, they had thought this would not be until March and therefore had not yet strengthened their defences as they planned to do. And secondly because the French troops – ex-convicts for the most part – lacked the stomach for a fight. The casualty figures tend to support this. The English lost twenty men, including one officer, with seventy wounded. The French suffered just one fatality – an African soldier – and three wounded.

Commodore Keppel wrote to Secretary of State Pitt from Gorée on 3 January,[98] a letter carried home on the sloop *Saltash* and published in the London Gazette Extraordinary on January 29, 1759. The letter contained a brief account of the taking of Gorée and included a checklist of what was found on the island, rather more precise in regard to ordinance than men. Keppel listed:

---

97  Lindsay, p. 47.
98  Worge wrote his own letter on 1 January 1758, CO 267/12.

"French made prisoners of war, about 300.

Blacks in arms, a great number but how many I am not well enough informed as yet to say precisely.

The loss the enemy sustained, as to men, is so very differently stated to me by those that have been asked, that I must defer saying the number till another opportunity

Iron ordnance of different bores, ninety-three; one brass twelve-pounder; iron swivels, mounted on carriages, eleven; brass mortars, mounted on beds, two of thirteen inches; one of ten inches; and one of iron, of ten inches.

In the magazine: powder, 100 barrels, shells filled and empty, shot of different sizes, cannons cartridges filled.

Provisions of all species for 400 men, for four months."

With news reaching Worge that the garrison at Saint-Louis was short of provisions and in increasingly bad shape he and Keppel wasted no time in securing Gorée. The French soldiers were despatched to France on transport vessels on 5 January. Lt Colonel Newton was installed as Governor with a couple of hundred men and HMS *Experiment* and *Roman Emperor* were stationed at Gorée in support. Keppel also brought into His Majesty's service, and left at Gorée, a captured French brig which he named HMS *Gorée*. The squadron left Gorée on 12 January to a fifteen-gun salute. It arrived at Saint-Louis on 16 January, helped to ensure that Governor Worge was safely installed and departed for England on 23 January arriving in Portsmouth in early March.

The seizure of Saint-Louis and Gorée was warmly welcomed back home, the Annual Register of 1758 noting that "by these successes we have taken from the enemy one of the most valuable branches of their commerce."[99] It seems likely that the seizures led to the opening or at the very least renaming of the Senegal and Gorée Coffee House in St. Michael's Alley off Cornhill in the City of London. A bronze bust was

---

[99] Annual Register 1758, p.75.

put up in the Coffee House[100] in September 1762 with a blue plaque that read "George Dunk, Earl of Halifax, under whose conspicuous patronage the plan for conquering the French settlement of Senegal and Gorée, on the coast of Africa, was happily carried into execution in 1758". Presumably it was the same coffee-shop, but now named the Africa and Senegal Coffee House, which was included in an 1802 list of "respectable coffee-houses situated to the East of Temple Bar"[101] with the additional description that it was "frequented by merchants and captains trading to those parts". By the 1804 version it was said to be offering good wines and lodging. The Coffee House was still there, with the same name, until at least 1825.

We know quite a lot about Keppel's expedition because of an account made of the voyage by John Lindsay, who was Chaplain on HMS *Fougeaux*. He covers in some detail the squadron's journey south, the battle at Gorée and the situation on the island and at Saint-Louis. His account of his voyage constitutes the most detailed record made by an Englishman of their experiences in Senegambia since Francis Moore, twenty-four years earlier. It is full of local colour that must have delighted and intrigued its readership (even less familiar with Africa, especially Senegal, than the average British person today).

Like Jobson and Moore before him Lindsay devoted several pages to the people ("in the end, wonderfully civil"[102]), plants, fish and birdlife that he saw, including during some brief forays onto the mainland during his time in Gorée. Overall, he appears unimpressed by the flatness of the landscape and the poorness of the soil noting that he "could not meet with anything that afforded me great satisfaction". Nonetheless, he demonstrates a reasonable eye for detail, reeling out a list of the "common products" found on the mainland that would all be familiar to visitors to Dakar's markets today:

"...the millet, or maez, a sort of small grain pounded and made into either sanglet, or kuskus, a kind of bread much used by the

---
100 Annual Register 1762. p 103.
101 The Picture of London for 1802 by John Feltham.
102 Lindsay, p. 55.

negroes, the indian corn, the Banana, the Plantin, the kidney bean of various kinds, the pine apple, the cocoa nut, the guava tree, the lime and lemon trees, citrons, dates, tamarinds, yams, melons, honey, palm wines in varieties…"[103]

Lindsay's account is also notable for an early description of a baobab (though he does not call it that), Senegal's iconic tree. Lindsay describes a very stately tree "frequently found seven or eight feet in diameter at the root, which tapering for ten or twelve to a diameter of three, four or five feet, it then branches out into a great breadth as well as height". He noted that in winter (when he saw them) there was nothing remaining on the tree but the fruit "which the negroes as well as monkeys use" (in French the fruit of the baobab is called "pain de singe", monkey bread). He describes how the fruit "is usually about twelve inches in length… its skin is thick, hard like a shell, and covered with a coarse green down, like velvet; within the pulp is not unlike a fine white sugar cake, intermixed with a great number of seeds, somewhat resembling that of the tamarind, and in its taste has a very agreeable tartness."[104] [105]

Once in Saint-Louis, Lindsay has much to say about the local ladies ("for so I must call many of those in Senegal"[106]). Indeed, the good Reverend seems much taken with them: "they are in a surprisingly degree handsome, have very fine features, are wonderfully tractable, remarkably polite both in conversation and manners, and in the point of keeping themselves neat and clean… they far surpass the Europeans in every respect".

Having assured the reader that he possessed some expertise ("Negroes to me are no novelty") he gushes enthusiastically that "the appearance of the females on this occasion was to me a novelty most pleasing. They were not only pretty, but in the dress in which they

---

103 Lindsay, p. 57.
104 Lindsay, p. 56.
105 On the subject of fruit Duke, Worge's biographer, suggests it was Worge who introduced into England, from Senegal, the variety of strawberry known as a white-fruited Carolina (fragaria chiloensis). The plant, originally from Chile, had been introduced to France and from there to the French settlement in Senegal. p. 119.
106 Lindsay, p. 57.

appear'd, were even desirable."[107] The chapter ends however with a few words of warning: "There are few women who have not in their houses, ready hanging on a nail, the saw of the swordfish, with which in occasions of quarrel they tear and mangle each other in a manner most dreadful."[108]

Lindsay relates how the British were immediately faced with some delicate protocol challenges, when dealing with the local kings and their people. The King of Legiboli, who had come to pay his respects to the new governor, was offended to have two military officers arrive to escort him across the river whereas he had been accustomed, with the French, for the governor to come in person. Whether this unintended diplomatic snub was the reason for the King's failure to follow up on his promise to provide the garrison with livestock and other supplies, is unclear.[109]

Other misunderstandings proved more fatal. Lindsay records an incident that occurred under Governor Mason in July 1758, and which must have had a devastating impact on such a small and recently established garrison. Mason sent fifty marines down to the mouth of the river to secure the arrival of some new troops, some of whom had got into difficulty when their boat capsized crossing the bar. The marines pitched camp near a local village and were attacked at night losing over twenty men, including their commander Captain Rook in the ensuing action. It is possible that news of this disaster was a factor in the decision to replace Mason with Worge,[110] but we do not know for sure that news of the attack had made its way back to London by then.

Meanwhile Lt. Col Newton, newly installed as Lieutenant Governor on Gorée, was quickly recognising the need to be on good terms with the population of the island who might otherwise cut them off from the essential supply of wood and water from the mainland.[111] Many of the locals depended financially on the work of their slaves so Newton

---

107 Lindsay, p. 58
108 Lindsay, p. 80
109 Lindsay, pp. 71-72.
110 Lindsay, p. 92.
111 Letter from Newton to Pitt of 10 February 1759, CO267/12.

reluctantly employed them, commenting however that "four slaves will not do as much work as one of our labourers". He also reported receiving delegations from the Damel of Kayoor and another king "the purport of which was to get presents". Newton gave them goods to the value of £69 11s, mainly iron and brandy, reporting that his visitors had however been "greatly discontented" since they had been used to much more generous gifts from the French.

Back in London the authorities had received information that the French might try to seize back Saint-Louis and Gorée. In August 1759, Pitt wrote to Worge to inform him of this fact[112] and that he had sent 400 reinforcements (one hundred each from the 67th, 69th, 72nd and 75th Regiments of Foot). In October, Worge confirmed their arrival and that he had despatched half of the new troops to Gorée.[113] Meanwhile the garrison at Gorée was helpful to Britain's oldest ally. Newton reported back how he had bought the freedom of a Portuguese ship that had been seized by the local populations for the equivalent of £187 rather than the £884 the locals had been demanding.[114]

Although there were no French attempts to retake the settlements at Gorée and Saint-Louis – though many were planned – the west coast of Africa did not make for an easy posting. The climate was unhealthy, with dysentery commonplace and cholera a major killer of Europeans. If they had supplies of wine a garrison could avoid having to drink too much water, which was difficult to keep fresh. Worge reported that a French ship they had seized that was loaded with wine "was of great service to the garrison" but, the supply now exhausted, "the men have fallen very sickly".[115]

On New Year's Day 1760, Newton reported to Worge that seventy-four men had died since their arrival a year earlier.[116] Worge himself wrote back to London a few days later[117] that five

---

112 Pitt to Worge of 9 August 1759, CO 267/12.
113 Worge to Pitt of 19 October 1759, CO 267/12.
114 Newton to Pitt of 1 January 1760, CO 267/12.
115 Worge to Pitt of 19 October 1759, CO 267/12.
116 Newton to Worge of 1 January 1760, CO 267/12.
117 Worge to Lord Viscount Barrington of 3 January 1760, WO 1/319 folio 43.

of his lieutenants were already dead. Major Maule, who succeeded Lt. Colonel Newton as Lieutenant Governor of Gorée was already requesting, in a letter dated 25 November 1760, covering the garrison's accounts, to be sent home for health reasons.[118] He wasn't feigning. Less than a year later Governor Worge informed the Secretary of War that Maule had died at Gorée on 21 September 1761.[119] A couple of months later Worge wrote home to say how unhealthy Saint-Louis was as well.[120] And so it was to remain. Yellow fever regularly decimated the European populations on the coast whether British or French.

The garrisons also had their fair share of disasters. A fire on Gorée on 14 March 1761 consumed all but three houses in the town. Maule's successor, Lieutenant Governor Carey arrived in Gorée on 22 May 1762 with fifty men having dropped off just under 100 reinforcements with Worge in Saint-Louis.[121] His first letter[122] home focused on the disrepair he found, suggesting that neither his sick predecessor nor the interim Lieutenant Governor had done much to rebuild after the fire. Carey also comments that one of his priorities had been to appoint a chaplain as the locals had disapprovingly concluded that the English had no religion.

Later that year, Carey himself was reporting back on a further disaster. On 15 October 1762 a magazine containing 8,035 pounds of powder blew up, demolishing the eastern side of Fort Elizabeth. Quick action prevented another smaller magazine from exploding but the damage was considerable. In addition to the destruction inflicted on the fort the African part of the town was reduced to ashes. Fourteen members of the garrison were killed, and fifteen injured. The dead included the garrison's chaplain, the Reverend Doctor Berry, presumably the very man Carey had recently appointed.[123]

---

118  Maule to Lord Viscount Barrington of 25 November 1760, WO 1/319 folio 47.
119  Worge to Charles Townshend, Secretary at War, 29 September 1761 WO 1/319.
120  Worge to Townshend of 5 November 1761, WO 1/319 folio 131.
121  Worge to Townshend of 10 May 1762, WO 1/319.
122  Carey to Townshend of 8 June 1762, WO 1/319 folio 115.
123  Carey to the Earl of Egremont, 3 November 1762, CO 267/12.

But there were moments of celebration too. Worge reported how he had organised "public rejoycings" after being informed of the birth to the King and Queen of a son, later George IV, on 12 August, 1762.[124]

Throughout their occupation of Gorée the British garrisons kept good monthly accounts. An example,[125] signed off on 15 January 1761, itemises the month's expenditure (£98, 18s, 6d), and shows that a number of Africans including "12 black sailors" and "two black carpenters" were on the payroll. Accounts from the time also show the relative cost (and importance) of Senegal (including Gorée), the Gambia and British forts further to the east at Cape Coast. Annual expenditure on the Cape Coast forts at nearly £11,000 was almost double that of Senegal which in turn was three times more than the Gambia.[126]

Supplies sent out to the garrisons included butter, cheese, beef and pork as well as trading goods such as India cloth, beads, coral and amber; other supplies including "British brandy", flints and gunpowder could have been used both by the garrison and as trade goods. Worge recommended restricting the import of foreign baft noting how the locals – he estimated the market to be 14,000 pieces of sixteen yards each – had originally been happy to buy baft from Manchester but now wanted Indian imports dyed in Holland.[127]

Up in Saint-Louis Worge was having difficulty in establishing a presence higher up the Senegal River. In January 1760, he reported to London[128] that of a force of fifty men he had sent to take possession of the fort at Galam only six survived. Nonetheless he still had volunteers. Later that year he informed[129] London that an officer called O'Hara[130] was volunteering to chart the river and the mines

---

124 Worge to the Earl of Egremont, 12 November 1762, CO 267/12.
125 Accounts signed by Thomas Parker, agent for Governor William Newton, 15 January 1761, SP 78/260 folio 136.
126 £10,989.15s.1d for Cape Coast, £5287.1s.7d for Senegal and £1712.2s.8d for Gambia, CO 388/52.
127 Worge to the Earl of Egremont, 16 November 1762, CO 267/12.
128 Worge to Pitt of 14 January 1760, CO 267/12.
129 Worge to Pitt of 4 July 1760, CO 267/12.
130 I do not believe this to be the same O'Hara who later became Governor.

near Galam. This doesn't appear to have happened, however, because in January 1762, he informed Pitt[131] that he had sent three parties, each led by a captain, to Galam and that no one, officer or private, had ever returned. Despite his failure to establish a British presence at Galam Worge was upbeat about prospects for trade in Saint-Louis promising Pitt[132] in May 1761 that one thousand tons of gum and the same number of slaves would be exported that year. The garrison appears to have had a bit more luck establishing a presence at Podor, despite the hardships. A letter from Worge to London in 1761, refers to a Captain Hall who had spent twelve months at Podor "which is one of the most severe commands there can possibly be."[133]

Britain's third occupation of Gorée came to an end in 1763, just five years after they seized it. It was returned, controversially, under the terms of the Treaty of Paris signed in February 1763 following the end of the Seven Years War. Under Article 10 of the treaty it was agreed that "his Britannic Majesty should restore to France the Island of Gorée in the condition it was in when conquered; and his most Christian Majesty ceded in full right, and guaranteed to the King of Great Britain, the river Senegal, with the forts and factories of St. Louis, Podor and Galam, and with all the rights and dependencies of the said River Senegal".

Many commentators at the time could not understand why Britain, victorious in the war, had chosen to give up Gorée. Lord Chesterfield, a prominent member of the House of Lords, in a letter to his son a few months before the treaty was signed, opined that "Senegal is not worth one quarter of Gorée".[134] However, others disagreed. Governor Worge himself seems to have been unimpressed by the alleged strategic importance of Gorée, writing to Pitt in 1760 that the island could not possibly be of service to the English nation.[135] This is surprising. Saint-Louis may have been more significant in terms of its trade

---
131 Worge to Pitt of 11 January 1762, CO 267/12.
132 Worge to Pitt of 19 May 1761, CO 267/12.
133 Worge to (probably) Pitt of 19 May 1761, CO 267/1.
134 Letter from the Earl of Chesterfield to his son, dated 13 November 1762,
135 Worge to Pitt, July 4 1760, CO 267/12.

potential, but it had been recognised in 1758 that a British presence there would always be vulnerable to attack if the French were based at Gorée. The French presence also posed a threat to British interests on the Gambia.

Despite the hardship, illness and accidents the garrison at Gorée seems to have been in reasonable strength at the time the island was handed back to the French. An account[136] of the garrison on 12 September 1763 lists a total of 198 men (and they do all appear to have been men). In addition to the Governor there were one major, two captains, four lieutenants and "150 private men including sergeants and corporals". The rest were made up of two engineers, one "Inspector of Magazines and the Hospital", one storekeeper, one Captain of the Port, eleven volunteers and 24 "Artificers" (tradesmen). The document also included a short inventory of the boats at their disposal. These consisted of two large flat-bottomed boats each of which could carry two twenty-four pound cannon, three small vessels of about 40 tonnes and six large cutters, equipped with twelve oars. The document does not record the number of locals on the island. However according to a census carried out by the French when they regained the island the permanent population of Gorée was just 220: twenty-five mixed-race women, eighteen mixed-race men, sixteen African women, six African men and 131 slaves. By the 1776 census, the slave population had already increased to 1200.

While delighted to recover Gorée the French were far from happy with the state in which it was returned. The French Ambassador in London, the Count of Guerchy, complained to the British Government[137] of the poor condition of the forts, defences, stores and artillery, and the theft of items from the latter two. He blamed successive British governors and commanders at Gorée, accusing one, without naming names, of helping himself to whatever he took a liking to and noting that another had made no attempt to repair those wooden buildings damaged by the fire, instead using them as

---
136 An Account of the Garrison at Gorée 12 September 1763, p. 17, CO 388/52.
137 Letter from Compte de Guerchy to George Montague-Dunk, 2nd Earl of Halifax, Secretary of State for the Southern Department of 4 February 1764, SP 78/260, f. 99

firewood. He supposed this was because the British garrison's relations with neighbouring kings had been so poor that they dared not go to the mainland to cut wood. Recalling that under the Treaty of Paris, Britain was required to return the settlement to France in the state they had found it, or to pay for its repair, he suggested that the cost of repair be deducted from France's debt to Britain.

It may well have been the case that the French found the fort in poor condition, but the British appear to have had the best of intentions. The Earl of Egremont had written to Lieutenant Governor Carey[138] conveying the King's satisfaction that the front wall of the fort had been rebuilt and that the rear wall would be repaired by the time of the handover (originally fixed for 10 June,[139] though it slipped). Carey was told that should there not be time to finish the repairs he should make a note of what needed to be done (presumably to help deal with any subsequent claim for compensation from the French).

That the seizure of Gorée and Saint-Louis was carried out by regular troops and the occupation led by Governors appointed by the Government is noteworthy. Hitherto, from the Americas in the west to India in the east, most of England's (latterly Britain's) global expansion had been driven by trail-blazing individuals, or groups of individuals, rather than from the centre. Virginia, the first English colony, was founded by adventurers and the New England colonies by Puritans seeking a land untainted by "popery" and also by individuals and families attracted by the offer of more or less free land. Exploitation of the trading opportunities down the coast of Africa had been spear-headed by groups of investors in chartered companies, notably the Royal African Company. The most famous of these monopolistic companies, the East India Company, was still ruling its Indian settlements, now expanding under Robert Clive from its coastal trading outposts, and would continue to do so until the India Act of 1784 brought the East India Company's rule of India under the control of the British Government. The centre may have

---
138  Earl of Egremont to Carey of uncertain date, CO 267/12
139  Earl of Egremont to Worge of 18 April 1763, CO 267/12.

facilitated the early expansion of the English presence across the globe, through the granting of monopolies or tactical deployments of the Royal Navy, but by and large the Crown, Parliament and, once the exercise of power at the centre had evolved to this point, Government were happy to leave the risk to others.

This was to change as a result of the rivalry with France, whose ambition to expand the territory it governed overseas, at the expense of Britain, was unambiguous. So at the same time that France in North America was planning to limit the English to its coastal colonies by building a line of forts along the River Ohio, in India it was manouvering to install its own puppets on the local thrones, and on the coast of Africa France was seeking to gain greater control over the slave trade. The Seven Years War, a conflict between Britain and France played out on the global stage, was to end with Britain clearly holding the upper hand. On the back foot for much of the first four years of the war Britain's capture of Saint-Louis and Gorée in 1758 was to herald its "annus mirabilis" the following year, which turned the tide of the war. 1759 saw the seizure by Britain of Guadeloupe in the French West Indies, the holding of Madras, victory over the French at Minden in Germany, the capture of Quebec, the failed French invasion of England and a string of naval victories. At a time when the French were under-resourcing their colonies in order to achieve supremacy in Europe, Pitt deliberately sought an advantage by seizing French possessions overseas, including those at Gorée and Saint-Louis. Gorée may have been handed back under the Treaty of Paris, but Britain made signficiant gains. Under the Treaty the French ceded all their remaining possessions on the mainland of North America, and the Treaty essentially ended French ambition in India beyond their trading outposts at Pondicherry and other smaller enclaves.

# CHAPTER FIVE

# RULE BY COMMITTEE

1763-1765

Shortly after the signing of the Treaty of Paris in 1763[140] the forts at Saint-Louis, Podor and Galam were entrusted to the Committee of the Company of Merchants trading to Africa[141] with the consequence that Worge ceased to be Governor. He arrived back at Portsmouth on 24 September, 1763 and wrote from there to the Rt. Hon Welbore Ellis, Secretary at War, informing him of his return "with a soldier in confinement who had killed another at Senegal" and with Lieutenant Governor Carey "who has arrived in so low a state of health that he cannot write."[142] Worge's letter details how he had returned with fifteen officers, eight staff, fifty-two NCOs and 417 rank and file having left just 17 officers and NCOs and ninety-three rank and file at Saint-Louis, Podor and Gorée to complete the respective handovers to the Company and to the French.

---

140 Papers at the National Archives (CO 388/52) suggest that it was on 11 May 1763 that the Earl of Egremont "signified to the African Committee that it was His Majesty's pleasure that the Fort of St. Louis and its Dependencies should be delivered into their hands."
141 The Company of Merchants Trading into Africa, which was run by a 9 man Committee, was established by the African Company Act 1750 and in 1752 replaced the Royal African Company whose assets were transferred to the new company.
142 Letter from Worge to Welbore Ellis, Townshend's successor as Secretary at War, dated 24 September 1763, WO 1/319 folio 139.

The man appointed by the Committee of the Company of Merchants trading to Africa to be Governor of Saint-Louis was John Barnes. A record of the status of the garrison on 4 November 1763,[143] shortly after he assumed charge, lists just fifty-two men. In addition to the Governor and his Deputy (who was also the accountant) there was the Captain of the Fort (also double-hatting as the storekeeper), one sergeant, two corporals, one drummer and thirty-six private soldiers. There were also two surgeons, four writers, a carpenter, a smith and a cooper.

Unlike the Royal African Company which, once its monopoly ended, used the tax paid by independent traders to maintain its forts the Crown gave the new Company an annual grant for this purpose. On 27 July 1763 the Committee had received £7500 from the Lords of the Treasury for the administration of Saint-Louis and its dependencies (a further £7000 was received on 29 October 1764[144]). £2620 of this was intended for salaries with Barnes getting £200 a year and the private soldiers £25 each. The Committee spent £680 on goods for payment of customs and presents and £1200 was set aside for repairs, boats, insurance and other needs. Meticulous accounts were kept listing details of all the items purchased. On the list of stationery items bought, among the ledgers, reams of paper, blotting paper and red sealing wax were "four penknives of the best kind", "two best Dutch quills" and "three Almanacks for 1765".[145]

Barnes devoted a lot of his energy to trying to improve the state of the fort, including raising a bastion wall by four feet, covering the magazine and effecting various repairs to doors, windows and floors in the fort and to surrounding walls and enclosures. In a letter back to the Committee[146] he refers to having received supplies of lime, to having "a pretty good stock of firewood" as well as 30,000 bricks bought from a Mr Gibson. He was thoroughly unimpressed by the

---

143 C0 388/52.
144 CO 388/52.
145 Ibid.
146 Letter from Barnes to the Committee of the Company of Merchants Trading to Africa 9 July 1764, CO 388/52.

quality of the tradesmen sent out by the Committee. The carpenter was "worth very little" and the smith was "a good for nothing" and "an absolute stranger to his business". Fortunately, he could rely on the services of a good mason, but he was a Frenchman from Gorée rather than an employee of the Company.

A few weeks later[147] Barnes was begging the Committee "that there be no delay in sending our provisions, stores, crafts artificers" and reminding them of an earlier request to send him a surgeon since "I need not observe how precarious is the life of man here". Barnes' efforts do not however seem to have significantly improved the defensive potential of the fort. A Captain Vandeput, Commander of HMS *Gorée*, in a letter dated 13 September 1764 was of the opinion that the fort at Senegal was "of no use than to retire to if the natives are at any time troublesome."[148]

The British did not enjoy good relations with some local rulers, especially the king of neighbouring Waalo, Naatago Aram, who had come to power in 1757.[149] Naatago Aram sought to disrupt the inland trade routes that were important for the British at Saint-Louis and to divert trade from Senegal to Portendic in present day Mauritania. In the circumstances Barnes was "at a loss in what manner to act with regard to an annual custom paid by Worge to the chiefs of the Trarza and Elgibily Moors".[150] He told the Committee he assumed that Worge had decided to pay an annual custom in order to pacify them. "But we are very sorry to find that it has had a contrary effect; for these chiefs being so much stronger by the addition of the above goods to their Revenue are become daily more and more insolent and there has been hardly a season there these three or four years in which they have not killed some of our white men or Negroes employed in the trade". Barnes argued that trying to buy off the Moors was as good as throwing one's money away and that a better way to control them was to attack their trade. He similarly refused to pay a custom to Naatago

---

147 Letter from Barnes to the Committee of 27 August 1764 CO 388/52.
148 Letter from Vandeput to Stephens of 13 September 1764. CO 388/52.
149 Barry, *Kingdom of the Waalo*, p. 119.
150 Letter from Barnes to the Committee of 9 July 1764 CO388/52.

Adam leading the latter to block the trade of Saint-Louis on the river and to cut off supplies to the island.

Naatago Aram had earlier been in conflict with the kingdom of Kayoor to the south. He had taken advantage of the fact that civil war raged in Kayoor to extend his own influence, including to territory at the southern end of the Langue de Barbarie, the thin strip of land that separates the Senegal River, as it nears its mouth, from the Atlantic Ocean. As a result, he also claimed for himself the customary fees that the British paid to the Damel of Kayoor. His disagreement with the British coincided with a return to strength of Kayoor, under a new Damel, Makuudi Kumba Diiaring. With British support the new Damel pushed Naatago Aram back, recovering the villages of Gandiol, N'Diol, Mouite and N'Djelene, opposite the Langue de Barbarie.[151] In a letter back to the Committee Barnes described Kayoor as "the granary of this part of Africa" which also abounded with "good cattle, fowls, fruits and other refreshments and is capable of furnishing 100 to 150 fine slaves per annum."[152]

The British were also in conflict with the Brakna Moors, who controlled the interior north of the Senegal River. Governor Barnes reported disturbances at Podor in which the Brakna Moors damaged British vessels, seized canoes and slaves and destroyed the local fort.[153] Barnes's response was to decline to pay the Moors their customary dues and to spend the money he saved on strengthening the garrison instead.[154]

With the French reinstalled at Gorée, and French traders remaining on Saint-Louis, Barnes worried about how to ensure the loyalty of the local population. "It will never be in our power to attach the inhabitants of this place to our interests" he wrote to the Committee[155] "till such time as we can wean them in some measure from the French

---

151 Barry, *The Kingdom of Waalo*, p. 120.
152 Letter from Barnes to the Committee of the Company of Merchants Trading to Africa, 17 February 1765, CO 388/52.
153 Letter from Barnes to the Committee of 21 August 1765, CO 267/1.
154 Letter from Barnes to the Committee of 23 July 1765, T 70/37.
155 Letter from Barnes to the Committee of 9 July 1764, CO 388/52.

and from the superstition of their religion. We would therefore by all means recommend having a French Hugenot clergyman, or one well-acquainted with the French, and capable of teaching in that language, appointed for this establishment". Barnes thought it wouldn't cost very much because the Society for Propagating the Gospel in Foreign Parts would cover a good part of the costs.

He also recommended the appointment of a school master given that "there is an immense number of children on the island, whose parents would give any consideration to have them taught."[156] Here again he suggested the cost to the Company would be trifling because this time he thought the Society for Promoting Christian Knowledge would be happy to pay the salary of a teacher. Later correspondence[157] suggests that while the Society for Propagating the Gospel in Foreign Parts approved of the idea of sending a clergyman to Senegal they hadn't yet identified anyone to go.

Barnes lamented the absence of any judicial system in a town of over 3000 people arguing that without a judicial authority the settlement would earn the "extreme contempt" of both the white and African populations of Saint-Louis. He would not be the last either to complain about the drunkenness and disorder on the island blaming it on the fact that there was a brandy shop on every corner. There was no security on the island because the soldiers who were there to defend it were a "pack of drunkards". "The pay of our soldiers is generally drunk out at the brandy shop a month before they receive it". Meanwhile the sailors and the African population were "continually rioting and creating every kind of disorder in the place". "There hardly passes a day without theft, robbery, bloodshed or even murder". Barnes was clear, as were others that followed, that the drunken licentiousness that prevailed did nothing for the reputation of the British. Rather "it was to the scandal of the British nation rendering Englishmen through their irregularities here contemptible even in

---

156  Ibid.
157  Letter from Sam Poirier, Secretary to the Committee, to Barnes, 25 February 1765, CO 388/52.

the eyes of the most intemperate Negroes."[158] In a separate letter back to the Committee he lamented that "our soldiers are a set of the most mutinous, drunken and abandoned fellows I ever met with".[159]

Controversy also surrounded the allocation of land. After the peace treaty of 1763, Governor Worge had given anyone on Gorée with property at Saint-Louis time to come to claim it. This period to claim was extended by Captain Berry, who was in charge of Saint-Louis after Worge's withdrawal, and by his successor Captain Bunbury. After its expiry Bunbury apparently gave one of the forfeited houses to his brother (who had never set foot in Saint-Louis) and another "to the children of Lieutenant Philip Dixon", whoever he might have been. Barnes sought instructions from the Committee on how he should deal with these allocations as well as on the property gifted by Governor Worge.[160]

A list of the ships sailing from Saint-Louis between 25 July and 9 August 1764,[161] with their loading, gives a good indication of the trade (though Barnes admits "I only guessed at the loading as there is no believing the masters"). Seven ships sailed from Saint-Louis during this period. Four were London-bound with a total of 157 tonnes of gum on board. The other three crossed the Atlantic, one bound for Virginia with a cargo of eighty slaves and the other two for the Leeward Islands with cargoes of sixty and 160 slaves. Barnes also observed that the trade that season had been "remarkably bad". It appears to have got worse, at least for gum. Lists for the period between October 1764 and July 1765[162] indicate that only six ships left Saint-Louis bound for English ports with a total of 177 tons of gum. Slave ships, carrying a total of 1074 slaves, departed for St. Kitts, New York, Barbados, Antigua and other destinations across the Atlantic.

Saint-Louis appears to have been hit by fever at the end of 1764, with several soldiers in the garrison dying. Early the next year, Barnes

---

158 Barnes to the Committee of 9 July 1764, CO 388/52.
159 Barnes to the Committee, p16 T 70/37.
160 Barnes to the Committee of 9 July 1764, CO 388/52.
161 P 88, CO 388/52.
162 CO 267/1.

wrote back to inform the Committee that he himself had been "on the Point of Death."[163] A response from the Committee expressed the hope that the fresh supply of soldiers they had sent out would make up for those who had died.[164] However, a letter[165] the previous month from George Grant, the assistant surgeon at the garrison, indicates that five of the six new soldiers were already dead.

A list of the garrison dated 16 March 1765[166] suggests that it had not greatly expanded, comprising just forty-five British men, including the Governor, and ninety-three Africans.[167] Another list dated later the same month[168] records the names of all eighty-eight people sent out by the African Committee to Fort Louis since 29 October 1763, most of whom were on a three-year contract. The list includes James Ledgett and James Hayes who both deserted in Tenerife on the way out to Senegal, George Widdle who was discharged for mutiny on 21 March 1764, Hugh Collins who died of yellow fever on 17 June 1764 and Richard Fink who was "found dead in a brandy shop" on 1 May 1764.

The garrison list of 16 March, also indicates that the fort at Podor and Fort St. Joseph at Galam were unoccupied and in ruins though under the control of the respective local chiefs. It has been asserted[169] that the British relinquished control on the upper part of the river because they were more concerned with the gum trade than trade in slaves and other products from the interior. It is undoubtedly true that gum was the driving rationale for occupying Saint-Louis but Britain's relinquishing of control over the forts at Podor and Galam probably owes as much to the fact that the garrison at Saint-Louis was not resourced to secure and retain them, especially given the hostile attitudes shown by the Brakna and Trarza Moors.

---

163 Letter from Barnes to the Committee of 16 January 1765, CO 388/52.
164 Letter from Sam Poirier, Secretary to the Committee, to Barnes of 25 February 1765 CO 322/58.
165 Letter from George Grant of 7 January 1765, CO 388/52 f. 297.
166 CO 388/52.
167 It also had 45 cannon and 290 barrels of powder.
168 List dated 30 March 1765, CO 388/52 f. 250.
169 Barry, *Senegal and the Atlantic Slave Trade* p. 74.

The Committee seems to have been determined to keep the costs of the settlement down, presumably reflecting the fact that it was not yielding great profit. Writing in February 1765[170] the Committee cautioned Barnes that "we cannot but take notice that your Demands for Provisions are very large and exceed those for the supply of the whole Gold Coast for twelve months". Barnes was quick to justify himself[171] giving two reasons why that should be the case. First because of the "very large number of negroes we have been obliged to employ which is not the case down the coast". And secondly the fact that the garrisons in the Gold Coast found it cheaper to buy their provisions from American ships that came to the British forts to buy slaves.

With the French back in control in Gorée British trading activity on the coast at Joal and Portudal seems to have declined. Towards the end of 1764 Lord Halifax[172] wrote to the Lord Commissioners of Trade and Plantations to convey the King's wish that the Committee provide "positive information of the state in which Joually and Portudally were during the late war, in what state they are now, and whether during such periods his Majesty's subjects have been or now are in possession of the trade thereof."[173] In evidence given to the Committee[174] Captain Baird, Commander of the *Charming Molly*, reported that he had traded at Portudal and Joal in the years 1760, 1762 and 1763 and that neither the French nor the British had maintained a permanent trading factory on the coast during this time (although the ruins remained of a French one). He further gave evidence that "the English had the sole possession of trade" during this time "which they carried on by Boats and Sloops from Gorée, to the amount of about 200 slaves annually". He added that when he returned to the coast after the restitution of Gorée to France the local African population had not allowed him to land, considering the

---

170 Sam Poirier to Barnes of 25 February 1765, CO 388/52.
171 Letter from Barnes to the Committee 31 May 1765, CO 388/52.
172 Halifax was Secretary of State for the Southern Department, the predecessor to the Foreign Office.
173 Letter from Lord Halifax to the Lord Commissioners of Trade and Plantations, 14 December 1764, CO 388/5.2
174 CO 388/52.

French, who were in the process of rebuilding the ruins of the French factory, to now have the sole right to trade.

The French were also making a nuisance of themselves on the Gambia River, paying exorbitant prices for slaves in order to attract trade to Albreda. African traders would hold slaves upriver beyond the reach of the British traders while they established whether they could get a better price from the French.[175]

Saint-Louis and its dependencies were to remain under the control of the Committee of the Company of Merchants for just under two years before the Government, in response to French aggression, and conscious of the relative strength of Gorée in comparison to the British settlements at Saint-Louis and James Island, decided to retake control. A report by the Commission for Trade and Plantations in February 1765[176] noted with evident concern that:

- The French built fort at Saint-Louis, now under British control, was in a very poor state of repair and lacking in ordinance and other military supplies.
- No steps were being taken to secure the mouth of the Senegal River, as the French used to do.
- The "important establishments" of Podor and Galam had been abandoned even though Podor was a key market for gum, as well as being necessary to keep Saint-Louis supplied with grain and fresh provisions, and Galam an important market for slaves and gold.
- No attempt had been made to take possession of key trading points on the Gum Coast.
- The French garrison at Gorée, with 200 troops, was much larger and would shortly be increased to 500. They had also recently acquired two large flat-bottomed boats and were capable of embarking troops to any part of the coast. Meanwhile the English force in Saint-Louis numbered

---
175 Joseph Debat to Secretary of African Committee, 20 July 1764, CO 267/13.
176 Report to the Crown on the British Establishments on the coast of Africa by the Commissioners for Trade and Plantations, 21 February 1765 CO 389/31.

> only 4 NCOs and 36 privates, with just three officers and eight privates in Gambia. Moreover the troops were "under no military discipline, ill-cloathed and subject to every hardship and disease".

In short the report highlighted the precarious state of the King's possessions at Saint-Louis and on the Gambia River. The authors of the report noted the Committee's view that if things were in a bad way it was because of the limited grant voted to them by Parliament. But the authors cite other factors including embezzlement of supplies by officers of the Company whose accounts "seem imperfect and unsatisfactory" and the inadequate powers of the Committee itself.

Although the report covered British settlements further along the coast in Sierra Leone, Ghana and beyond its authors were of the view that the situation in Senegal required especially urgent attention. This was down to Senegal's relative size (Saint-Louis had over 4000 inhabitants at the time), the fact that the settlement was not confined to the coast (as was also the case with the Gambia), and to the "chief article of its production", a reference presumably to the fact that gum was uniquely exported from here.

> "It does appear to be absolutely necessary" the Commission concluded "both for the preservation of this important part of your Majesty's Dominions, and for the advancement and improvement of its Commerce, that the Districts of the Senegal and Gambia should be taken out of the hands of the Company of Merchants Trading to Africa; that they should be placed under your Majesty's immediate direction; and that a Civil Constitution and a Plan of military establishment should be formed for the Government and Protection of them."

The Commission was of the opinion that the Province could be made to finance itself. They estimated that the annual cost of the province would not exceed £10,000, with start-up costs of £2,000. They noted that the annual average of gum exported between Christmas 1760 and Christmas 1763 had been 400 tonnes. They calculated, perhaps rather too tidily, that with a tax of thirty shillings per hundredweight an annual revenue of £12,000 could be achieved. Ironically, about the time the report was being finalised Barnes was writing back to the Committee to tell them the garrison owed £1500 to Moorish and African chiefs and did not have the means to pay its staff.[177]

The day after the report issued, on 22 February 1765, the Privy Council decided "to take the Districts of Senegal and Gambia out of the Hands of the African Committee and to erect them into a Province under the immediate Authority and Direction of His Majesty."[178] This was later approved by Parliament and followed on 1 November 1765 by a further Order in Council deciding that "all His Majesty's Territories upon the Coast of Africa, from Cape Blanco to Cape Rouge and all his Majesty's Islands, Forts, Territories and Establishments within those limits... should be erected into one Government under the immediate authority and direction of His Majesty, and that it should be called the Province of Senegambia".[179] So it was that Senegambia – not Kenya, Ghana, Sierra Leone or other anglophone African countries more closely associated with Britain – was to become the first Crown colony in Africa.

George III never visited his African possessions, but had he done so he might have been surprised, given the contrary impression conveyed by the Order in Council, just how tenuous a foothold Britain had on the coast between Cape Blanco (in present day Mauritania) and Cape Rouge (Guinea-Bissau). In 1765, having withdrawn from Podor and Galam, the British were only present at Saint-Louis and at Fort James and other "factories" on the Gambia River. Later in his reign, they were to recover Gorée, briefly settle on Bolama – in what is today Guinea-Bissau – in the 1790s, and to trade at Arguin on the Mauritanian coast. But the reality never quite lived up to the impression of dominance and authority conveyed by official documents.

---

177  Barnes to the Committee of 16 February 1766, CO 267/13.
178  A copy of the decision can be found on PC/1/7/140 folio 3.
179  National Archives, Treasury Papers T 1/440 folios 334-339.

The first Governor of the Province of Senegambia, Charles O'Hara was to arrive in Saint-Louis on 19 April 1766. Outgoing Governor John Barnes was there to meet him. Hoping to depart in dignity and style on a Company ship he was to be disappointed. Writing on the day of O'Hara's arrival[180] he admitted "we find it a little hard that we are obliged to beg for a passage to England having flattered ourselves with hopes that the Committee would at least for their own honour have made some provision for us in that respect."[181]

---

180 Letter from Barnes to the Committee of 19 April 1766, CO 267/1.
181 At the time of his departure Barnes headed a garrison of 37 Europeans (Governor, Deputy Governor/Accountant, Captain of fort/storekeeper, surgeon, clerk, overseer of the works, smith, mason, Assistant Governor, carpenter, cooper, two drummers and 24 private soldiers). There were also 38 Africans (including 1 mason, 1 carpenter, 3 linguists and 32 labourers). State of garrison on 17 February 1766, CO 267/13.

CHAPTER SIX

# GOVERNOR O'HARA AND THE PROVINCE OF SENEGAMBIA

1765-1775

According to the "Propositions for forming a civil Constitution and a Military Establishment for the Government of Senegambia" submitted to King George III on 15 November 1765[182] the new Province of Senegambia was to have its capital at Saint-Louis and to be administered by a Governor. An earlier proposal[183] that Saint-Louis be renamed St. George appears to have been quietly dropped. In addition, a Superintendent of Trade, later to be known as Lieutenant Governor, was to be posted to James Island, with responsibility for the Gambia River, but accountable to the governor at Saint-Louis. The arrangement generally didn't work well and relationships between governors in Saint-Louis and lieutenant governors in the Gambia were frequently poisonous.

---

182 "Propositions for forming a civil Constitution and a Military Establishment for the Government of Senegambia", under cover of a letter to King George III of 6 February 1766 from the Commissioners of the Board of Trade (Lord Dartmouth, Soame Jenyns, J Dyson, William Fitzherbert and Lord Palmerston), CO 268/2.
183 Letter from the Commissioners of the Board of Trade to King George III 21 February 1765, CO 389/31.

The powers of the governor were explicitly based on those held by governors in Britain's American colonies except that the Governor of Senegambia did not have the right to make any grant of land without the express direction of the King. The Governor was to be assisted in his administrative and legislative responsibilities by a nine-person Council in which the Chief Justice, Commandant of the Troops, the Secretary of the Province and the Secretary of Trade would also sit. The Propositions also envisaged that security would be provided by three companies of seventy men, specifying that Africans could be recruited but were not to exceed one third of each company.

The Privy Council agreed a budget of £12,050 for the new Provincial Government for a one-year period from 25 March 1765. The Governor was to receive a salary of £1200 (a hefty increase on the £200 paid by the Committee to Barnes) while the Chief Justice was to be paid £400 and the Secretary to the Province £200. The Superintendent of Trade based at Fort James was also to receive £200. The Privy Council decision envisaged the appointment of two ministers of the Church with a salary of £100 each, and "a school master" on £50 (but this was soon doubled). £6000 was set aside for "subsistence, clothing, provisions and other contingent expenses", £2000 for repair of the forts and a total of £1500 for the purchase, equipping and maintenance of two flat-bottomed boats – to defend the entrance to the river Senegal – and a sloop.[184]

The Propositions, subsequently approved by the King, envisaged that the Governor and Council would occupy themselves with the "welfare of the inhabitants and the advancement of trade" and clarified that until proper laws and a constitution could be made, government and justice were to be administered under the Laws of England. The job of the Secretary to the Province was to prepare all acts and documents of government for the Governor's signature. The budget also provided for the recruitment of a Secretary conversant in the Moorish language (at a salary of £100) "for the better and more

---

184 "Estimate of the Expense of supporting the civil and military Establishment of the proposed new Government of Senegambia on the coast of Africa from the 25th of March 1765 to the 25th of March 1766, CO 267/1.

easy transacting of affairs with the Moors". The Propositions also authorised the appointment of a Collector "for laying certain duties on Gum Senega and Gum Arabic imported into or exported from Great Britain, and for confining the Exportation of Gum Senega from Africa to Great Britain only."[185]

Such was the significance of His Majesty's new province that the governor was to be equipped with a new seal. Lord Dartmouth, President of the Board of Trade, explained to the King[186] the form this would take. The seal would have "on the one side a representation of a large spreading tree, of that species which produces the Gum Senega with bales of gum lying under it" and underneath the motto "Ramis felicibus Arbos."[187] The seal was to be used in authenticating all public instruments in Senegambia.

Charles O'Hara, the first Governor of Senegambia, was one of a number of colourful figures to serve in the province. Born in 1740 in Lisbon, he was the illegitimate son of General O'Hara, Lord of Tyrawley, then Ambassador to Lisbon, and his Portuguese mistress. Having joined the army aged twelve he served in Germany and Portugal during the Seven Years War before being appointed commandant of the Africa Corps in Senegal at the age of about 26. O'Hara was to survive nearly ten years as Governor in Saint-Louis, surprisingly long given the unhealthy climate and his evident ambition. He later fought in the American Revolutionary War, as General Cornwallis's second-in-command and gained a place in history for having surrendered both to George Washington (at Yorktown in 1781) and to Napoleon (in 1793). He also served as Governor of Gibraltar from 1795 until his death in 1802.

O'Hara was commissioned as Governor on 28 December 1765 and his instructions were signed on 6 February 1766.[188] His Commission gave him full power and authority to establish courts,

---

185 T 1/440 folios 334-339.
186 Dartmouth to George III of 15 November 1785, CO 268/2.
187 This could be translated as "A tree with prosperous branches" or "A tree with fine branches". Virgil used this phrase in Book Two of his Georgics.
188 CO 268/2.

appoint judges and other judicial officers, to imprison or put to death "enemies, pirates and rebels at sea" and to build forts, castles and other fortifications for the defence of the province. His instructions gave him three clear objectives: the establishment of an administration and the maintenance of order; the defence of the province, and the protection and security of its inhabitants and their property; and the extension of trade.

If Their Lordships had expected regular reporting from O'Hara on his performance against these objectives, they were to be disappointed. He started well, corresponding regularly for his first six months. For the next three years (1767-69), he wrote infrequently, and no correspondence exists at all for the years 1770 and 1771. 1772 and 1773 were also lean years with only four letters from O'Hara.[189] It is possible perhaps that some letters went astray. But a more likely explanation is that he was a poor correspondent. The main evidence for this lies in the fact that their Lordships frequently lamented the lack of communication from O'Hara and that having been warned O'Hara became a frequent correspondent again in his last two years.

O'Hara's failure to do much to advance his first objective – the establishment of governing institutions and the maintenance of order – contributed to his eventual dismissal. His instructions had specified that O'Hara should choose the nine-member council "from amongst the most considerable of our Protestant inhabitants". He was to submit his recommendations for Council members for the approval of the Commissioners for Trade and Plantations along with a reserve list of eight persons. Within a few months of his arrival[190] O'Hara was writing back that "for want of a sufficient number of proper persons the Council is not so numerous as was directed".

Thereafter his correspondence makes little reference to the proceedings of the council. Nor is there any mention of a judicial system having been put in place, despite the fact that his instructions make explicitly clear that appointing a Chief Justice and establishing

---

189 Eveline C. Martin, Chapter VI.
190 Letter of 28 May 1766 from O'Hara to Henry Seymour Conway, Secretary of State for the Southern Department, CO 267/1.

a system of courts "should be a very essential and immediate object of [his] attention". It seems likely that even if courts and a council were established, they struggled to operate, and O'Hara exerted sole executive authority. His decisions were not always popular. A merchant and MP, Anthony Bacon, complained to the Secretary of State for Colonial Affairs that O'Hara had refused to let a French ship that he had contracted land at Saint-Louis. O'Hara stood his ground, arguing that such use of foreign vessels by British merchants was specifically forbidden by the Navigation Acts, which restricted trade between Britain and its colonies to British vessels.

O'Hara's bosses in London were acutely conscious that the Committee of the Company of Merchants' running of Senegal and Fort James on the Gambia River had been shambolic. His instructions underlined therefore the urgent need for a civil administration to restrain "that licentiousness which has so long continued without control and which has produced almost every abuse and evil practice."[191] They were clear what was to blame.

> "Among many other Disorders and Irregularities which have been taken notice of, that of the excessive use of spirituous liquors sold by retail in every Part of the Town, has been fully represented and the evil consequences of it, destroying the health of the soldiery and encouraging profligacy amongst the inhabitants are so obvious that it will be your particular duty… to restrain so dangerous a licence, by limiting the number of public Houses, and by allowing none to be opened without a licence".

London also thought that greater practice of Christianity would both civilise the African population and encourage better behaviour on the part of the civil administrators and military. O'Hara's instructions were unmistakably clear that it was in no way the Government's intention

---

191 Instructions to O'Hara under cover of a letter to King George III of 6 February from the Commissioners of the Board of Trade (Lord Dartmouth, Soame Jenyns, J Dyson, William Fitzherbert and Lord Palmerston), CO 268/2.

that any of the inhabitants should be denied liberty of conscience or the right to exercise their own religion. Nevertheless they also stated clearly that the Church of England should be established in principle and practice and that the inhabitants of the Province should be encouraged to embrace the protestant religion. Hence the provision in the budget for two Ministers. Needless to say, given the persecution of the Catholic Church in England at this time, O'Hara was told he should not "admit any ecclesiastical jurisdiction of the See of Rome."[192]

As for his second objective – defence of the province – O'Hara was not impressed by the state in which he found the fort on his arrival.[193] The walls of the fort were "in a very ruinous condition" and too narrow and weak for even the garrison's small cannons to be mounted upon them. "The fort has not even the appearance of strength and is in reality nothing more than very indifferent houses ranged in the form of a fort". Few of the garrison had any military experience – "I doubt much if there was science enough in the whole garrison to load a gun."[194] He highlighted the settlement's vulnerability to attack, commenting that between July and November any hostile force would not need to negotiate the natural defences of the bar but could land on the sea coast and march the short distance across the narrow peninsular. "I think it cannot be reasonably expected," he concluded, "that I can answer for the security of this place".

O'Hara recommended rebuilding the fort and increasing the size of the garrison to 500 soldiers. He did not however support the Privy Council's view that Africans could provide up to a third of a company's strength. "I am apprehensive the soldiers would think themselves very ill-used, being obliged to do Duty with them, besides, it would be very impolitic to put them upon a footing with white men, which would at once destroy that subordination to which the Negroes submit and is so essentially necessary in this country". O'Hara also argued for a settlement on the mainland opposite the island of Saint-Louis where crops could be grown, grain stored and livestock kept.

---

192 Instructions to O'Hara of 6 Feb 1776, CO 268/2.
193 Ibid.
194 Letter from O'Hara of 27 January 1767 to Lord Germain, CO 267/13.

It was his third objective – extending trade – that clearly motivated O'Hara the most. He needed no convincing of the benefits of trading with the interior and was quick to describe the opportunities offered by inland trade in the hyperbolic language favoured by many early travellers. From his earliest letters back to London O'Hara advocated establishing a settlement at the mines of Galam, "which are said to be the richest in the world". He argued that "there is no part of Africa where there is so great a consumption of manufactures as in the Kingdom of Galam". The fact that 70,000 slaves a year were being exported from Senegambia showed, he argued, just how populous Africa was and therefore the potential market for British goods (which he estimated already to amount to £40,000 a year). He was convinced that travelling by river to Galam would make the British much more competitive than Moorish traders who travelled by land.[195]

O'Hara's ambitions did not stop at Galam. He suggested that once the settlement at Galam had grown, which it would do quickly, the British should establish settlements further afield "to the Eastward of the mountains of Gavina",[196] "and by these means we might in time extend every part of this continent that was worthwhile to settle". Future desirable settlements included the Kingdom of Saltique[197] which, the exuberant O'Hara proclaimed, "abounds in prodigious quantities of rice, wax, cotton, indigo and tobacco", the cotton, "repeatedly proved to be the finest in the world". Senegambia would, he confidently predicted "in time be one of the richest colonies belonging to His Majesty".

O'Hara's instructions put a lot of emphasis on the need to ensure an English monopoly over the gum trade, with a view to stabilising prices, and the desirability of limiting the trade to Saint-Louis. In the event that this was not possible consideration was to be given to building a fort on the Mauritanian coast at Arguin or stationing a ship at Portendic to discourage interlopers. Ship owners picking up gum in Saint-Louis were to be required to show evidence that

---
195  O'Hara to Secretary of State Southern Department of 25 July 1766, CO 267/1
196  ibid
197  It's not clear where O'Hara meant either by Gavina or Saltique.

previous consignments had been delivered to England and not sold to the French. While gum was undoubtedly the priority, O'Hara was also tasked to establish how "the commerce for slaves, ivory and gold [might be] greatly extended and improved".[198] He was also asked to advise on the expediency of re-establishing forts at Podor and Galam, though his instructions noted that any new forts would need to be funded from within the budget already set by Parliament.

O'Hara's first annual budget (minus start-up costs) in 1766 was £5,500. It was still the same, after O'Hara's departure, in 1777 and 1778. In between, there had been some variation but not much. Ever conscious of the cost of maintaining settlements on the coast of West Africa the authorities in London were to suggest, in 1778,[199] that savings could be made by sending local Africans from Senegal and the Gambia to garrison the forts on the Gold Coast and Whydah to work there as soldiers, craftsmen and labourers. The note pointed out that if any of them deserted they would quickly be picked up by local tribes – with whom they shared neither language or culture – and sold back to the fort they had fled as slaves. The note further suggested that Africans from the Gold Coast could similarly be used in Senegal.

Within a matter of weeks of his arrival O'Hara was setting out in detail both how a fort might be constructed at Galam[200] – he did not want to rebuild the French fort at Fort St. Joseph as it was in a marshy area – and the build required for vessels to go up the river. O'Hara was commended[201] for the clarity of his proposals and for his diligence.

O'Hara's instructions also referred to detailed instructions that had issued earlier to the Superintendent of Trade who would be based at Fort James.[202] These made clear the need to keep a watchful eye on the French, especially at Albreda "seeing that they do nothing which

---

198 Instructions to O'Hara of 6 Feb 1876, CO 268/2.
199 Note on the Annual estimate of charges for the military establishments on the coast of Africa, from ?Lord Lewisham, dated 28 October 1778, CO 267/6.
200 Letter from O'Hara of 25 July 1766, CO 267/1.
201 Letter from Lord Shelburne to O'Hara of 17 October 1766, CO 267/6.
202 Instructions to the Superintendent of Trade in the Province of Senegambia, 6 December 1765, CO 268/2.

may be inconsistent with the terms upon which they are suffered to remain in that establishment". The Provincial authorities were also put on guard to counter any measures the French might take "to alienate the affections of the Natives from the British interests" or otherwise to frustrate and disrupt British commercial interests in the region. The British authorities were particularly concerned that the French at Gorée might seek to communicate with their former citizens on the island of Saint-Louis, or with the Moors, to the detriment of British trade.[203]

Although the Committee of the Company of Merchants no longer controlled Saint-Louis the private sector was still very much present and securing good business from His Majesty's Government. Businessmen such as William Bishop and John Lang, agents to Samuel Smith of London, would charge £20-£25 a trip to ferry soldiers over the bar at the mouth of the Senegal River.[204]

Governors at Saint-Louis would also send provisions (flour, rice, beef) and supplies (pitch, tar, turpentine) by private ship to their colleagues at Fort James in the Gambia.[205] Sometimes the supplies would include slaves. A letter survives from Joseph Debat, a Superintendant of Trade, explaining how materials sent from Saint-Louis had been used to repair the fort at Fort James and thanking Governor O'Hara for having purchased for him "seven castle slaves who he had put to work repairing the fort, enlarging the island and removing the negro huts to a distant part of the island."[206]

There was also good business in feeding the garrisons. Governors were required to submit regular detailed accounts. The victuals list for the period 21 July 1768 to 15 January 1769 shows[207] that the garrison at Saint-Louis was charged for 54,106 man days, 46,042 of which at 5/-, and 8,064 (presumably the officer class) at 6/-, for a total of £1989.19s 1½d. The total of 430 people this covered included, in

---

203 Instructions to O'Hara of 6 Feb 1876, CO 268/2.
204 T 1/474 folio 227 and T 1/478 folio 161.
205 Letter from O'Hara to Joseph Debat of 28 August 1770, T 1/478 folio 317.
206 Letter from Debat to O'Hara of 28 May 1770, T 1/478 folio 319-320.
207 T 1/474.

addition to the Governor, his household staff, officers and soldiers, 184 local residents – including translators, craftsmen and sailors – as well as "Moor and Negro visitors". Some of the positions were long-term. Two of those listed as linguists in the 1768 victuals list – Charles Thevenot and Amady Compagnie – were still present on the victuals list for the period 1 January – 31 March 1775.[208] This later list reveals that local Africans were also employed as boatmen, sailors, hospital attendants, cooks and labourers, as sweepers, for burning lime and, in one case, as a "gum woman". Africans were also used to crew a boat kept near the mouth of the river to deter Moors from crossing the river. The January 1775 list shows that twenty-eight people were employed at Fort George in Podor. A victuals list from the third quarter of 1775 however suggests that the garrison at Fort George was evacuated that year.[209]

Local business people also did well. According to Searing[210]

"British preference for using African merchants to carry on trade with the interior, which contrasted with the [French] company's direct management of the trade, accelerated the process which transformed the inhabitants of St. Louis into a powerful slave-owning merchant class in the second half of the Eighteenth Century".

Britain's seizure of Saint-Louis from the French in 1758 enabled the local inhabitants, especially the signares (mixed-race women entrepreneurs), to acquire assets in slaves, boats and houses which had belonged previously to the French. Under British rule the inhabitants of Saint-Louis also developed increasing political autonomy, with the British recognising the mixed-race Charles Thevenot as the mayor. A French census in 1779 showed that the population of Saint-Louis had increased from 2,500 in 1754 to 3,018. Most of the increase was accounted for by the increase in the slave population which stood

---

208 T 1/516 folios 3-4.
209 T 1/516 foilos 7-10.
210 Searing, p. 106.

at 1858. Women slaves were employed in the preparation of food (especially the pounding of millet), cleaning, fetching wood and water, as washerwomen and as concubines. Men slaves were often slave sailors, known as "laptots", who were used to defend the slave ships as they sailed down the Senegal River. In 1784, the French tried to re-impose monopoly conditions, fixing the price of the slaves they would buy from the local populations.

As noted earlier, the Waalo King Naatago Aram had been a particular thorn in the English side during the early days of their occupation of Saint-Louis, with the king intercepting trade on the Senegal River and blocking supplies on the island. O'Hara advocated the disarming of the African populations living near Saint-Louis and the construction of a blockhouse, close to the bar in the river, which would help to protect communication between Kayoor and Saint-Louis.[211]

Naatago Aram's death in 1766, heralded two decades of civil war. The Moors took advantage of this, with the active support of Governor O'Hara, to overrun the Kingdom of Waalo and secure control of both sides of the Senegal River. Barry[212] sees O'Hara's intervention as decisive in triggering a decline in the fortunes of the Kingdom from which it was never to recover. The Moors' southward swoop also forced the British to give up Podor.[213]

A French source[214] holds O'Hara and Le Brasseur, the French Governor at Gorée (and subsequently Saint-Louis), responsible for encouraging the Moors to take more captives from their wars with the rulers of Waalo and to sell them to Saint-Louis. The source suggests that the Moors took over 8,000 prisoners in a six-month period, selling them to the British in exchange for guns and blue linen. O'Hara's role in bringing about the destruction of the Kingdom of Waalo was confirmed by Charles Maxwell, Governor of Saint-Louis at the beginning of Britain's final occupation of the island in 1809-

---

211 Barry, *The Kingdon of Waalo*, p. 121.
212 Barry, p. 124.
213 According to Barry, p. 124 based on letter from O'Hara of 18 August 1775, CO 268/4.
214 Colonies C6 18 according to Barry, *The Kingdom of Waalo*, p. 59.

1817. Giving evidence to a Commission of Inquiry into the Forts and Settlements of Africa in 1811 he wrote:

> "During the period that Senegal was in our possession after the peace of 1763, the inhabitants of [Waalo] then exceedingly powerful were [giving] trouble [to] some [of] the settlements and threatened to prevent communications with the upper part of the river. General O'Hara then Governor entered into a treaty with the Trarza Moors and King damel to assist him in attacking that nation, which they did most effectually and the Wa[a]lo country received a blow from which it has never since recovered. Its villages on the Senegal River's bank are yet deserted and abandoned; its people have been carried into captivity and those who remain are constantly subjected to the plunder of the Moors who treat [them] as a dependent and tributary state. O'Hara's name is still used by the Waalo mothers to frighten their crying children.[215]"

Although the two countries were no longer at war relations between Britain and France were becoming increasingly fractious in the early 1770s and suspicions about French activity in the region were running high. With English merchants complaining, the Colonial Office reprimanded O'Hara for having done nothing to secure the gum trade at Arguin and Portendic as he had been instructed to do and for failing to provide them with regular and thorough reports.[216]

Eager for information on the Province of Senegambia – or perhaps just aware that they didn't know much about the place – the Colonial Office sent O'Hara in August 1773 a long list of topics he should cover in his reports.[217] They asked for information on its size, population, geography and climate; on its boundaries and whether they were disputed; on its rivers and whether they could be used

---

215 Referenced in Barry, The Kingdom of Waalo, p. 125.
216 e.g letters from Lord Dartmouth to O'Hara of 10 August 1773, CO 267/6 and 27 October 1773, CO 268/3.
217 Lord Dartmouth to Charles O'Hara, 18 August 1773, CO 268/3

for commerce; the depth of its harbours; and on the local produce, its mines, the extent of British trade and the competition. They never received a reply. Over two years later Lord George Germain, who succeeded the Earl of Dartmouth as Secretary of State for the Colonies, sent the same list of questions to the new Governor, John Clarke.[218] This also did not receive a reply but for the better reason that Clarke was already dead.

Clarke had served as O'Hara's deputy in Saint-Louis and towards the end of 1774, in O'Hara's absence on leave, he exchanged correspondence with the French governor in Gorée, M. Le Brasseur, in which they disagreed on whether Britain – as it claimed – enjoyed exclusive rights to trade in gum at Arguin and Portendic.[219] Le Brasseur argued that the Treaty of Paris provided in Article 23 for all possessions other than those explicitly mentioned to revert to France, that is that Arguin and Portendic should now be under French control.

At the same time trouble was also brewing between Britain and France over whether the French had the right, without permission, to take on water at Jufureh on the Gambia River. Incidents there were sufficiently serious for the Earl of Rochford, Secretary of State for the Southern Department, to send several letters on the subject to M. St. Paul, the French Ambassador in London and for the despatch of two frigates to enforce the ban on French trading in the Gambia. A Royal Navy vessel, HMS *Weazle*,[220] was also stationed off Portendic, in 1774, to discourage French activities during the gum season.[221]

In February 1775, O'Hara was making excuses for why he had not kept London adequately informed, saying that he could not "sufficiently lament my long continuance of ill-health which has prevented me from having the honour of obeying your Lordship's commands in laying before you the state and condition of His

---

218 Germain to Clarke of 28 August 1778, CO 268/3.
219 Brasseur to Clarke of 15 November, 11 and 28 December, Clarke to Brasseur of 3 and 28 December, SP 78/295.
220 sometimes spelt HMS *Weazel*
221 CO 268/4.

Majesty's Province of Senegambia in Africa."[222] By 20 June 1775, he was desperately trying to defend himself against accusations from his bosses that he had been vague in his reporting, alleging many encroachments by the French but only mentioning specifically the disputes over Portendic and Jufureh.[223] O'Hara in reply: "It is with infinite chagrin that I have the mortification to find your Lordship's letters are filled with reprimands couched in the severest terms of neglecting my duty."[224] He went on to explain that the French had established settlements at Portudal, Joal and Rufisque and that "they used their vessels into all the rivers and creeks on the sea coast of this Province, the river of Senegal excepted and that by those unwarranted practices they carry on a very extensive and profitable commerce highly prejudicial to the interests of His Majesty's subjects". Having failed to keep his Lordships informed of the threats to British interests in this part of the coast of West Africa, and then painting such an alarming picture, O'Hara's job must have been on the line.

O'Hara also tried to blame the authorities in London, arguing that he had never been given any instructions defining French rights on the Gambia or elsewhere in the province and that he had therefore had to exercise his own judgement. He explains that except at their factory at Albreda, the French had not been allowed to procure anything from the locals such as wood, water or timber without the express permission of the Commandant at Fort James. That permission had always been given until the British realised that under the pretext of provisioning themselves with water the French were conducting other business and trying to lure the locals to Albreda and away from British factories.

Rather disarmingly O'Hara says that if the French were allowed to trade on the Gambia River the British would have to leave "as the French Merchandise is not only far superior in Quality and

---

222 Letter from O'Hara to the Earl of Dartmouth dated 10 February 1775, SP 78/295 folio 204.
223 O'Hara refers in fact to Gillifree, a reference to Fort Jillifree at Jufureh.
224 Letter from O'Hara to Lord Dartmouth of 20 June 1775, SP 78/296 folio 259.

consequently much preferred to the English Goods by the natives, but the French, by being supplied with their Manufactures in general at Thirty per Centum and in some Articles at One hundred per Centum cheaper than the English Trades could therefore afford to give a much greater price for the slaves, ivory, wax and other productions of the Gambia and would consequently monopolise the whole of that trade". He also accused the French, barred from Portendic, of getting the Moors to deliver trade direct to Gorée. British merchants had also raised this concern in London,[225] and held O'Hara responsible. They said his decision not to pay customs to the Damel had caused the latter to allow the Moors passage through his territory on their way to Gorée.

O'Hara was being somewhat disingenuous in suggesting that London had not sent instructions in respect of French rights along the coast. Indeed, the intentions of the French seem to have been a constant preoccupation during the English occupation of Gorée and Saint-Louis. On 10 August 1773, for example, the Earl of Dartmouth wrote to O'Hara[226] about their suspicions that the French wanted to establish themselves at Arguin and Portendic in order to recover control of the gum trade. He noted that any attempt of that nature "will be a violation of the King's rights and must have the consequence to deprive us of that commerce which is the great object of our possessions in that part of the world". He informed O'Hara that he had been commanded by the King "to signify to you His Majesty's Pleasure that you keep a very watchful eye upon the Proceedings of the French at Gorée" adding pointedly that O'Hara didn't appear to have done much to secure Arguin and Portendic as his original instructions had tasked him to do.

Later, when O'Hara did attempt to position a robust British presence at Arguin he faced resistance from the Navy. O'Hara wanted Captain Cornwallis, Commander of His Majesty's Squadron on the coast of Africa, to remain on the coast at Arguin during the season of

---

225 Letter from Messrs Rofs, Mills and Bradley, from the Senegal Coffee House, 12 December 1774, CO 268/4.
226 Earl of Dartmouth to Charles O'Hara of 10 August 1773, CO 267/6.

the gum trade but Cornwallis refused on the grounds that he needed to send one of his two ships down the coast and the remaining ship – HMS *Weazle* – would be able to achieve little by itself.[227]

If O'Hara was already in trouble with his bosses things got worse. On 22 August 1775, the Mayor of Saint-Louis Charles Thevenot and other leading members of the community submitted a petition to the King detailing the abuses they had suffered under O'Hara.[228] Whether this received the immediate attention of the authorities in London is unclear but after O'Hara departed on leave to England in November 1775, the Acting Governor Matthias MacNamara made sure the allegations against him were addressed.

MacNamara was Lieutenant Governor at Fort James and O'Hara's deputy. Described by Edward Morse, later Chief Justice of Senegambia under Governor Clarke, as "a man without education, extremely brutal, vulgar, and avaricious"[229] MacNamara was insubordinate and gave O'Hara a hard time. His appointment as Lieutenant Governor, despite being the youngest lieutenant in the regiment with only two years service, had gone down badly with more senior officers, some of whom had served over twenty years.[230]

Both Charles O'Hara and the Government in London considered some of MacNamara's actions towards the French in the Gambia to be poorly judged, confrontational, and at risk of seriously escalating tensions between the two countries. Such was the animosity between O'Hara and his deputy that when he set off on leave to England in November 1775, he made no effort to inform MacNamara of his departure. Instead he left his senior military officer Captain Joseph Wall in command, with instructions not to hand over control of the province to MacNamara. That at least is MacNamara's version of events.[231] MacNamara turned up in Saint-Louis to take charge and

---

227 Exchange of correspondence between O'Hara and Cornwallis in January 1775, CO 267/16.
228 Petition dated 22 August 1775 (which appears to have been signed and submitted again on 1 February 1776), CO 267/1.
229 According to Gray, Morse to Lord Townshend, 12 August 1782 CO 267/20.
230 Letter from O'Hara to Lord Dartmouth of 13 May 1775, CO 267/16.
231 MacNamara to Lord Germain of 26 January 1776, CO 268/4.

proceeded to gather information to indict O'Hara for brutality and repression, fraud and mismanagement of the province's affairs.

Writing back to London early in 1776,[232] MacNamara painted a bleak picture of the settlement at Saint-Louis, putting the blame for this firmly at O'Hara's door. Echoing O'Hara's own comments on his arrival he lamented the ruinous condition of the fort and claimed many of the inhabitants had left because of O'Hara's severity. He went on to explain how under O'Hara relations with local tribes were bad: the Trarza Moors refused to come to Saint-Louis, meaning provisions were scarce; and the Peuls were angry because so many slaves had been taken in the wars that O'Hara encouraged. MacNamara arranged for further depositions to be taken from Charles Thevenot and the signatories of the August 1775 petition[233] and other disgruntled residents and forwarded these to London. Shortly afterwards O'Hara, still in England, received a letter from one of his colleagues in Saint-Louis warning him of what was afoot so that if called upon he could "refute their vile and false accusations". The author of the letter considered the accusations malicious given the "many great benefits, services and protection" they received from O'Hara.[234]

On the command of the King[235] the Board of Trade investigated the allegations made against O'Hara and presented their report in June 1776.[236] This summarised five main charges:

i. That he had governed arbitrarily without the advice and consent of a Council.
ii. That he had interrupted the inhabitants in their religious observance.
iii. That he had invaded the property rights of the inhabitants both by compelling their slaves to work for him without

---

232 Ibid
233 Minutes of the Council meeting held on 26 January 1776, CO 267/1.
234 Letter from John Lang to Charles O'Hara of 3 February 1776, CO 267/1.
235 Lord Germain to the Board of Trade of 23 April 1776.
236 Letter from the Board of Trade to King George III of 10 June 1776, CO 268/2.

pay and by taking away the lands of several inhabitants against their consent.
iv. That he had made it difficult for the inhabitants to obtain fresh provisions through certain prohibitions (e.g. on the sale of beef on the island).
v. That he had engaged extensively in private trade.

The report did not dwell on some of the other more colourful accusations that Thevenot and his fellow residents had levelled against O'Hara. These included that he had regularly insulted them, calling the men rascals and blackguards and the women whores and bitches, and that he frequently threatened to enslave them. They also accused him of particular cruelty to the lover of one of his concubines, with whom she had a child. The child was either stillborn or died soon after birth, but the residents alleged that O'Hara had the body dug up to establish whether the child was white or black.

The Board of Trade opened their report to the King by saying that this was the first complaint against O'Hara in ten years (though this forgets Bacon's grievance) and noting a fulsome testimonial[237] recently received from the Merchants of London Trading to Senegal expressing satisfaction with O'Hara's administration of the colony. In relation to the first charge the Board noted that within a short time of his arrival O'Hara seemed no longer to consider the Council as forming an indispensable branch of the constitution, preferring instead to administer "at his own despotic will". They noted too the complete absence of a Court of Judicature and any Judges, Justices of the Peace, a Sheriff or other judicial officers.[238] They found no evidence either that he had done anything to establish the Christian religion as he had been instructed to do. On the first charge therefore, they found him "justly liable to reprehension".

---
237 Dated 13 May 1776.
238 A letter dated 17 August 1782 from Edward Morse, who had been Chief Justice under Clarke, indicates that O'Hara had attempted to appoint a Chief Justice – a Mr Miller – but they had been unable to establish a Court of Justice due to there not being enough white people on the island outside the military, CO 267/20

The Board found that the second charge related to decisions by O'Hara to ban the ringing of bells by the local population during religious ceremonies and a further ban on burials on the island. The Board found that O'Hara had indeed been guilty of a breach of the clear instruction on freedom of religion, while giving him credit for having revoked his decision within a matter of days.

In respect of the third charge the Board found that O'Hara had compelled others' private slaves to work for him, while noting that this had been for public works – e.g repairing holes in the roads – and that the slaves had been paid "in brandy and beads". No compensation, however, had been paid to their owners. They also established that O'Hara had evicted some members of the local population from their land or dwellings on the crowded island in order to free up space for traders. But they found that in each case he had paid compensation or found alternative sites (though presumably the compensation was considered inadequate or the new site inferior). The Board dismissed the fourth charge on the grounds that all the evidence suggested the markets on Saint-Louis were constantly open and well-provisioned. On the final charge the Board concluded that he had not himself engaged in private trade, while noting that he was a shareholder in a partnership importing slaves into Dominica where he co-owned a plantation.

The Board considered the first charge the most serious and concluded that had O'Hara faced difficulties or obstructions in establishing the Council, the Courts or other elements of the civil administration he should have reported them in order to be given new instructions. For this reason, they recommended, and the King agreed, that O'Hara should be dismissed.

There is little in the report to suggest that the Board put much store by MacNamara's allegations. No doubt they considered him an unreliable witness. Nor, as far as I can tell, did they consider a document entitled "Remarks on Governor O'Hara's Accounts" prepared at around that time (though the exact date is unclear) by an official in London. These suggested that O'Hara's detailed accounts were fraudulent, noting that most of the money was allegedly spent either on repairs to the fort, which nevertheless seemed to be in a permanent state of ruin; on boats, though there was little evidence of their existence; and on essential presents for the local kings. The accountant noted however that O'Hara had claimed in 1773 for eight years of arrears of gifts to the King of Trarza, querying how essential they could be if they hadn't been paid for so long and pointing out that O'Hara's successor had been told by the King of Trarza that the annual presents had never been paid.[239]

—

The story of British colonisation in the eighteenth century is as much about the actions of individuals as the policies of companies or governments. The committee managing the interests of a chartered company of merchants, or a Secretary of State for the Colonies might have set clear objectives for their "man on the spot" and provided detailed guidance on how the trading outpost or colony should be run, and how they and those they led were expected to behave, including on matters of financial propriety. However once they arrived they were more or less on their own. Distance from London meant communications, in the days before the telegraph, were poor. New instructions were infrequent, sometimes intercepted or lost at sea, and frequently overtaken by events. Often the centre's expectations of what should be possible did not match the reality on the ground and the man on the spot would have to make do the best he could. Some leaders lived up to the expectations of their superiors back home, others didn't.

In India, news from London could take six to twelve months to arrive. When war broke out between Britain and France in May 1756 the news only reached India in December. The death of 123 British prisoners in a Calcutta dungeon ("The Black Hole of Calcutta") in June 1756 apparently only reached London in June the following year.

---

[239] "Remarks on Governor O'Hara's Accounts", anonymous and undated, C0 267/10.

While the supplying of provisions or reinforcement of troops could be scheduled, urgent and unexpected requirements could not be expeditiously met. The coast of West Africa was far closer than India, three to five weeks sailing away, but far enough for a governor, in the absence of any effective supervision, to do more or less as he pleased. Charles O'Hara seems to have decided early in his tenure what was realistic and achievable from the instructions he had been given and to have prioritised actions that contributed to his own personal gain. No other British governor came close to his ten-year tenure. He was far from being the worst of the British governors, but it is hard to identify many achievements during his tenure. Perhaps a different leader would have used their ten-year term to build a solid platform for an enduring British presence in Saint-Louis. But this was not to be Charles O'Hara's legacy. O'Hara's career does not however appear to have suffered unduly as a result either of his dismissal from the post of Governor or the suggestion that he was guilty of fraud. Having made his mark in the American Revolutionary Wars he was later promoted to General, ending his career as Governor of Gibraltar.

CHAPTER SEVEN

# THE PROVINCE OF SENEGAMBIA: DESCENT INTO INFAMY

1775-1783

Notwithstanding the concern in London at his behaviour, MacNamara was not immediately recalled or replaced but stayed on in Saint-Louis as Acting Governor of Senegambia. One of his first actions was to get rid of his rival Joseph Wall by sending him off to James Island as Lieutenant Governor. Their relationship deteriorated rapidly and when Wall turned up unannounced one day in Saint-Louis MacNamara had him arrested, returned to James Island and confined there for ten months, as he gathered evidence against him.

Meanwhile, MacNamara appears to have lived up to his reputation for brutality in his heavy-handed administration of Saint-Louis, allegedly guillotining an African for not showing sufficient respect.[240] Under MacNamara a brutally repressive law, enacted under his predecessor, was further strengthened.[241] The "Act for the Better Ordering and Governing of Negroes and punishing offences relative to them," based on a model in force in some of Britain's American colonies, set out the punishments for slaves striking others. The law

---

240 According to Gray, this was "for not raising his hat to him" , quoting Le Brasseur in letter to (unknown) of 31 August 1776, CO 267/6.
241 Minutes of Council held at St. Louis on 10 April 1776, CO 267/16.

provided that a slave should be severely whipped for a first offence and be severely whipped and have his nose slit and face burnt for a second offence. The penalty for a third offence was death, or any other punishment at the discretion of the Chief Justice. Under MacNamara the law was amended to make clear that it applied also to "free negroes" and that the offences in question related specifically to the striking by blacks of white persons. On the other hand, the Act clarified that the offspring of white men or "free negroes" and female slaves should be free and that the penalty for killing a slave out of wilfulness, wantonness or bloody mindedness should be increased from six months in prison and a maximum £100 fine to death.

MacNamara also appears to have continued his overly confrontational approach to French ships, provoking diplomatic protests by Paris in London about his high-handed behaviour in respect of a French ship *la Grue*. The incident seems to have arisen after an English captain complained to MacNamara[242] that the French had prevented him from purchasing corn on the mainland. As a result, he had been forced to buy it from Gorée at a higher price. MacNamara firmly believed that under the Treaty of Paris the French only had the right to trade at Gorée and at Albreda on the Gambia River and that the factories that they had illegally established at Portudal and other places on the mainland were diverting trade from the Gambia River. He fired off a letter of protest to the French Governor at Gorée, ordering him to withdraw the French factories at Joal and Portudal. This went unanswered. MacNamara wrote again, making clear to the Governor his determination to enforce the English trading monopoly in His Majesty's Province of Senegambia. This elicited a response from the Governor[243] that he could not withdraw from Joal and Portudal without the approval of the French King. He added that he was "ignorant of what is meant by the Province of Senegambia" but was clear that Portudal and Joal were dependencies of Gorée and therefore part of the French sphere of influence. At around the same

---

242 Letter from MacNamara to Lord Germain of 18 July 1777, CO 267/6
243 Dated 11 September 1776

time MacNamara bet a visiting Frenchman (the bet withdrawn the next day according to MacNamara) that he would get rid of all French ships trading on the coast of the mainland.

Shortly afterwards *la Grue* was seized on his orders. According to the French[244] it had a cargo of eighty slaves. MacNamara disputed this saying there were only three slaves on board (one boy and two women) and a free boy used as an interpreter. An inventory done of *la Grue* by the English, presumably for the purpose of compensation, assessed that the ship "was in want of a thorough repair."[245] The inventory listed all the rigging and fittings on the ship as well as the merchandise on board which included India baft, laced hats, scarlet cloth, handkerchieves, knives, beads, coral, combs, guns as well as a "prime girl slave" (there was no mention of any other slaves on board), a lioness and "an indifferent old French mare". The British Government eventually decided that *la Grue*'s owner, Joseph Lodin de Mauvoir, should be compensated £4,106 and ten shillings including £1000 for the expenses he had occurred in presenting his claim, though he had to wait until 1786 to receive his money.[246]

With the British Government nervous about the prospect of the French joining the American Colonies in their War of Independence they decided to replace MacNamara, who was ordered to return home to face the charges made against him. In addition to complaints from the French Ambassador,[247] these included complaints from merchants who compared MacNamara unfavourably with his predecessor. A Memorial submitted by James Mather and twenty other "Merchants and Other Adventurers of London in the trade to Senegal" stated that trade was "free, secure and unmolested" under Charles O'Hara but that they had been treated by MacNamara "with the utmost cruelty, tyranny and oppression" and accused MacNamara

---

244 Letter from M de Noailles, dated 5 November 1776, CO 267/6.
245 Inventory dated 2 May 1777, CO 267/6.
246 Journal of the House of Commons, Volume 41, 10 May, p 785 and Resolutions of the Committee of Supply, General Index Volumes XXXV to Volume XLV under Supply, entry 228.
247 Lord Germain to MacNamara of 5 February 1777, CO 268/3.

of carrying "a considerable trade, contrary to his duties" exporting slaves to Albreda.[248]

Nevertheless, MacNamara had his supporters, particularly among the locals. Some of these submitted an Address to the King thanking him for his "bounty and goodness" in removing Charles O'Hara for his "arbitrary, oppressive and unjust behaviour", applauding the appointment of MacNamara "to whom we are bound by the most boundless gratitude for his most humane and tender behaviour"; and lamenting his departure and the charges against him which they found most unjust.[249]

Fortunately, there never seems to have been any suggestion that MacNamara should permanently replace O'Hara. Instead, they appointed John Clarke[250] who had earlier served in Saint-Louis under O'Hara. Clarke's instructions[251] were not markedly different to those given to O'Hara, though the fact that MacNamara had upset the French, English and Africans, and concern that the French might seek to avenge their loss in the Seven Years War by supporting the US against the British in the American War of Independence, no doubt influenced the additional responsibility given to him by Lord Germain. Writing to him about the evident state of disorder of the Province Germain told Clarke[252] that "it will therefore be your Duty to apply your utmost diligence to remove every just ground of uneasiness or discontent among His Majesty's subjects, or the natives, and to cultivate a friendly and cordial correspondence with the commanding officers of the neighbouring European settlements, but you will at the same time be extremely careful to keep a watchful eye over their conduct and suffer no encroachment to be made on

---

248 Memorial of James Mather and twenty others, dated 19 September 1776, CO 267/2.
249 Address to the King from "the Natives and Inhabitants of Senegal", 17 November 1777, signed by the Mayor of Saint-Louis and 34 others.
250 Note to King George III from the Board of Trade (Lord Germain, Bamber Gascoyne, William Eden and Whitshed Keane) with draft Commission, 13 September 1776, CO 268/2.
251 Submission from the Board of Trade (Soame Jenyns, Whitshed Keene, Charles Greville and William Eden) to King George III, 26 November 1776, CO 268/2.
252 Lord Germain to Clarke, 5 February 1777, CO 267/12.

His Majesty's rights without remonstrating against it in the strongest possible terms".

Clarke arrived at Saint-Louis on 8 April, 1777. He was the most diligent and competent of Senegambia's three governors. But he was also the shortest-lived dying, most probably of yellow fever, on 18 August 1778. On arrival Clarke discovered the colony to be in complete disorder. Reporting back to London[253] he said how he had "found matters so circumstanced that they could not have continued in the same situation much longer without some fatal consequence: licentiousness and a total lack of discipline among the soldiers; public embezzlement openly encouraged – every necessary institution, civil or military neglected – in short equal disorder in every department and the natives themselves much altered for the worse by the bad examples constantly before their eyes"

Soon after his arrival[254] he instigated an Enquiry, before the Council, into the allegations made by MacNamara against Wall.[255] These numbered twenty-five and included insubordination (including a threat to sever MacNamara's head from his shoulders), dereliction of duty, embezzlement and the conducting of private trade. The enquiry opened on 2 June 1777 with Wall conducting his own defence and MacNamara, who had refused to return home,[256] also present. On 30 July, the Council concluded that the charges against Wall were "frivolous, groundless and vexatious"[257] and acquitted him, awarding damages[258] amounting to £1527.14s.6d.

MacNamara was subsequently detained on a charge of subornation of perjury at the request of his creditors to whom he was in considerable debt.[259] He also faced charges levelled against him by

---

253 Letter from Clarke to Richard Cumberland, Secretary to the Board of Trade of 26 July 1777, CO 267/3.
254 Ibid.
255 Memorial from MacNamara to Governor Clarke of 2 June 1777 with 25 Articles setting out complaints against Wall, CO 267/3.
256 According to MacNamara, Clarke despatched the Weymouth Packet, the ship on which he arrived, before MacNamara had time to board it.
257 CO 270/1, according to Gray.
258 Memorial of Edward Morse, 28 February 1778, CO 267/4.
259 Clarke to Lord Germain of 7 July 1777.

the Merchants in England trading to Senegal to which he was asked to prepare his defence.[260]

Three charges were levelled against MacNamara.[261]

- That he assumed a power of raising money from the inhabitants and levied heavy fines.
- That he cruelly treated several masters of vessels and men of respectable character engaged in trade.[262]
- That he engaged in private trade, specifically that he traded with the French at Albreda.

The Board of Trade, who conducted the investigation, reported to the King[263] that MacNamara had come up with various explanations for why he had traded privately in slaves. MacNamara claimed that he had had to trade slaves in order to raise money to buy provisions for the garrison which, on arrival, he had found lacking (the loss of a ship with supplies on the bar at Saint-Louis may have given him some hope this excuse would be accepted). He also said that he had bought slaves, on his own account, to reinforce the garrison, pending approval to do so from London and that when that approval had not been forthcoming, he had been forced to sell them.

The Board of Trade rejected these explanations as implausible and recommended to the King that MacNamara be dismissed as Lieutenant Governor at James Island. The King approved this recommendation[264] and subsequently Joseph Wall – who was never to take up the

---

260 Letter from the Board of Trade (Bamber Gascoyne, Robert Spencer, Whitshed Keene and Charles Greville) to MacNamara, 11 November 1776, CO 268/2.
261 Report on charges against MacNamara, 31 March 1778, CO 268/2.
262 One complainant was William Nicholson, the local agent of Robert Browne who had the contract for provisioning the garrison. In addition to accusing MacNamara of obstructing his business he claimed that he was "at sundry times cruelly kicked, pulled by the Nose and otherwise personally ill-used" by MacNamara who also abused him "in the most scurrilous and vilifying language". He allegedly called Nicholson a rascal, a scoundrel and a villain. CO 267/3
263 Letter from the Board of Trade to King George III, 3 March 1778
264 MacNamara appealed the decision but this was rejected and he was informed of his dismissal in a letter from Lord Germain of 20 August 1778, CO 268/3

post – was appointed in his place. In informing Clarke[265] of Wall's appointment Lord Germain said how "the most ample testimonies of Captain Wall's good services and abilities, as an Officer, particularly when in the West Indies, seems very fully to justify his appointment". Given the infamy Wall was later to acquire it is reasonable to believe Germain would come to regret this ringing endorsement.

MacNamara, presumably in revenge, in turn accused Clarke of malpractice. On 7 April 1778, the Board of Trade wrote to Clarke[266] enclosing petitions against him by MacNamara and four of his close associates[267] requesting him to prepare his defence.

Governance of the province was of sufficient concern that Lord Germain wrote to Governor Clarke on 28 August 1778 – ten days after his death, news of which had yet of course to reach London – to inform him that the condition of the province, in particular its finances and the use of its armed sloop, was to come under Parliamentary consideration in the following session.[268] While there was good reason for Parliament to be concerned – and not before time – Clarke himself appears to have done his best, during his short tenure, to bring order to the affairs of the province.

As we have seen the Council, to which London attached so much importance, appears never to have been properly constituted during O'Hara's ten-year governorship. Under MacNamara the Council met four times in 1776, though he appears to have used the meetings to serve his own ends. Presumably as part of the investigation into his behaviour four members of the Council signed a declaration saying that under MacNamara "we never had the power therein we were entitled to, or ever had a free voice during the whole time of his being President thereof but were constrained by threats, personal

---

265 Lord Germain to Governor Clarke, 28 August 1778, CO 268/3
266 Letter from the Board of Trade (Soame Jenyns, Robert Spencer and Thomas de Grey) of 7 April 1778, CO 268/2
267 Francis MacNamara, Thomas Wallace, Thomas Sharpless and Benjamin Duley, CO 268/2,
268 Lord Germain to Clarke of 28 August 1778, CO 267/17.

abuses and severe contradictions to every proposal we made...".[269] Two of the four Council meetings MacNamara chaired related to the petitions which MacNamara had instigated against O'Hara and two were held to pass ordinances compensating people dispossessed of their properties by O'Hara. These ordinances were not approved by the King and had to be revoked.[270]

Under Clarke however things were different. The Council met nineteen times between his arrival on 8 April 1777, and July of the same year.[271] And whereas MacNamara used the Council to pursue his vendettas, under Clarke it addressed diverse administrative matters including trade with Gorée (still held by the French), rules governing visiting ships, debts among the black populations and restrictions on the amount of time visiting marabouts were allowed to spend on the island (forty-eight hours).

Notwithstanding the parlous state in which he found the colony Clarke remained optimistic that something could be made of the place.[272] Like others before him however he thought there would be more chance of success if the French were to be removed from Gorée. "In the hands of the French" he wrote to Lord Germain[273] "the trade of the province was very considerable and they still look upon it with a jealous eye. But Gorée by its natural situation is such a thorn in our side as to prevent its thriving, as it otherwise would, and is of such consequence that I will venture to assure your Lordship that in any case of Misunderstanding with France the only way to save this Province would be to take Gorée immediately, which might be easily affected, if unprepared, by two or three ships of war".

Although gum remained the commodity of most importance to

---

269 Declaration, dated 19 July 1777, signed by William Bishop, William Lacy, Henry Mallard and one other. However it should be noted that three of these signatories also signed a Declaration from the Council Chambers to the King, dated 4 December 1776 describing MacNamara as "a most loyal prudent and courageous commander", CO 267/3.
270 CO 268/2.
271 CO 268/2.
272 "I cannot but think the situation to be retrievable" he wrote in a letter to Lord George Germain on 12 September 1777, CO 267/3.
273 Ibid

the English at Saint-Louis, and the reason the French were so keen to regain control, slaves also offered lucrative business and Clarke took steps to ensure that business was not diverted to the French at Gorée. Clarke commented on arrival that he "found a new Trade of carrying slaves to Gorée by land, openly practised and encouraged, but I put a stop to it."[274] On 13 May 1778, by which time France and Britain were again at war, France having formally recognised the United States in February of that year, Royal Approval was given to an Act "to prevent the sale and delivery of Negroes exported from His Majesty's Province of Senegambia in Africa to any foreign part and to oblige Masters of Vessels to deliver their cargo of Negroes exported from Her Majesty's Province of Senegambia in Africa in some English port or place in the West Indies or elsewhere."[275]

Although the Province's budget had remained largely flat – an increase of £100 to £5650 was approved for 1779 to reflect the appointment of a Provost Marshall, a position created by MacNamara to provide employment for his brother Francis – London were looking for savings to help fund the war in America.[276] The total estimated annual cost of maintaining the Senegambia was about £20,000. In addition to the annual budget directly attributed to the province (which as we have seen hovered around £5500 for most of Senegambia's existence) the cost of the military establishment, victualling and "contingencies" each cost about £4-5,000 a year.

By way of example goods sent to Governor Clarke in 1778 for the payment of "duties, presents and contingencies"[277] included 1000 Mexican dollars, 550 pieces of blue long cloth, sixty-five yards of scarlet cloth, 1600 gallons of brandy, similarly prodigious quantities of wine, eight tonnes of iron as well as quantities of sugar, molasses, coral, amber, agate and beads. He also received 200 kegs, each thirty hundredweight, of gunpowder.

---

274 Letter from Clarke to Richard Cumberland, Secretary to the Board of Trade of 26 July 1777 CO 267/3.
275 CO 268/3.
276 CO 268/2.
277 CO 268/3.

Germain informed Clarke that the aim was to reduce the cost of the Province to about £14,000 by removing the element for contingencies and cutting the cost of victualling the garrison to £3,000.[278] Though there was no suggestion that he personally was at fault, Clarke was warned that there needed to be tighter controls of rations, his predecessors having considerably expanded the list of those eligible to receive them. Germain had earlier informed Clarke[279] of plans to abolish the position of Secretary for Moorish Affairs it "never having been found of any use".

Having still not received the news of his death Lord Germain continued to write to Clarke through October. The absence of correspondence from Clarke would not have unduly concerned London. They were used to it. In a letter written on 10 October 1778[280] Germain expressed regret that letters from Clarke had been lost when an English ship had been seized by the French and that they had not as a result heard anything from him since 12 September 1777. Germain said that he kept himself up to date on events in the Senegambia by talking to merchants, but clearly news of Clarke's death took several months to filter back to London.

While London were trying to make savings, they were also looking to invest in the security of the province now that England and France were again at war. In mid-October 1778, Germain wrote to Clarke[281] to instruct him to buy fifty male and twenty female slaves at a cost of £1,100 in order to make improvements to six forts. The slaves were to be paid at a monthly rate of 15s 3d to 18s 9d for men (with a few receiving 20 shillings), 11s 3d for women and 1s 10 ½ d for children.

In 1778, the garrison at Saint-Louis was hit by a yellow fever epidemic that killed off half the European population including, as we have seen, Governor Clarke.[282] Fevers were commonplace during the

---

278 Lord Germain to Clarke of 10 October 1778, CO 268/3.
279 Lord Germain to Clarke of 28 August 1778, CO 268/3.
280 Lord Germain to Clarke of 10 October 1778, CO 268/3.
281 Lord Germain to Clarke of 16 October 1778. CO 268/3.
282 Curtin raises the possibility that that year's deaths could have been malaria-related since at that time many fevers were loosely described as "yellow fevers".

rainy season, their severity deemed to be linked to the heaviness of the rains. An English doctor based in Saint-Louis in the second half of the 1770s, John Peter Schotte, was to write an account of the epidemic of 1778,[283] prefaced by a meteorological journal. He recorded that:

> "During the first rainy season, that I resided there, viz in the year 1775, when the rains were pretty heavy and frequent, many were seized with the bilious fever, which in some few was attended with very bad symptoms, and might be called, from the yellow colour, which it induced on the skin, yellow fever. The next year, viz 1776, we had but a few showers of rain, and they fell at intervals of many days; for which reason the season was remarkably favourable, and passed over without occasioning any mortality. In the year 1777 the rains were not quite so heavy as in the year 1775, and, therefore, the fevers were milder, but in the year 1778 the rains set in early, they were frequent and heavy, and continued for a long time; in consequence of which the island became partly overflowed, and the very dreadful disease… made its appearance."

According to Schotte the garrison had been remarkably healthy in July 1778. At the time, the white population of the island numbered ninety-two. By the time the French seized the island back on 28 January 1779 only thirty-three were left, eight of whom were essentially bed-ridden. Transmission of the disease was intense with most victims dying within four or five days. Four Europeans "died on the 23rd of August, four on the 26th, three on the 27th, five on the 5th of September, and there was hardly a day between the 9th of August, and the 18th September, without one or two."[284]

On Clarke's death Ensign Fall took up command and sent a message to William Lacy, in charge at James Island, to inform him of the Governor's death. Lacy ordered Fall to give the command to a

---

283 Schotte, J.P A Treatise on the Synochus Atrabilosa, a Contagious Fever which raged at Senegal in the year 1778, pp. 36-37.
284 Schotte, p.41.

Lieutenant Stanton but Fall refused. In January 1779, Fall came into conflict with some of the garrison, they shut him out of the fort, and Lieutenant Stanton assumed command. A murderous confrontation ensued within the garrison between those who supported Fall and those who preferred Stanton. Afterwards what was left of the garrison got drunk, mutinied and fired on the African population killing eight or nine of them. Schotte, who was there at the time, later wrote that the African population were so incensed that they would probably have massacred the remaining white population had the French not arrived two days later.[285]

The French had gone to the effort of assembling a sizeable squadron commanded by the Marquis de Vaudrevil and a land force commanded by the Duc de Lauzun to take Saint-Louis. They needn't have bothered. They met little resistance and took over Saint-Louis on 30 January 1779. By one account by the time of the French attack the British had just one bed-ridden officer and thirty-one men.[286] Soon after it was the turn of the French at Gorée to be decimated by yellow fever. Sixty out of ninety Europeans died and the rest were evacuated to Saint-Louis, then clear of the disease. The disease however was to return to Saint-Louis – only 180 of de Lauzun's battalion of 600 men were to survive. With the majority of the civilian population evacuated from Gorée the French left just a small contingent of soldiers – about twenty – to guard it. The French fleet continued on to the Gambia River, soon taking possession of James Island and razing the fort to the ground.

Aware that Gorée was poorly defended the English made plans to seize it back. Lord MacLeod, shortly to embark with his troops for the East Indies was given additional "secret instructions"[287] to "reduce and take possession of" Gorée en route and to leave four companies of the 75th Foot/Prince of Wales Regiment and a detachment of artillery to defend it. MacLeod embarked on a fleet commanded by Rear Admiral

---

285 Ibid, p. 168.
286 Maillat, p.42.
287 Secret instructions to Lord MacLeod, 9 December 1778, CO 267/12 (also in CO 267/6).

Sir Edward Hughes and arrived off Gorée on 8 May 1779. There he found a handful of French troops and four small vessels laden with guns, stores and brandy, which he seized.[288] Having successfully executed his additional instructions MacLeod continued on his original mission to the East Indies, acting under his Commission to appoint a governor for Gorée by the name of Lieutenant Colonel Rooke.[289]

According to Daniel Houghton, appointed fort-major of Gorée by Rooke, the garrison struggled to establish itself due to disease. Four hundred men had remained behind in May after Lord MacLeod's departure. By August a hundred of these had died and of the rest only a hundred were fit for duty.[290] Houghton's answer was to train up Africans to do the job, "on the same plans as the seapoys are in India". Africans, he argued, were better seasoned to the climate. "They are a hardy, strong nation and bear much fatigue which a European in this climate cannot". This bravery "only wants British discipline". He recommended that they be brought in from further afield, venturing that if they were well-treated and given good food they would soon forget their home. He suggested a salary of twenty guineas a man, a "trifling" expense in comparison with the cost of European troops. A day after Houghton wrote his letter Lieutenant Colonel Rooke was writing his own back to London informing them that he was returning home for health reasons and that he had left Captain George Herbert Adams as Lieutenant Governor in his absence.[291]

In November 1779, the French attempted to retake Gorée though strangely the garrison do not appear to have reported this until March the following year.[292] They then reported that three French warships had anchored off Gorée on 13 November. There had been an exchange of fire over three hours – English guns were outnumbered fifty-two to

---

288 MacLeod to Lord Germain of 10 May 1779, CO 268/4. In this same letter MacLeod refers to a sketch of Gorée, enclosed with his letter, "taken by Mr Hodges, the same ingenious gentleman that accompanied Captain Cook in his discoveries of (Tahiti)."
289 Annual Register vol 23 page 11.
290 Letter from Daniel Houghton, 14 August 1779 to Lord Germain, CO 268/4.
291 Letter from Rooke, 15 August 1779 to Lord Germain, CO 268/4
292 Letter from Lieutenant Winter to Lord Germain of 1 March 1780 and from Captain Adams to Lord Germain of 10 March 1780, CO 268/4

three – at the end of which three English soldiers were dead, two of them killed in an accident when the gun they were loading exploded. In addition, three Africans were wounded, "several… having voluntarily offered their services with the Batteries, and behaved with uncommon spirit". From their letters it appears that in the ten months since Lord Macleod seized the island neither Rooke nor Adams had received any instructions from London. They also complained of being about to run out of stores though later in March a ship was to arrive bringing flour, wine and brandy.[293] They happily unloaded the ship and got on with life, enclosing the front part of the hill on Gorée and erecting batteries on the back.

At this point, Joseph Wall reappears on the scene. Appointed Lieutenant Governor at James Island on the dismissal of MacNamara he had not yet left England when James Island was lost to the French. After Gorée had again fallen into English hands in May 1779 Lord George Germain, Secretary of State for the Colonies, decided to appoint Wall as Governor of Gorée.

Wall arrived at Gorée in early July 1780 and anchored offshore.[294] Adams, it seems, was reluctant to cede his place[295] on the basis that he had received no instructions to that effect (or indeed any instructions at all), precipitating an angry exchange of threatening letters between the two men. The stand-off lasted a good two months. On 25 August, around sixty of the garrison even tried to seize one of the transport ships carrying Wall's men by force of arms.[296] Tired of waiting Wall prepared to sail away to Saint-Louis, which he had been instructed to retake. But as he did so he spotted Adams making a run for it on a couple of private ships with everything he could take from Gorée, including ordinance and stores. Wall captured Adams, took him back to Gorée, and had him court-martialled (for which he was later

---

293  Letter from Adams to Lord Germain of 21 April 1780, CO 268/4
294  Adams to Lord Germain of 10 August 1780, Wall to Lord Germain of 17 July, CO 268/4.
295  Wall to Lord Germain of 22 August 1780, CO 268/4.
296  Wall to Lord Germain of 6 October 1780, CO 26/4.

reprimanded,[297] not having the authority to do so). Having settled in, Wall sent off a wish-list to London. He requested that a house be built for the Commanding Officer (i.e. himself), and also asked to be supplied with a seventy ton vessel that could be used to ferry supplies between Gorée and further down the coast, two or three others smaller boats and furniture for the government house.[298] In a later letter, Wall reports that some of the mixed-race and free Africans on the island had petitioned him for the same liberty to trade as the English merchants "yet they have refused to take the oath of allegiance to his Majesty or bear arms as required to do."[299] Meanwhile Wall was being told to reduce his budget (other papers suggest that he was under suspicion for falsifying accounts and inflating costs)[300] and to "banish all notions of a government or civil establishment and think [rather] of what is fitting for a garrison of 200 men."[301] With US and French troops joining forces against the British Army in North America, leading a few months later to the surrender of British forces, led by the now Brigadier General Charles O'Hara, at Yorktown on 17 October, it is perhaps not surprising that the authorities in London were thinking less of investing in Gorée as a colony for the long-term and more of keeping it defendable in the short-term against any French attack. Had Lord Germain already been anticipating the defeat of British forces in America he may also have assumed that it wouldn't be long until they would be returning Gorée to the French.

The rainy season in 1780 was particularly sickly with over 100 deaths on the island. The French at Saint-Louis suffered even worse, which contributed to high rates of desertion. At one point, over thirty French deserters were encamped on the mainland trying to get to Gorée. According to Wall[302] it was difficult for these men to get the locals to take them to Gorée as the French had offered a reward for

---

297 Letter from Lord Germain to Wall of 30 May 1781, CO 268/3
298 Letter from Wall, 6 October 1780, CO 268/4.
299 Letter from Wall to Lord Germain of 3 July 1781, CO 268/4.
300 CO 267/7.
301 Letter from Lord Germain to Wall of 30 May 1781, CO 268/3.
302 Letter from Wall to Lord Germain of 3 July 1781, CO 267/20 (also).

their return. Although Wall had been acquitted of the charges levelled against him by MacNamara he had been an unduly severe commander at Fort James and had been unpopular with his men. Wall's ten-month incarceration on James Island by MacNamara appears to have affected him considerably and as time passed his reputation for cruelty gained ground. On his voyage out to Gorée Wall ordered one of the convict-soldiers to be flogged. The man died from his wounds and it is said that witnessing his brother's cruelty, contributed to the death of Patrick Wall soon after their arrival at Gorée.[303] Wall was also involved in a controversial incident in 1781, when he was required to resolve a dispute between two officers on a Gold Coast bound boat that had called in at Gorée. He recommended a duel – generally not fatal by the 1780s – but one participant was mortally shot.

But Wall's real notoriety dates from the following year. On 11 July 1782, the day of Wall's departure on leave, the soldiers gathered to be paid. Some demanded Wall also pay what they were owed by his predecessor. If the troops were in rebellious mood it was hardly surprising. As well as not being paid, the conditions in which they lived had deteriorated considerably. Wall himself had earlier reported back that they were on two thirds rations of beef and the wine had turned sour and was only fit for vinegar. And they had no bedding of any kind.[304] Faced with this demand for pay Wall identified Sergeant Benjamin Armstrong as a troublemaker and ordered him to be tied to a gun carriage and given 800 lashes. Over the next couple of days six others received similar punishments, inflicted by slaves with a one and a quarter-inch rope. Armstrong, Captain Thomas Upton and Private George Paterson died from their wounds. One man present recalled that "during the flogging of these poor unhappy Men their Flesh was torn off by the Ropes & flew about in large pieces and a great part of it stuck [to my clothes]". [305]

---

303 An Authentic Narrative of the Life of Joseph Wall by a military gentleman.
304 Letter from Wall, from London, dated 26 August 1782, enclosing the return from Gorée of 11 July 1782, the day of his departure from the island..
305 Christopher, A Merciless Place, p. 221.

Charges were brought against Wall on his return to England[306] but were subsequently dropped when a ship with many of the witnesses to appear at the court martial was lost. A new arrest warrant was issued a short while later, but Wall managed to escape from those sent to arrest him and fled to Europe, only returning in 1797. It was not until 1802 that he was brought to trial. He was found guilty, sentenced to death and executed by hanging on 28 January 1802. The Newgate Calendar, a monthly bulletin of executions, and a popular read in the eighteenth century records how "from the knot of the rope turning round to the back of the neck, and his legs not being pulled, at his particular request, he was suspended in convulsive agony for more than a quarter of an hour".

Few of those who served under Wall will have lamented his fate. One of his lieutenants, Thomas Poplette wrote to Lord Shelburne[307] about the floggings and other abuses of power by Wall adding that "there is not a person, black, white or brown that does not abhor his name and character". Although it is clear from the same letter that Poplette was looking to replace Wall as governor he seems to have had little need to exaggerate Wall's crimes.

Several months before Armstrong's murder Poplette had also written to Daniel Houghton, the former fort-major of Gorée, of Wall's "villainous conduct" and the murderous and abusive environment that prevailed. He accused Wall of allowing prisoners to starve to death, of not paying the soldiers with money and selling to them at extravagant prices. He concluded his letter with the belief that "our inquisition here exceeds, for perfidy and cruelty, any ever known in Spain."[308] Houghton had an even longer list of grievances,[309] accusing Wall of false accounting, of selling government property for his personal gain, of terrible punishments meted out on both soldiers and local inhabitants, of

---

306 Having been asked by the King on 27 July to consider a response to the allegations against Wall the Privy Council decided the following day that he should be arrested to face charges, PC 1/16.
307 Letter from Poplette to Lord Shelburne of 1 August 1782, folio 230, CO 267/20.
308 Letter from Poplette to Houghton of 7 April 1782 folio, 373, CO 267/20.
309 Folio 367, undated, CO 267/20.

defrauding the soldiers of pay or paying them with drink, of neglecting the sick, antagonising local kings, plundering captured ships, allowing the French authorities from Saint-Louis to freely roam the island and of misrepresenting what was happening in the settlement in his reports to London. A petition signed by five deserters[310] – two of whom were subsequently hung – said that they had not been paid in money since they arrived in Gorée but instead in goods "such as beads, powder, bale, flints, brandy, wine, kettles, snuffboxes, looking glasses and Gambia soap, for which he makes his own price as he pleases."

However brutal Wall's administration may have been, there were nevertheless those in the region who preferred to see the British in control rather than the French. Alicorie, King of the Trarza Moors, wrote to King George III in 1782 inviting him to retake Senegal and promising 5000 men in support.[311] There was no appetite in London however to invest in recovering Saint-Louis, nor it seems in consolidating their presence in Gorée.[312]

Early in 1783, Captain Lacy, now in charge at Gorée, informed London that the settlement had no salt or any merchandise to purchase fresh supplies and were "obliged to beg from the offspring of the French".[313] It's fair to say that Lacy did not appear to enjoy his posting. It would be hard to surpass the brevity and succinctness of his letter to the Prime Minister, Lord Shelburne, of 2 December 1782. "Dear Lord", it read, "I beg leave to acquaint you that this island is in the greatest distress in every department. The European feels nothing but want in so inhospitable a climate. I have the honour to be my Lord your Lordships most obedient humble servant."[314] That was all it said and for Lacy, one imagines, it said it all.

Britain's brief occupation of Gorée at the beginning of the 1780s was notable too for a decision that was arguably decisive both for the

---

310 Petition of 19 March 1782 folio 361, CO 267/20.
311 Letter forwarded to Colonial Office on 10 October 1782, CO 267/20.
312 Presumably because they knew they would soon be returning Gorée to the French –a preliminary draft of the eventual Treaties of Versailles had been signed in Versailles on 20 January 1783.
313 Lacy to Lord Shelburne of 25 February 1783, CO 267/20.
314 Lacy to Lord Shelburne of 2 December 1782, CO 267/20.

development of Gorée as a town and for the development of the narrative that has led Gorée to be one of the most famous examples of a slave post in West Africa. Before the British occupation it was not allowed for houses to be built directly on the seafront. Largely for security reasons houses were set back with a strip of open land between them and the coast. French maps[315] produced when Gorée was once more under French occupation indicate areas of land "given up" by the British, i.e. made available for construction, with a distinction made between land that had already been built upon, and areas where construction had yet to take place. Gorée's most famous building, the House of Slaves, with the much photographed "Door of No Return" giving directly onto the sea was most likely built during this period of British occupation.

A Peace Treaty signed at Paris on 3 September 1783 between Great Britain and the United States of America brought an end to the American War of Independence with defeat for Britain. The same day a further Treaty, known as the Treaty of Versailles, was signed between Britain and the USA's ally in the war, France. Under Article 9 "the King of Great Britain cedes in full right, and guaranties to His Most Christian Majesty, the river Senegal and its dependencies, with the forts of St. Louis, Podor, Galam, Arguin and Portendic and His Britannic Majesty restores to France the island of Gorée, which shall be delivered up in the condition it was in when the conquest of it was made". In return, the British recovered possession of Fort James and the Gambia River. Under the same treaty the two Governments also agreed to appoint commissioners to be "charged with the settling and fixing of the boundaries of their respective possessions". I have seen no evidence that such work was carried out and the boundaries between Senegal and Gambia were not fixed for another hundred years (see Chapter 12).

Several months before the Treaty of Versailles was signed Lacy received a letter[316] to inform him that it was the King's intention to

---

315 Plan de L'Ile de Gorée levé lors de la prise de possession, par M. le Marquis de Lajaille, Lieutenant de Vaisseau, Commandant de la Corvete la Bayonnaise, 25 March 1784 in Durand, Jean-Baptiste Léonard, Atlas pour server au voyage du Senegal 1802 (Royal Society).
316 Letter to Lacy (sender not known) of 3 June 1783, CO 267/20.

restore Gorée to France, that a Captain Wilson would soon arrive on a sloop called HMS *Racehorse* and that Lacy should hand over command of the island to Wilson who would have the responsibility to hand it over to the French. Lacy was also commanded "to give strict instructions to the officers and men under your command that they do not wantonly deface or destroy any of the fortifications, buildings or stores" and that any soldiers sentenced to serve on the coast of Africa for a given period, or for the rest of their lives, should not return with him to England but be left with Wilson who would arrange for them to be sent to Cape Castle on the Gold Coast. Lacy replied[317] to confirm that he would act on these instructions, but was clearly irritated that a navy man should be entrusted to hand over an island that for so long had been under the command of the army.

The 1783 Treaty of Versailles also provided for Britain to be allowed to conduct trade in gum from the mouth of the river St. John (in today's Liberia) north to the bay and fort of Portendic provided that they did not establish a permanent settlement of any kind in the river St. John, on the coast or in the bay of Portendic. This was an important article for the English. In 1777, when Saint-Louis was still under English control, gum arabic was sold in London at between £30 and £35 a tonne. By 1782, when Saint-Louis was again in French hands the price had risen to over £240 a tonne.[318] The French however never had any intention of allowing the British to participate in the gum trade. On 2 May 1785 Durand, the Director-General of the Compagnie du Senegal signed a Treaty[319] with the marabouts of Armankour, under article 1 of which the marabouts "out of the particular affection they had and would always retain for France"[320] promised to have no communication, direct or indirect with the English; and promised to do everything in their power to stop the English trading at Portendic, whether for gum or anything else. Under

---

317 Letter from Lacy (recipient not known) of 10 September 1783, CO 267/20.
318 Schotte, p.167.
319 Traité avec les Maraboux d'Armankour, au sujet de la gomme (held by Royal Society).
320 "par une suite de l'affection particuliere qu'ils ont et conserveront toujours pour les Francais."

Article 3 the marabouts promised to get as much gum as possible for the French company. Durand signed a similar agreement with the King of the Braknas eight days later and a third with the King of the Trarzas on 20 May 1785 – this one covering in addition to gum, slaves and ivory. French intentions were clear, they wanted a monopoly on the gum trade along the entire coast and up the Senegal River.

Before the end of 1783, in accordance with the Treaty of Versailles, both Gorée and Saint-Louis were back under the control of the French. The same year an Act of Parliament was passed[321] in the British Parliament returning Gambia to the Committee of the Company of Merchants Trading to Africa, thus bringing to an end the Crown colony of Senegambia.

The colony hadn't been a glorious success. A raft of reasons can be found for why this should have been the case. The province of Senegambia attracted very few settlers and never gained the critical mass that would have allowed the key components of the civil administration – notably the Council and judiciary – to function effectively. The climate was inhospitable with many soldiers and other visitors dying within months of their arrival. Leadership was lacking. O'Hara, Governor for ten years, and while not without some merit, was idle, corrupt and self-serving. Some of his successors – notably MacNamara and Wall – appear to have revelled in brutality and violence.

The authorities in London must also take their share of the blame, including for some terrible appointments. For the most part they showed only desultory interest in the first Crown colony in Africa, notwithstanding its supposed strategic location (though this view was not universally shared as we have seen) and its importance to the UK economy as a source of gum arabic and slaves. Lord Germain's view[322] that Senegambia was a settlement "from which little hitherto has resulted but embarrassments and complaints" was probably widely shared within government and among the political classes as a whole.

---

321  23 Geo III, c65.
322  Letter from Lord Germain to Governor Clarke of 28 August, CO 268/3.

Another factor that undoubtedly played a part in the woeful administration of the province, and the culture of drunkenness and violence that often prevailed, was the poor quality of the troops sent out to garrison the settlements. Many were convicts, sent out as soldiers to Senegambia instead of going to prison. In the early days prisoners were encouraged to volunteer in the Royal African Corps, in lieu of sentence. But as Africa's deadly reputation gained ground courts began to pardon convicts on condition of them serving there. Deserters were also sent to Senegal. The Annual Register in 1778 reports how a deserter, on the point of being executed, had his sentence commuted at the last minute to serving as a soldier until he died in Senegal.[323]

Dr Schotte was very clear that this policy was a mistake, arguing that "the present mode of sending convicts for soldiers to the island of Gorée does more harm to the English nation …than is generally imagined. These fellows continue to exercise their old villainous tricks, and if many or even a few of them are concerned in malpractices, the punishing of them may be attended with sedition and mutiny".

Schotte admitted, however, that some of the normal recruits were just as bad.[324] Convicts appear not to have been sent to Saint-Louis while he was there and nevertheless discipline deteriorated to the point of mutiny, leaving the province, already weakened by the plague, at the mercy of the French. Schotte was concerned at the reputational risk of sending convicts as soldiers, not least in terms of how the English were then seen by the local populations.

> "The blacks, who are neither so void of sense nor irrational, as they are imagined by many to be, are apt to judge of the English nation in general by those out-casts; for the greater part of them do not know, that they are sent there for horrid crimes. The soldiers themselves will certainly not reveal it, and

---

323 Emma Christopher p. 93.
324 The Duke of Wellington famously described his soldiers as "the scum of the earth" in 1813, the year before Waterloo, and in 1831 wrote that "English soldiers are fellows who have enlisted for drink".

it is not much to the honour of the officers who command them to declare it. On the other hand, those of the inhabitants, who know it, think themselves very hardly treated by the English government that they should send such wretches among them. To prevent, therefore, any false prejudices the natives may form and entertain of the English in general, to gain their affection, and to insure the possessions in that country, the sending of convicts there for soldiers should, in my opinion, be dropped by a nation deservedly ambitious of its good fame, laws and government."[325]

His concerns do not appear to have been shared by the Government. Indeed, towards the end of the 1770s the architects of Britain's penal policy began to take an interest in Senegal as a possible place to send criminals instead of incarcerating them at home. Sending convicted criminals abroad was a popular way of dealing with crime (if the crime did not warrant the gallows). It got the criminals out of the way. And they rarely came back. Convicts had been transported to the Americas since the beginning of the seventeenth century and by the 1770s over 50,000 criminals had been sent there.[326] Many had ended up working in plantations, where subsequently slave labour was to prove more popular among employers. For a while in states such as Virginia, African slaves and British convicts would stand side by side on the auction block and could end up working side by side in Virginia's tobacco fields. But there was increasing opposition among American colonists to the sending of convicts, who were blamed for committing crimes in America and sowing dissent among the slaves.

After the outbreak of the American Revolution it became harder to ship criminals to America and the practice ended in October 1775. Policymakers in London therefore started looking for a new destination. Captain James Cook had only set foot in Botany Bay five years earlier, in 1770, and prisoners were sent to Australia only from

---

325 Schotte, pp. 168-169.
326 Christopher p. 31.

1788. Attention in the meantime turned to Africa and the Crown colony of Senegambia with the Government giving serious thought to establishing a penal colony there. Podor was put forward as a possible location but ruled out on the grounds of health and vulnerability to attack. Gambia found favour, including with Lieutenant Governor MacNamara, with Bintan and Nyanimaru suggested as possible sites upriver. The plan was to acquire land on the river and to despatch 200 prisoners, with food and equipment, to fend for themselves. Guards would base themselves down the river to prevent escape.[327] For a while the scheme was put into action, with Lemain Island (later to become MacCarthy Island) bought as the site for the penal colony. But it was soon abandoned as other voices argued for the colony to be established on the Gold Coast instead. While Gorée was never used as a penal colony there is evidence of civilian prisoners, women as well as men, being abandoned there during the four years (1779-1783) the island was again under British control.[328] With food hard to come by even for the garrison some prisoners perished but a couple at least are known to have secured passage on ships back to Britain.

The brutality, corruption and licentiousness that often characterised the Crown colony of Senegambia was in stark contrast to the lofty aspirations of the Government in London that the colony should be governed in accordance with the rule of law and with the local populations treated in a fair and just manner.[329] Once the Governor arrived at his post however the distance and poor communication meant it was difficult for the centre to know whether their instructions were being followed. They were often reliant on the news they received from ships' captains who traded between British ports and Senegal, or who participated in the triangular transatlantic trade, and the news they received was invariably several weeks if not months out of date. What the history of the Province of Senegambia does show however is that London, despite these challenges, was

---

327 Christopher, Chapter 4.
328 Christopher p. 224.
329 To the extent that is possible in a territory where slavery exists and from where slaves were exported.

determined to hold governors accountable for their actions. Charges were brought against both O'Hara and MacNamara leading to their eventual dismissal. Even Clarke was required to prepare a defence against allegations made against him. Wall, was eventually brought to justice, convicted and hung for his crimes. Demonstrating that allegations of fraud and brutality would be investigated and crimes punished was one of the few ways the authorities could hope to exert any control over their man on the spot, who otherwise may have felt they could act with impunity.

## CHAPTER EIGHT

# IN SEARCH OF THE NIGER

Twelve years after Britain's departure from Gorée in 1783, a young Scotsman set out on arguably the most famous exploration by a Briton in West Africa. And while his starting point was the Gambia and Mali was his initial destination much of his arduous journey took place in Senegal.

It was from Pisania on the Gambia River that Mungo Park set off on horseback in search of the Niger. The year was 1795. At that time, very little was known in Europe about inland Africa, in contrast to the coast where the Portuguese, Spanish, Dutch, French and English had been trading, building forts and establishing settlements since the 1450s. European nations were also venturing inland via the main rivers. The British had established factories upriver on the Gambia River as had the French at Podor and Galam on the Senegal River, but beyond these main rivers the maps of Africa were short on detail, and what detail they had was often fairly speculative.

Several of the great and the good in London at the time considered that when so much was known about the world, more ought to be known about what many then called the Dark Continent. One of those was Sir Joseph Banks, a botanist who had accompanied Captain

Cook on the first of his three circumnavigations of the world[330] and was to hold the position of President of the Royal Society for forty years. Others included General Conway, a former politician and intimate of Charles O'Hara, the then Lord Rawdon (later Marquess of Hastings) who was to be appointed Governor-General of India in 1812 and Sir John Sinclair, a Scottish politician and financier who was the first President of the Board of Agriculture. They were twelve in total, eight of them Members of Parliament. In the beginning they met as an informal supper club, known as the Saturday's Club, three or four times a year. However, they came together in London on 9 June 1788 to pass a resolution:

> "That as no species of information is more ardently desired, or more generally useful, than that which improves the science of Geography; and as the vast Continent of Africa, notwithstanding the efforts of the Ancients, and the wishes of the Moderns, is still in a great measure unexplored, the Members of this Club do form themselves into an Association for Promoting the Discovery of the Inland Parts of that Quarter of the World."

Very soon the Africa Association, as it was better known, decided to focus its attention on the interior of West Africa, which in comparison with other parts of Africa remained largely unexplored. At the time the reading public were eagerly awaiting publication of Paterson's explorations in Southern Africa (his *A Narrative of Four Journeys in the Country of the Hottentots, and Caffraria* was published in 1789) and Bruce's *Travels to Discover the Source of the Nile*, an account of his travels in Ethiopia in 1769-1771 was published a year later.

In the 1780s, people knew of the existence of Timbuktu, an almost mythical city said to be full of gold and other riches, on the River Niger, and of Housa, capital of a great Empire further to the East. But no Westerner had ever been to either city and no one knew very much

---

330 1768-1771

at all about the Niger, including its source, its direction or where it flowed into the sea. Popular theories were that it ran from east to west, connecting with the Senegal and Gambia Rivers to flow into the sea. By way of example the Annual Register of 1758 which reported the successful seizure of Saint-Louis and Gorée included a footnote on the Senegal River,[331] the first part of which read as follows:

> "The river Senega, or Senegal, is one of those channels of the river Niger by which it is supposed to discharge its waters into the Artantic (sic) ocean: the river Niger, according to the best maps, rises in the east of Africa; and after a course of 300 miles, nearly due west, divides into three branches, the most northerly of which is the Senegal as above; the middle is the Gambia or Gambra; the most southern, Rio Grande."

Those who had the Niger River flowing east had the river petering out in the Sahara Desert.

The African Association, which was both motivated by a desire for scientific knowledge and to open up African markets for British goods therefore decided to finance expeditions to discover the Niger. Mungo Park was the fourth explorer selected for the task. The first, an American called John Ledyard, set foot in Africa at Cairo, fell ill and in an attempt to self-medicate, accidentally poisoned himself. This was a rather anticlimactic end for a man who had accompanied Cook on his last expedition (he was with him in Hawaii when Cook was killed) and attempted to walk across Siberia. The second, Simon Lewis, fared only marginally better. Having started his African journey at Tripoli he journeyed along the coast to Misrata before his guides abandoned him and he was forced to turn back. Lewis also had a noteworthy past. Son of a wine-merchant he was learning the family business in Cadiz when he was abducted at sea, spending three years as a slave in the Imperial Court of Morocco. He was to become Vice-Consul in Morocco and later Oriental Interpreter at the Court of St. James. A

---

331 Annual Register 1758, p. 75.

few years after his ill-fated trip in search of the Niger he returned to Tripoli as Consul, dying there in 1801.

In 1790 the Association decided the Niger should be approached from a new direction, via the Gambia River, and commissioned an Irish major in the British Army to lead the expedition. Major Daniel Houghton already had some experience of the region having served, as we have seen, as fort-major on the island of Gorée under the brutal Joseph Wall between 1779 and 1781. Back in London he wrote to General Conway, asking him to recommend him to the King "to the command of the province of Senegambia". He lamented that the province had not been effectively governed since the demise of Governor Clarke and that with his knowledge of the coast, its kings and languages he was the right man for the job.[332] It's unclear whether General Conway did recommend him for the job of Governor. But nine years on he and the other members of the African Association clearly thought that Houghton had the right skills to attempt to reach the Niger.

Houghton's instructions were to "ascertain the course, and if possible the rise and termination of that mysterious river [the Niger]; and after visiting the cities of Tombuctoo and Houssa, to return by the way of the Desert, or by any other route which the circumstances of his situation at the time should recommend to his choice."[333] The Honourable Gentlemen of the Association made it sound easy. Presumably they knew all too well that it wouldn't be.

Houghton set sail from England on 16 October 1790, arriving at the mouth of the Gambia River on 10 November. He was kindly received by the King of Barra and proceeded by river to Junkiconda, where he purchased a horse and five donkeys. He was fortunate to get wind of the fact that local traders, suspicious of his intentions and fearing loss of their trade, planned to kill him. He fled to the other side of the river – probably not easy with six animals in tow – and made his way along its southern bank before recrossing higher up, once

---

332 Houghton (from London) to General Conway of 7 August 1782, CO 267/7.
333 Proceedings of the Association for the Promotion of the Discovery of the Interior of Africa 1792.

he was opposite the Kingdom of Wooli. There he received a warm reception from the king in his capital of Medina. It is possible that the king's welcome to Houghton (and subsequently to Park) reflected a familiarity with white people. He would no doubt have met a few English traders from the nearby Gambia River and an Englishman by the name of Captain Littleton had recently lived there for four years, trading in wax and slaves.[334]

Houghton seems to have liked Medina, at least initially. He wrote, in a letter to his wife on 10 March 1791 "You may live here almost for nothing…ten pounds a year would support a whole family with plenty of fowls, sheep, eggs, butter, honey, bullocks, fish and all sorts of game". However, his comfort was to be short-lived as a fire broke out in Medina, destroying many of his possessions. His interpreter ran off with his horse and two donkeys. And a trade gun blew up in his hands, wounding him on the face and arms.[335]

Leaving Medina on 8 May Houghton, and his remaining two donkeys, journeyed from Wooli to Boundou with a slaver, reaching the border of Boundou five days later. On they travelled, crossing the dry river Falémé before reaching the border of the Kingdom of Bambouk. Houghton noted that while the chief occupations of the people of Bambouk were agriculture and livestock they were also adept at smelting iron ore, and using this to make both agricultural equipment and weapons. In a recent war, Boundou had got the better of Bambouk and the King of Boundou now controlled the area of Bambouk where Houghton had arrived. Houghton hastened to see him. Unfortunately, in contrast to the warm welcome he received from the King of Wooli, the reception he received from the King of Boundou was distinctly chilly.

The day after his arrival, and an awkward meeting with the king, the king's son visited Houghton at the house in which he was staying and helped himself to whatever, among Houghton's possessions, took his fancy. To Houghton's dismay this included a fine blue coat,

---

334 Hallet, p. 221.
335 Proceedings of the Association for the Promotion of the Discovery of the Interior of Africa 1792

which he had planned to wear for his meeting with the King of Timbuktu. Houghton had hoped to proceed swiftly on to Timbuktu but was delayed by his slaver guide who had to attend to some family business. He used the time to visit the defeated King of Bambouk in the town of Ferbanna. The king, who received him warmly, attributed his defeat to lack of ammunition. He explained that the French, who normally supplied him with ammunition, had abandoned Fort St. Joseph and had not sailed upriver for a while. His enemy, the King of Boundou, however had received a steady supply of arms from the British. Houghton set off from Bambouk towards the end of July having swapped his two donkeys for a horse.

Houghton's last correspondence back home was dated 24 July. But the very last that was heard of Captain Daniel Houghton was a pencilled note dated 1 September 1791 and sent, probably from the village of Simbing in Ludamar (in present day Mali), saying that he was "in good health on his way to Timbuctoo (but) robbed of all his goods" by the son of the local potentate.[336]

The circumstances of his death are unclear. The Association's own records[337] suggest that he died a natural death, probably from dysentery. They also suggest that Houghton brought upon his own death by ignoring the advice of friends who urged him to travel lightly and with no items of value. "The Major had encumbered himself with an assortment of bale goods, consisting of linens, scarlet cloth, cutlery, beads, amber and other merchandise, which presented to the immoral Negroes such temptations as savage virtue could not resist". They remained convinced that travels into the interior could be made successfully and that "a traveller of good temper and conciliating manners, who has nothing with him to tempt rapacity, may expect every assistance from the natives, and then fullest protection from their chiefs". Mungo Park, travelling through the region six years later, heard that Houghton had been robbed and either killed or left to die.

---

336 Proceedings of the Association for Promoting the Discovery of the Interior Parts of Africa, Volume II, page 5.
337 Ibid p. 6.

While Mungo Park is one of the most well-known British explorers, Houghton's name is known but to a few. Yet he had managed to penetrate deeper into the interior in this part of Africa than any European before him and it was he who established, through the information he collected, and passed back in his letters, that the Senegal River did not link up with the Niger and that the Niger flowed west to east.

We know a lot more about Mungo Park's journey for the simple reason that he made it back home. His *Travels in the Interior Districts of Africa performed under Direction and Patronage of the African Association in the years 1795, 1796 and 1797* was published in 1799 and constitutes the first detailed and reliable account of the experiences of a British traveller in inland Senegal.

Park was just twenty-three years old at the time of his appointment. He became known to Banks through his brother-in-law, who shared Bank's passion for botany. It was Banks who secured Park (who had studied medicine at Edinburgh University) the job of surgeon on an East India Company ship bound for Bencoolen (a British settlement in Indonesia later to be swapped in a deal with the Dutch[338] for the port of Malacca in present day Malaysia).

Park's instructions from the African Association were very similar to those given to Houghton. In his "Travels" he says that he was directed, on his arrival in Africa "to pass on to the river Niger, either by the way of Bambouk, or by such other route as should be found most convenient. That I should ascertain the course, and, if possible, the rise and termination of that river. That I should use my utmost exertions to visit the principal towns or cities in its neighbourhood, particularly Timbuctoo and Houssa; and that I should be afterwards at liberty to return to Europe, either by the way of the Gambia, or by such other route as, under all the then existing circumstances of my situation and prospects, should appear to me to be the most advisable."

Park sailed from Portsmouth on 22 May 1795, arriving in the Gambia on 21 June and reaching Pisania on 5 July. At Pisania he stayed

---

338 As part of the Anglo-Dutch treaty of 1824.

with a Dr Laidley, an English slave-trader who was one of three white residents of the village (the other two brothers by the name of Ainslee). He had intended to linger there a short while to learn Mandinka but ended up contracting severe fever and staying many months longer. It was only on 2 December 1795 that he finally set off from Pisania with an interpreter called Johnson,[339] a slave boy of Dr Laidley's, who was promised his freedom on his return, a horse and two donkeys. The Association having concluded that to carry lots of trade goods would invite robbery and death (one of the lessons learned from Houghton's expedition) Park, by his own account, travelled with little more than "a small assortment of beads, amber and tobacco".

It may have been later the same day that Park first entered Senegal. He refers to crossing the Walli Creek, probably a reference to the river Sandougou. The following day he was stopped by local people and asked either to accompany them to Peckaba[340] to present himself to the Mandinka King of Walli, or to pay customs to them. Four "bars" of tobacco secured his onward passage.[341] By 5 December they had reached Medina, the capital of the Kingdom of Wooli whose chief products, Park noted, were "cotton, tobacco and esculent vegetables"[342] with corn grown on the higher ground. His first encounter with a Senegalese ruler, appears to have gone rather well. The King of Wooli, by the name of Jatta, the same king it is said who met Houghton, gave permission for Park to travel through his country and prayed for his safety. By the following morning however the king, concerned for his safety, was encouraging him, unsuccessfully, not to go on.

Contrary to some of his predecessors Park's initial impression of the Mandinkas seems a generally positive one. He comments favourably on the system of government; a monarchy with circumscribed powers, taking the advice of a council of elders, based on Sharia law, noting that "in the forensic qualifications of procrastination and cavil, and

---

339 Johnson was to be paid 10 bars per month; with 5 bars a month for his wife in his absence and 2 prime slaves if he accompanied Park as far as Segou.
340 Presumably the modern day village of Pakeba Maka Sisse.
341 Park, *Travels in the Interior of Africa* (Wordsworth Classics), p. 30.
342 Ibid, p. 29.

the arts of confounding and perplexing a cause (local lawyers) are not always surpassed by the ablest pleaders in Europe". Mandinkas themselves he describes as being "of a mild, sociable and obliging disposition. The men are commonly above the middle size, well-shaped, strong and capable of enduring great labour; the women are good-natured, sprightly and agreeable."[343]

Later in his account, as he reflects back on his journey, he sums up the Mandinkas as "a very gentle race; cheerful in their dispositions, inquisitive, credulous, simple and fond of flattery."[344] He adds however, borne of bitter personal experience, especially in areas of modern-day Mali, that "perhaps the most prominent defect in their character was that insurmountable propensity which the reader must have observed to prevail in all classes of them, to steal from me the few effects I was possessed of". This however was the men. He hasn't a bad word to say about Mandinka women. "I do not recollect a single instance of hard-heartedness towards me in the women".

The villages Park says he passes through on those first few days – Kootacunda, Tabajang, Medina, Konjour, Malla and Kolor – bear little resemblance to the villages marked on a modern day map. He mentions spending the night of 9 December at "Tambacunda" but has no more to say about the town that was later, if indeed it is the same, to become an important town on the Dakar-Bamako railway and a post-Independence regional capital.

But even if the names of the villages do not survive into the modern day much of what he observed still does. Throughout his journey Park was witness to the beliefs and superstitions of the local populations, how they used fetishes and gris-gris to ward away evil spirits, and how these animist traditions and rituals, were retained even by those who had adopted Islam. In Konjour, he had to resolve a quarrel between two of his companions over who would keep the horns of the sheep they had had for supper. The horns were prized as containers for "keeping secure certain charms or amulets called

---

343 Ibid, p. 17.
344 Ibid, p. 242.

saphies".³⁴⁵ Saphies, Park explained, were bits of paper on which Imams had scribbled phrases from the Koran, and which protected the holder against danger.

Shortly after leaving Koojar (which he had reached via Kooniakary from Tambacunda) and entering the "wilderness that separates the kingdoms of Kooli and Bondou", one of his companions ensured that no harm would come to them on the way by spitting on a stone and throwing it on the path before them. "The same ceremony was repeated three times, after which the Negroes proceeded with the greatest confidence; every one being firmly persuaded that the stone… had carried with it everything that could induce superior powers to visit us with misfortune". ³⁴⁶

It was in Koojar, it seems, that Park first saw Senegalese wrestling. His short account may also be one of the first references to shea butter, whose moisturising powers are so much prized in the cosmetic industry today (though it is later in his journey, in the Bambara region of Mali, that he extols at length on the economic importance of trade in shea which he considered "of a richer flavour than the best butter I ever tasted made from cow's milk"). ³⁴⁷ Whereas Senegalese wrestlers today face each other on two feet Park notes how "Stripped of their clothing, except a short pair of drawers, and having their skin anointed with oil or shea butter, the combatants approached each other on all fours, parrying with and occasionally extending a hand for some time, till at length one of them sprang forward and caught his rival by the knee." He concludes that few Europeans would be a match for such wrestlers.

Park entered Boundou at Tallika where he encountered a small caravan "with five asses loaded with ivory."³⁴⁸ His journey across Boundou to its capital at Fatteconda was largely uneventful compared with the hardships and deprivation he was to endure later in his journey, in what is now Mali. From Tallika he continued to Ganado,

---

345 Ibid, p. 33.
346 Ibid, p. 37.
347 Ibid, p 187.
348 Ibid, p. 40.

crossed the Neriko River, reached Koorkarany ("a Mahometan town surrounded by a high wall"), and passed through the small villages of Dooggi, Buggil and Soobrudooka before arriving at the unmistakable landmark of the Falémé River. The next day (21 December) they crossed the river and entered Fatteconda.

In Fatteconda, Park was soon brought before the king, a man he understood to be pagan rather than Muslim. The king, based on his previous knowledge of white travellers, assumed Park to be a trader, interested in slaves or gold, and found it hard to believe that Park's motivation was one of discovery. Park clearly approached his meetings with the king with much apprehension knowing that the very same man "had acted towards Major Houghton with great unkindness". But some well-chosen gifts, including his umbrella which delighted the King, and the judicious surrendering of his only good coat, a blue one with appealing yellow buttons, appears to have won over the King to the point that he presented him on departure with five drachma of gold.

Unlike Walli and Wooli Boundou was sufficiently known to be included in the 1831 edition of Brooke's Gazetteer with its description as "an interior country of North Africa, lying between the rivers Senegal and Gambia, inhabited by the Foulah race of negroes, who are industrious and social in their habits, and Mahometans in religion."[349] Park describes Boundou as a place of trade, principally conducted by Mandinkas and Serahulis (or Serawoolies as he calls them). Salt, corn and indigo cloth appear to have been the main items traded.

Park describes the local people, the Foulahs (Peul), as being "naturally of a mild and gentle disposition, but the uncharitable maxims of the Koran have made them less hospitable to strangers, and more reserved in their behaviour than the Mandingoes."[350] Although the prejudice of his own Christian beliefs leads him to make some dismissive comments towards Islam, he is impressed both by the strength of the Foulahs' faith, and their tolerance towards

---

349  Brookes Gazetteer (London, 1831), p. 97.
350  Park, *Travels in the Interior of Africa* (Wordsworth Classics), p. 53.

non-believers. He comments favourably on the education system, the teaching of the Koran to young boys, on the hard-working nature of the Foulahs and upon their dairy farming skills, praising the excellence of their milk.

Mungo Park, according to his account, crossed the Senegal River at Kayes on 28 December 1795. Robbed, imprisoned for several months and weakened by sickness Park eventually reached the Niger River –as far as we know the first European to do so – on 21 July. He staggered on, making it as far Silla, two days short of Djenne before deciding to turn back, increasingly unsettled by the hostility of the Moors, and convinced that ill, destitute, and with the rains making travel ever more difficult, he would die attempting to go on.

Park owed his safe return to the coast to the hospitality of a slave trader, Karfa Taure, who offered to take Park with him when he next led a convoy of slaves to the Gambia River. Park arrived in Karfa's town of Kamalia, west of Bamako on 16 September 1796, staying there until the convoy set off on 19 April the following year. Karfa fed and watered Park for these seven months against a promised payment of the value of one slave that Park would get on credit from Dr Laidley, against a draft from the Association.

While in Kamalia Park drew up notes on the gold and ivory trade that was widespread at that time. He describes in meticulous detail the techniques used by the women – for the role fell to them – for gold-washing and how "the gold-dust is kept in quills, stopped up with cotton: and the washers are fond of displaying a number of these quills in their hair."[351]

Gold appears to have been traded for salt with traders of desert salt and sea-salt both converging on south-western Mali. In contrast, ivory appears to have been a trade very much driven by European demand with Park noting that "nothing creates a greater surprise among the Negroes on the sea-coast than the eagerness displayed by the European traders to procure elephants' teeth; it being exceedingly

---

351 Ibid, p. 270.

difficult to make them comprehend to what use it is applied."³⁵²  Although elephants were enthusiastically hunted, for both the meat, popular with local populations, and for the tusks, much of the ivory traded at the time was obtained through non-lethal means. Elephants were so numerous it was possible to find tusks that had broken off as they tried to uproot trees.

Park re-entered Senegal on 12 May 1797 by crossing the Falémé River, further down this time at Satadoo, lodging for a night "at a small village called Medina, the sole property of a Mandinka merchant, who, by a long intercourse with Europeans has been induced to adopt some of their customs. His victuals were served up in pewter dishes, and even his houses were built after the fashion of the English houses on the Gambia".³⁵³

Park proceeded to Baniserile, the capital of Dentila, continuing on through a number of villages including Sibikillin and Komboo, both well-known for their inhospitality towards strangers. We pick up a clearer reference to his progress as he crosses "a considerable branch of the Gambia, called Neola Koba,³⁵⁴ overnighting at Kola Tenda and reaching on 30 May Jalacotta³⁵⁵ "a considerable town, but much infested by Foulah banditti, who come through the woods from Bondou and steal everything they can lay their hands on."³⁵⁶

Park records crossing the Nerico, and, the following day, reaching the Gambia River (still in Senegal at this point). The final leg of his journey passed back through the Kingdom of Wooli though with the slavers impatient to reach Pisania Park did not have the opportunity to pay his respects to the old King, instead sending him greetings via the customs officers.

By 12 June, Park was back in Pisania, looking more Moor than British and understandably delighted to discover that Dr Laidley, although believing him dead, had hung on to his European clothes.

---

352  Ibid, p. 272.
353  Ibid, p. 321.
354  i.e Nioloko Koba.
355  Presumably today's Djalocoto.
356  Park, *Travels in the Interior of Africa* (Wordsworth Classics), p. 327.

Having drawn off his African Association account with Dr Laidley, and paid Karfa with two slaves rather than the promised one, Park took the first ship to leave, an American slave ship called the *Charleston*, that called at Gorée on the way across the Atlantic. Park comments that the "mode of confining and securing Negroes in the American slave-ships... ...being abundantly more rigid and severe than in British vessels employed in the same traffic, made these poor creatures to suffer greatly, and a general sickness prevailed amongst them."[357] A total of 130 slaves, were embarked on Park's ship in the Gambia and Gorée. "Besides the three who died on the Gambia and six or eight while we remained at Gorée, eleven perished at sea and many of the survivors were reduced to a very weak and emaciated condition".[358] After an eventful journey via Antigua, Park eventually arrived back at Falmouth on 22 December 1799. He had become the first European to reach the Niger but also one of the first British people to explore inland Senegal.

Park's discoveries contributed to a major change in the way key members of the British Establishment, including the African Association, viewed Africa. While scientific curiosity and trade had long been the principal drivers of exploration, thoughts now turned to conquest. Park was present at the Association's General Meeting in May 1799 when Banks advocated the despatch of a force of "five hundred chosen troops" to the Niger arguing that "If this Country delays much longer to possess themselves of the Treasures laid open to them by the exertions of this Association, some Rival Nation will take possession of the banks of the Joliba[359] and assert by arms the right of Prior possession."[360] The Scramble for Africa didn't start for real until the 1880s but some of the seeds were sown here.

A short while later Banks wrote to Lord Liverpool, then President of the Board of Trade, to encourage the Government to "secure to the British throne, either by conquest or by Treaty, the whole of the

---

357 Ibid, p. 335.
358 Ibid, p 335-336.
359 i.e the name of the Niger River in the Manding language.
360 Resolution of the African Association of 30 May 1799, CO 267/10.

Coast of Africa from Arguin to Sierra Leone; or at least to procure the cession of the River Senegal as that River will always afford an easy passage to any rival nation who means to molest the Countries on the banks of the Joliba".[361]

But it was not until autumn 1803, by when Britain was again at war with France, and once again occupying Gorée, that the Government started planning seriously for a follow-up expedition to the Niger. They sent for Park[362] but then put their modest plans for him on hold as they developed a much more ambitious three-pronged plan for West Africa. This involved re-establishing a presence on Bolama (in present-day Guinea-Bissau), sending a detachment of soldiers north from Freetown to the Futa Djallon and, while Park was securing the agreement of local chiefs to establish trading posts in Segu, Timbuktu and other major towns on the Niger, building forts in Bambouk to secure the route between the Niger and the Gambia River. These ambitious plans were shelved following a change in government.[363]

Lord Camden, the new Secretary of State for the Colonies, and the African Association reverted to a more modest expedition and again turned to Park. Although by all accounts happily married, and with three young children, the life of a quiet country doctor seems to have left Park unfulfilled and he was itching to return to Africa. By 28 March 1805, he was back in Gorée and on his way to the Gambia River. Promising double pay and a discharge on return there were no shortage of volunteers among the soldiers in Gorée to accompany Park on his second expedition "but no inducement could prevail on a single Negro to accompany me."[364]

They left Gorée on 6 April "in high spirits"[365] and sailed up the Gambia River to Kayee from where they headed off overland. The expedition consisted of Park, his brother-in-law Alexander Anderson

---

361 Hallet, p. 321.
362 Park, *Travels in the Interior of Africa* (Wordsworth Classics), p. 340-341.
363 Hallet, p. 328-329.
364 The explanation given by Governor Lloyd for the local population not volunteering to join Park's expedition was "the dread which all neroes here entertain of a voyage into the interior". Lloyd to Earl Camden of 9 April 1805, CO 267/23.
365 Lloyd to Earl Camden of 9 April 1805, CO 267/23.

as second-in-command, a friend from Scotland called George Scott and, recruited in Gorée, a Lieutenant Martyn and thirty-five soldiers. The expedition also included two sailors and four carpenters, also recruited in Gorée, to build and sail the boats on which they intended to sail down the Niger.

Park's plan had been to get to the Niger well in advance of the rainy season, but repeated delays meant he set off what was to prove disastrously late. The rains came on as he was crossing south-eastern Senegal, washing out their camps, swelling the rivers they had to cross and weakening his men with fever. By the time they reached Bamako in late August only ten Europeans were left alive and when they eventually put to sail in a patched-up canoe from Sansanding in mid-November the entire expedition consisted of Park, Lieutenant Martyn, three soldiers, three slaves and their guide. Before setting sail from Sansading Park wrote a number of letters including to Sir Joseph Banks, to his father-in-law and to his wife.[366] Park informs his wife of her brother's death from fever and writes encouragingly of his own likely return, via the West Indies, in May. However, no more was heard from the expedition and in the course of 1806 news began to filter out that Park and his companions had been killed.

Early in 1810 Lieutenant Colonel Maxwell, then Governor of Senegal, recruited Park's former guide, Isaaco, to try to find out what had happened to him. Given that nearly five years had passed without news of Park Maxwell remained oddly optimistic, reporting to Lord Liverpool, that "the general opinion in this Country… is that Mr Park has not fallen victim to his dangerous voyage, but that he is detained in captivity, or prevented by poverty, sickness or other such causes from effecting his return."[367] Isaaco managed to track down Amadi Fatoumi, who had been Park's guide from Sansading to the Kingdom of Hausa, but who had not been with him at the time of his death. Fatoumi recounted the details of their long and hazardous journey down the river from Sansading and of Park's death along with

---

366 Park, p. 380-381.
367 Maxwell to Lord Liverpool of 8 March 1810, CO 267/33.

Martyn and the two remaining soldiers at the Bussa rapids near Yauri, in today's Nigeria. Attacked with pikes, arrows and stones by local warriors from a broad rock that lay across the river Park and his men jumped into the Niger and were drowned.[368] One of the slaves had survived to tell Fatoumi the story of how Park died.

Another of Britain's great Africa explorers also visited Senegal, though only fleetingly. Alexander Gordon Laing was to gain fame as the first European to visit Timbuktu, the fabled Saharan city of gold and other riches. Laing reached Timbuktu from the north after a journey of almost indescribable hardship and despite having been the victim of a savage and violent attack on route that left him wounded in twenty-four places. He recovered, made it to Timbuktu, spent a month there but was murdered on his return journey in September 1826. However, in October 1820, on his way to Sierra Leone, he had stopped at Gorée. The French commander there had given "unwilling permission to land" and Laing seems to have spent less than twenty-four hours on the island. His principle observation was that "the people are hospitable, the negroes the strongest and most powerful I have ever seen"; conversely however "the French soldiers stationed there are both lazy, indolent and slovenly".[369]

A number of overlapping factors drove the epic jouneys of discovery undertaken by Mungo Park and others at the turn of the eighteenth century. One certainly was the ambition, articulated at the inception of the African Association in 1788, to discover what lay in the interior of Africa, hitherto largely unexplored by European nations and therefore unknown even to the educated elite. It was a desire for learning, to extend the boundaries of science and of geography, and to answer the questions about this mysterious continent- such as which way the Niger flowed – that captivated the finest minds of the day. Wrapped up in the idea of "the Dark Continent", mysterious and inaccessible, was the growing desire too among moralising Europeans to protect and educate races they considered backward, and therefore

---

368 Park, p. 388.
369 *Notes, Mementos and Memoranda* by Alexander Gordon Laing.

in need of the enlightened guidance that only Europeans, they believed, could provide.

As had been the case from the very earliest days of European exploration down the coast of Africa explorers were also interested in opening up new areas of the continent for trade. The waterways of Africa, whether the Niger, Senegal or the Gambia, were of most interest to European explorers as means to bring trade items to and from the coast. Even if the British Parliament and public were turning against the slave trade – the Slave Trade Act of 1807 was to prohibit the slave trade in the British Empire – the promise of gold and other undreamt riches in the interior of Africa spurred on those intent on pushing back the boundaries of the unknown. It was also a time of global expansion of Britain's Empire, despite the loss of the American colonies in 1783. 1788, the year when the Africa Association was established, was also the year that Arthur Philip landed at Botany Bay, where Captain James Cook had set foot eighteen years earlier, and founded the first permanent British presence in Australia. A year earlier, in 1787, the British had founded a settlement in Sierra Leone, intending to resettle there some of the black population in Britain, as well as people of African descent who had fought with the British in the American War of Independence and escaped to England at the end of the war. And in India General Cornwallis was laying the foundations of British rule, having succeeded Warren Hastings as Governor-General in 1786.

But the rivalry with France was another factor in wanting to push into the unknown interior. Prime Minister William Pitt the Younger had declared war on Revolutionary France in 1795 and after a brief peace in 1801-1802 Britain was back at war again with France in 1803, this time against Napoloeon. Although the Scramble for Africa was not to take place until the 1880s the history of the second half of the eighteenth century is one of Britain and France vying to extend their influence globally. This was evident in the Americas, in India, and in Africa, where the French were more successful than elsewhere in establishing a permanent presence.

Thomas Jefferys — *The Western Coast of Africa from Cape Blanco to Cape Virga, Exhibiting Senegambia Proper.* This map, published in 1786, is a copy of a map drawn by the French cartographer Jean-Baptiste Bourguignon d'Anville in 1751.

*Portrait of Ayuba Suleiman Diallo, called Job ben Solomon by William Hoare of Bath, 1733.*

*Commodore The Honourable Augustus Keppel (1725-1786) who seized Gorée in December 1758. Painted by Sir Joshua Reynolds in 1749.*

*The British Attack on Gorée, 29 November 1758 by Richard Paton (1717-1791). The painting hangs in the British Ambassador's Residence in Dakar.*

*View of Gorée Island from the British Ambassador's Residence, Dakar.*

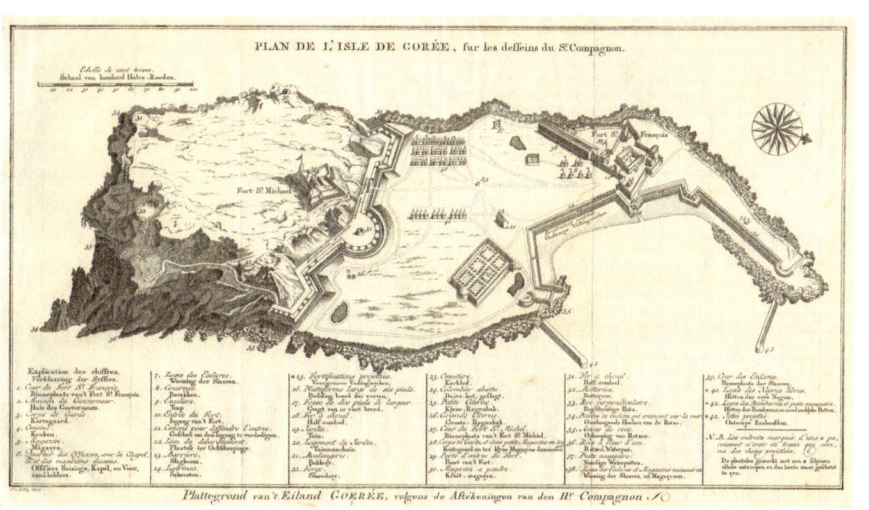

*Plan of Île de Gorée, from the drawings of Compagnon. 1747. Artist/engraver/ cartographer: Jakob van der Schley & Jacques Nicolas Bellin. Showing the forts and fortifications on the island.*

*Aerial view of Gorée island today.*

*The Goree Warehouses, George's Dock, Liverpool. Date: 1820 The warehouses suffered extensive damage during World War II and were demolished in 1958.*

'A View of the Fort at Senegal taken from the Road', a watercolour by Gabriel Bray (1750-1823) dated Jan-Feb 1775 showing the Union Jack flying over the fort at Saint-Louis during the governorship of Charles O'Hara.

Pont Faidherbe, which has linked the island of Saint-Louis to the mainland since opening in 1897.

"Governor Wall contemplating on his unhappy Fate, in the condemned Cell' by an unknown artist.

Mungo Park(1771-1806), the Scottish explorer who travelled through Senegambia to become the first European to reach the Niger River.

Le Radeau de la Méduse by Théodore Géricault (1791-1824), painted in 1819, three years after the tragic shipwreck of la Méduse on the Banc d'Arguin off the coast of Mauritania.

*The River Gambia at Génoto, Senegal, in the vicinity of the Barrakunda Falls.*

*Map of West Africa that shows both the approximate routes taken by Mungo Park (Chapter 8) on his two journeys to the Niger (red line from the Gambia River to the Bussa rapids) and, in light blue, the French territories on the Ivory Coast, Slave Coast and at Gabon that were all considered as possible swaps for British Gambia (Chapter 12).*

General Charles de Gaulle, Leader of the Free French Forces (second on left) and General Edward Spears (far right), Head of the British Government's Mission to de Gaulle, on board the Westernland, with its Dutch captain, on the way to Dakar, September 1940.

Old postcard showing the view of the island of Gorée from the British Consulate, now the British Ambassador's Residence.

British Ambassador's Residence Dakar 2015.

CHAPTER NINE

# ENDING THE SLAVE TRADE

1800-1807

In 1800, just seventeen years after Britain returned Gorée to the French, they seized it back. The two countries had been at war again since 1793, following the execution by revolutionary France of Louis XVI, and the British had made a number of half-hearted and unsuccessful attempts to recover Gorée in the following years. But in March 1800, Sir Charles Hamilton, Captain of HMS *Melpomene*, having learnt of the presence of three French frigates at Gorée, picked up HMS *Ruby*, then at Praia in Cape Verde, and set off in pursuit.[370] On his arrival at Gorée on 4 April Hamilton found the French frigates were no longer there but realising the island was poorly defended he seized the opportunity to attack. The French fort commander, with only ten reliable men at his disposal, surrendered after a brief exchange of artillery fire. A few days later Hamilton sent two boats and thirty men to Joal, a dependency of Gorée 100km down the coast, seizing this trading post and two French ships at anchor there.

Having recovered Gorée, British thoughts immediately turned to seizing Saint-Louis. Captain Thomas Tidy, left in interim charge of Gorée after Hamilton's departure, offered London enthusiastic

---

370  Letter from Hamilton to Evan Napien of 23 April in London Gazette of 8 July 1800.

advice on how this might be done given that the French garrison at Saint-Louis, according to his information, numbered only twenty Europeans under a governor called Blanchot.[371] London meanwhile appointed a governor for Gorée, a Colonel John Fraser, instructing him before his departure from England[372] to seize Saint-Louis, if he had the chance.[373] Henry Dundas, Secretary of State for War, was also keen that Fraser should investigate the possibility of enlisting Africans as soldiers both to serve on Gorée – where he suggested they should be paid no more than three-quarters what was paid to British soldiers – but also in black regiments in the West Indies.[374] He proposed that those recruited to serve in the West Indies might be trained in Gorée, so that they were ready for duty on arrival. Here the authorities in London were learning the lessons of India where from the mid-eighteenth century the English East India Company had been recruiting Indian sepoys into its armies at Calcutta, Madras and Bombay. Entire regiments were made up of Indian soldiers, led by European officers. What had been a guardforce of 3,000 in the middle of the eighteenth century, when the Company's ambitions were still focussed on trade rather than territory, grew with Indian recruits to become a private army of over 250,000 soldiers by the end of the century. Might the model work in Africa?

Fraser, who had lost a leg in the defence of Gibraltar in 1780-82, lost no time in planning an attack on Saint-Louis.[375] After a twenty-day passage from England and before even arriving at Gorée, he pulled into the bay near the mouth of the Senegal River. It was Christmas Day 1800. Encouraged by Tidy's positive report on the weak state of the French garrison at Saint-Louis Fraser decided to send a flag of truce to the French governor, proposing terms for the garrison's capitulation. Unfortunately, the boat carrying the flag was lost in the surf and the officers and crew were taken prisoner. Governor Blanchot

---

371 Tidy to Dundas of 1 June 1800, WO 1/351.
372 Fraser also sailed on HMS *Melpomene*.
373 Dundas to Fraser of 11 November 1800, CO 268/6.
374 Dundas to Fraser of 15 November 1800, CO 268/6.
375 Fraser to Dundas of 5 January 1801, WO 1/351.

further ruined Fraser's plans for a swift transfer of power by refusing to surrender.

Anxious to secure at least some material advantage from his visit Fraser decided to attack a French brig and schooner lying at anchor in the river. Fifty-five volunteers from HMS *Melpomene*, five from an accompanying transport vessel and thirty-six members of the African Corps, a regiment raised in England from convicts and deserters, successfully crossed the bar without being seen and, after a twenty-minute fire fight, seized the brig. Sailing back down the river they ran aground and were forced to abandon their prize, having first disabled it. The expedition suffered eleven dead, including two officers, and eighteen wounded for no gain.

With the French garrison seemingly reinforced since Tidy's intelligence Fraser decided not to make a further attempt on Saint-Louis and continued on to Gorée. He reported confidently back to London that the inhabitants there appeared relieved from considerable anxiety by the arrival of the British and happy to find themselves once more under their protection.[376] Prisoners captured by the British from the French brig were later exchanged for those taken by the French during the failed mission at Saint-Louis.[377]

Having put aside, for the moment, any thought of taking Saint-Louis Colonel Fraser focused on establishing the garrison at Gorée on a proper footing.[378] He acquired a schooner to run between Gorée and the mainland in order to ensure there was always two months supply of wood and water on the island. He identified that savings could be made by buying fresh beef (rather than imported salt beef), and he reduced the daily allowance of brandy for his men from half a pint to one gill per person. Fraser was convinced of the health benefits of sugar and wine and ensured the garrison was well supplied with both. He recruited locals to the African Corps, as he had been asked to do, paid them four pence a day, and was impressed by their ability to learn English. Initially doubtful that it would be possible to enlist

---

376  Fraser to Dundas of 23 January 1801, WO 1/351.
377  Fraser to Dundas of 24 January 1801, WO 1/351.
378  Fraser to Dundas of 23 January 1801, WO 1/351.

Africans for service in the West Indies Fraser subsequently revised his opinion when local kings gave their view that 200-400 men could be "recruited" annually at a cost of £30 a head.

For the local kings the arrival of the British at Gorée was to prove a disappointment since the British were not as generous with their presents as the French had been.[379] Fraser's assessment of the different tribes echoed that of Jobson and Moore before him. Wolofs were "tall, stout and hardy, reckoned brave and faithful even as slaves". Mandinkas meanwhile were "more remarked for deceit than any good quality."[380]

Within a year or so of Fraser's arrival[381] it seemed that Gorée would revert to the French in accordance with a peace treaty signed at Amiens in March 1802 to bring an end to the French Revolutionary Wars. Initially, the British appeared ready to press ahead with implementation of the Treaty of Amiens. Lord Hobart, Dundas's successor as Secretary of State for War and the Colonies,[382] wrote before the month of March was out instructing Fraser to publish the treaty "with the least possible delay".[383] A printed copy of the treaty was sent to him on 1 May with similar instructions. But Hobart chose to delay sending the Warrant for Evacuating Gorée, signed by George III on 3 May, until the end of July on the grounds that the French had not been in touch to discuss preparations for the return of the island.[384]

Fraser was now instructed to evacuate to Sierra Leone[385] and he sent a message to Freetown asking for an appropriate vessel to be sent. However, on 26 October Lord Hobart issued further instructions telling Fraser that because of changing circumstances – rising alarm

---

379 Letters from Fraser to Dundas of 23 January, 23 April, 11 and 17 October 1801, WO 1/351.
380 Fraser to Dundas of 23 April 1801, WO 1/351.
381 On 8 January 1801.
382 In 1801 the position of Secretary of State for War became Secretary of State for War and the Colonies.
383 Lord Hobart to Fraser of 31 March 1802, CO 268/6.
384 CO 268/6.
385 Letter from Fraser to Hobart of 11 October 1802, WO 1/351.

over Napoleon 's behaviour – restitution of Gorée should be delayed. But the two countries were not at war, that was to follow in May 1803, and Hobart was keen that Fraser should explain the delay in such a way as "not to incite jealousy or be seen as a hostile act."[386]

The length of time it took for letters to reach their destination meant that instructions were often out of date by the time they were received. Hobart's letter of 26 October, instructing Fraser to delay the return of Gorée to the French, only reached the governor on 21 December.[387] Fortunately HMS *Agreeable,* despatched from Sierra Leone to evacuate the troops from the island, had only just arrived and Fraser explained to Blanchot, the French govenor in Saint-Louis, that he wouldn't be able to embark with his men on HMS *Agreeable* for Sierra Leone until a ship arrived at Gorée from England to collect the garrison's stores.

But on 15 November Hobart had sent another letter saying that notwithstanding the instructions in his letter of 26 October Fraser should immediately proceed with the restitution of Gorée to the French.[388] For reasons that are unclear Fraser does not appear to have received this letter until 28 April 1803,[389] ironically less than a month after HMS *Agreeable*, which Fraser had detained five months at Gorée, had returned to Freetown. No damage was done however because by early June Fraser was aware of the probability that war with France would resume. Later that month he received confirmation that Britain had declared war on France in May. This ruled out an evacuation. Instead he seized six French ships that lay in Gorée harbour.[390]

In early November 1803 Fraser was informed by London[391] that a detachment of 200 men would soon be sent to him to bolster the garrison at Gorée "or by employing them to dislodge the enemy from any establishment they may have formed and which you think

---

386  Hobart to Fraser of 26 October 1802, WO 1/351.
387  Fraser to Hobart of 27 December 1802, WO 1/351.
388  Hobart to Fraser of 15 November 1802, WO 1/351.
389  Fraser to Hobart of 29 April 1803, WO 1/351.
390  Fraser to Hobart of 11 July 1803, WO 1/351.
391  Hobart to Fraser of 5 November 1803, CO 268/6.

it prudent to attack with so small a force". This can only really have meant Saint-Louis.

Unfortunately for Fraser this letter crossed with one of his own[392] informing Hobart proudly of the garrison's health and the fact that they had not lost a man in eight months (a notable achievement at that time). Hobart therefore decided[393] to postpone sending out the additional 200 troops until mid-December when they now planned to send a larger force of 5-600 men to take Saint-Louis. Fraser was instructed[394] to raise one or two companies of native troops to take part in the attack on Saint-Louis. However, the British troops' departure from the UK was delayed when it was thought likely that additional men would urgently be required for the war against Napoleon in Europe. Eventually Fraser was informed[395] that "it has been judged advisable under existing circumstances to defer taking any measures against the French settlement upon the Senegal". But a short while later he was told that reinforcements of 320 men were being sent to him on HMS *Inconstant*.

While the British were planning to seize Saint-Louis the French were plotting to recover Gorée. Fraser feared an attack and must have been looking forward to the arrival of the promised reinforcements. On 18 December 1803, a French warship, *L'Egyptienne*, approached Gorée, initially flying English colours. Its captain asked Fraser to hand over Gorée which by rights was French, he said. Fraser refused. The French captain warned Fraser that if he was forced to attack, he would have to supplement his soldiers with sailors "whose enthusiasm it was difficult to restrain,"[396] but no attack came that day.

Then, on 17 January 1804, a French squadron arrived off Gorée.[397] It was an impressive force. Blanchot, still the French Commander-in-Chief at Saint-Louis, had summoned up four schooners from

---

392 Fraser to Hobart of 11 July, CO 268/6.
393 Hobart to Fraser of 30 November1803, CO 268/6.
394 Letter (unclear from whom, but on Hobart's instructions) to Fraser of 1 December 1803, WO 1/351.
395 Sullivan to Fraser of 4 February 1804, CO 267/23.
396 Fraser to Hobart of 26 December, WO 1/351.
397 Fraser to Lord Hobart of 5 February 1804, CO 67/23.

Cayenne in French Guyana with a combined forty guns and 342 men. To this he was able to add a schooner of his own with a further two guns and thirty men and a commandeered private ship with twenty guns and 230 men. The fleet was commanded by Chevalier Mahé who had a landing force of a further 240 men at his disposal. Fraser, on the other hand, commanded just fifty-four British troops, though some local inhabitants had agreed to assist in defending the island.

Unlike earlier confrontations between the two sides real battle now took place. Very early on the morning of 18 January, one of the French schooners moved towards the beach on the west side of Gorée. It came under immediate and heavy bombardment from the British guns. At the same time, 130 French troops landed from eight small boats on the rocky east side of the island and overran the main guard post. The British successfully counter-attacked, recovering the position. But at dawn they realised both that the French had taken the hill overlooking the settlement and just how outnumbered they were.

The British had nine dead and ten wounded and only twenty-five men and three officers in a fit state to continue the fight. The local population, recognising where the balance of power lay, withdrew. Outnumbered and surrounded Fraser proposed terms of capitulation, which were agreed. According to Fraser French losses had been heavier than their own, with three officers and forty men killed and a further two officers and thirty men wounded. Had the promised reinforcements arrived earlier he was confident the garrison could have held Gorée.[398] In the event, the French occupied Gorée for less than two months. As it had been won in a hard-fought battle it is surprising perhaps that Blanchot left only a garrison of twenty men under the command of a retired cavalry major called Montmayeur to defend the island.

On 8 March 1804, HMS *Inconstant*, despatched by Lord Hobart to reinforce and supply Fraser's garrison, finally arrived at Gorée. Montmayeur quickly ran up the Union Jack. *Inconstant*'s commander, Captain Edward Dickson, suspecting something was amiss sent ashore

---
398  Fraser to Lord Hobart of 5 Feb 1804, CO 267/23.

his First Lieutenant, a man called Pickford. When Pickford failed to send the signal they had agreed upon Dickson knew the island to be under the control of the French and this was subsequently confirmed by an English supercargo on a Prussian ship in the harbour. The next morning *Inconstant* pretended to leave but returned at night planning to attack the island. Dickson then postponed the idea when he realised that he only had boats to land 130 men and did not think this would be enough. But the French, knowing themselves to be outnumbered, surrendered.[399]

Dickson appointed Captain William Murray as Commandant of Gorée. Murray quickly sought to win over the local chiefs though he does not relate[400] whether the King of Barbasin[401] was satisfied with his present of rum, four guns and a trumpet, or whether he too was disappointed compared to what he received from the French. Murray also set about repairing the defences on the island, making bricks to rebuild the barracks, hospital and sentry boxes as well as constructing new platforms for the guns.

Concerned about the effect of the heat on his men Murray confined them to barracks between nine and four in the afternoon, stipulating that no workmen should be employed outside during those hours. Like others before him, he was soon advising Lord Hobart that Saint-Louis could easily be retaken. All that was needed, he said, was one frigate, a sloop of war, two gunboats, a few flat-bottomed boats to get over the bar and two hundred men. He reckoned the French garrison was no more than one hundred men strong and that the locals would be favourably disposed to British rule and would welcome an attack.[402]

With Gorée changing hands so often and news of each new seizure travelling slowly it was understandable that English ships approached Gorée with caution. Francis Spilsbury, a surgeon on HMS *Favourite* recounted[403] how on approaching Gorée in late 1805 they sent a cutter

---

399 Murray to Lord Hobart of 15 March 1804, CO 267/23.
400 Murray to Lord Hobart of 30 March, CO 267/23.
401 A name sometimes used by Europeans for the king of Sine.
402 Murray to Lord Hobart of 28 April 1804, CO 267/23.
403 Spilsbury F.B. *Account of a Voyage to the Western Coast of Africa…*

with a flag of truce fearing that the French might have possession of the island. Gorée at the time was governed by Lieutenant Colonel Richard Lloyd, who had succeeded Murray in August 1804, and had been reinforced by 190 members of the Royal African Corps, a unit that had evolved from Colonel Fraser's initial recruitment in 1800 and which was officially established, with George III agreeing to the addition of the "Royal" to the Corps' name, on 25 April 1804.

Spilsbury paints a colourful picture of life on Gorée – notwithstanding that it was "almost a barren rock". He describes a ball given during his stay "at which there was certainly a numerous and beautiful assemblage". The women were "excessively fond of gold". Otherwise the riches of the inhabitants consisted of slaves "each house having a slave yard". Weddings were frequent including between the British and local signares. "If any officer or settler of respectability wants a wife he must court the girl a month, and then give what they call a great dinner; inviting all her relations and keeping open house for some days." According to Spilsbury weddings seldom cost less than £200 and, once married, women were not allowed to leave the island. For another traveller of the time, Joseph Corry, "the ceremony of marriage is too offensive for delicacy even to reflect upon, much less for me to narrate". Corry's short stay in the region included a meeting with "King Marraboo" in his, to Corry's taste, less than palatial accommodation in his capital of "Decar."[404]

While today open water swimming competitions take place between the mainland and Gorée Spilsbury notes how he and his companions were obliged to use the utmost caution in transferring from their ship to the island "for fear of the sharks, which are of a large size and swarm round the island." Spilsbury relates too how for fear of infection no one was buried on the island but on the mainland "where they are generally dug up and devoured by the tigers and other wild beasts". Like other travellers before him, Spilsbury was also fascinated by the superstitions of the local African populations and their use of

---

[404] Corry, J. *Observations upon the Windward Coast of Africa* (Bulmer and Co, London 1807). Chapters 2-3

gris-gris noting that they would never admit to mistakes "but attribute everything to the ill conduct of those who have offended them".

An American, visiting Gorée a few years later, when it was still under English occupation painted a genteel picture of life on the island. Invited by a mixed-race family for lunch he marvelled how they enjoyed "French soup, fricasseed and baked fowls, fried eggs, fried plantains, sweet potatoes, yams etc besides wines of different kinds, and all the various fruits that could be obtained…such as oranges, pine-apples, bananas, guava etc."[405] After lunch the ladies retired and the gentlemen moved to the piazza where they enjoyed cigars, looking out onto the Atlantic. Carnes was enraptured by everything he saw especially the head wraps worn by the women. "But O! What enormous turbans, more than a foot high, in the shape of a bee-hive and composed of muslin or cotton of various colors, red, yellow and blue predominating, twisted or folded together and coiled upon the head somewhat in the manner of a ship's cable on the deck!" The headscarves worn by Senegalese women today are as striking, colourful and worthy of appreciation as those worn in the early 1880s.

Whether it was Murray's advice that proved decisive is unclear, but Lloyd assumed the governorship with instructions from London to take Saint-Louis as soon as the opportunity arose. He waited[406] seven weeks off Cape Blanco for reinforcements until countermanded by Hobart's letter of 7 November postponing the attack. Lloyd was himself eager to retake Saint-Louis not only because of its own trade potential – an estimated 1000 tonnes annually in gum exports plus wax, gold and ivory – but also because he was concerned at the risk posed to British commerce in the region, especially in the Gambia River, by French privateers who operated out of Saint-Louis. Lloyd had ambitious plans to ensure the safety of British interests in the region. He called for a warship to be based at Gorée,[407] and advocated extensive works,[408] at a cost of £10-12,000 in order to make Gorée, with

---

405 J.A. Carnes, *Journal of a Voyage from Boston to the West Coast of Africa* p 47.
406 Lloyd to Lord Hobart of 14 January 1805, CO 267/23.
407 Lloyd to Lord Hobart of 16 August 1805, CO 267/23.
408 Lloyd to Edward Cooke of 23 November 1805, CO 267/23.

a garrison of 300 soldiers, "one of the strongest fortresses belonging to Britain".

Lloyd got his wish of a warship based at Gorée but may have regretted it. Correspondence between the protagonists and with London[409] reveals an intense and destructive departmental rivalry between Lloyd, as Commander of the Royal African Corps, and Captain Keith Maxwell, Captain of HMS *Arab*, who took his instructions from the Navy Department. Maxwell went so far as to threaten war between the two departments. However once matters were brought to the attention of the Navy Department Maxwell was swiftly relieved of his command.[410]

In order to encourage British traders Lloyd scrapped the six dollar anchorage fee imposed on British ships (neutrals continued to pay fourteen dollars as had been the practice under his predecessor). Instead he introduced a one dollar a head tax on slaves exported on neutral ships.[411] In the early 1800s, an estimated two thousands slaves were being exported each year from Gorée and Saint-Louis. Lloyd used the money raised from the new tax to employ a secretary. A complaint was made by British merchants and he was told that he did not have the authority to levy a new duty and it should not be continued.[412]

—

The British were still occupying Gorée in 1807 when the British Parliament passed a law abolishing the slave trade. At the beginning of the nineteenth century Britain was still exporting 50,000 slaves a year from the coast of Africa. Profitable though the trade remained those opposing it on moral grounds began to make more headway among public opinion and in Parliament. Getting to the point of abolition had however been a long battle.

---

409 Lloyd to Lord Castlereigh (and attachments) of 20 May 1806, CO 267/23.
410 Windham to Lloyd of 11 July 1806, CO 268/6.
411 Lloyd to Cooke of 23 November 1805, CO 267/23.
412 George Shea to Lloyd of 11 July 1807, CO 268/6.

The abolitionist movement only began to gain traction in the 1770s. In 1775, at the instigation of the Quakers, a parliamentary commission was set up to take evidence on the slave trade. The following year a debate was introduced in Parliament on the theme "that the slave trade is contrary to the laws of God and the rights of men". About that time, in 1779, the last public sale of a slave in the UK took place in Liverpool.

The first real momentum in England for abolition was in the 1780s (ironically the only decade in the second half of the eighteenth century when slave exports out of Senegambia, otherwise in decline, briefly rallied). In 1787, a Committee for Effecting the Abolition of the Slave Trade was established in London. The same year the politician William Wilberforce assumed the political leadership of the abolition movement. In February 1788, a committee of the Privy Council was set up to investigate the slave trade and its report[413] was debated in Parliament the following year.

One of the witnesses who gave evidence to the committee was Captain Wilson, commander of HMS *Racehorse*, whose responsibility it had been to hand Gorée over to the French in 1783. Wilson had spent six months on the coast between Cape Blanco and the Gambia River based mainly at Gorée. He said that slaves were procured through inter-tribal wars, by local kings breaking up villages, by crimes or imputed crimes or by kidnapping. He recalled how a courier of Captain Lacy, his predecessor, was kidnapped and sold to a French vessel even though he was a Moor, a free man, a native of Senegal, fluent in French and having in his possession documents that showed he was on British Government business.

John Barnes, Governor from 1763-66 when Saint-Louis was run by the Committee of Merchants also gave evidence. Unlike Captain Wilson he was directly involved in trading, including of slaves. By his account slaves were rarely captured in war nor, to his knowledge, seized by kings breaking up villages or through kidnap. Instead they

---

413 Abridgement of the Minutes of the Evidence taken before a Committee of the Whole House to whom it was referred to consider of the Slave-Trade, 1789

were largely criminals convicted of crimes including theft, murder, adultery, witchcraft or debt. He thought it unlikely that crimes would be imputed. A slave-trader, Captain William MacIntosh, of the East India Company gave similar evidence. He had traded in slaves in the 1770s, including from Senegal. He had once walked from Saint-Louis to Gorée and back. He too said that most slaves were individuals convicted of crimes and claimed never to have heard of villages being raided for slaves or of Africans kidnapping Africans. Both testimonies are difficult to believe. Numerous commentators from the Venetian Cadamosto in the fifteenth century, to Francis Moore in 1730, as well as contemporaries of Barnes and MacIntosh, held that most slaves sold to European traders were prisoners taken in tribal wars, or were kidnapped, with those who had been convicted of a crime and condemned to slavery a minority.[414] I can only think Barnes and MacIntosh, in an attempt to head off any criticism of their roles, sought to equate the transatlantic slave trade with the transportation of British criminals as indentured labour to the American colonies.

In 1791, Wilberforce managed to introduce a bill into Parliament to abolish the slave trade. It was defeated by 163 votes to 88. Encouraged by a decision by the Danish Government to abolish the import of slaves into their three small West Indian colonies,[415] he tried again the following year to introduce a bill to abolish the slave trade into the House of Commons. On 3 April 1792, after an epic and high quality debate, the House of Commons voted 230 to 85 in favour of an amended motion, tabled by Henry Dundas, at that time Home Secretary, "that the slave trade ought to be gradually abolished". Dundas's amendment was an attempt to kick abolition into the long grass, and geopolitical events conspired to divert attention from this agenda: in 1793 Britain went to war against revolutionary France, occupying the attention of Prime Minister Pitt the Younger who had hitherto given Wilberforce consistent support in taking forward his private members bill in the House of Commons.

---

414 Thomas, pp. 370-371.
415 The ban was to come into force only in 1803.

Wilberforce, however, kept up the pressure pushing abolition to the vote in 1795, and each of the following four years, being defeated each time. But Wilberforce's patience began to be rewarded, as a new and more abolitionist-inclined generation entered Parliament. In 1804, his bill was actually passed in the House of Commons before being defeated in the Lords. Finally, the bill passed on 23 February 1807 by 283 votes to sixteen and received royal assent on 25 March. This made the slave trade illegal from 1 May 1807.

The British were not the first to abolish the slave trade. The Danish ban on the slave trade, enacted in 1792, had come into force in 1803, though the volume of trade they engaged in was small by comparison with Britain and other European nations. In March 1807, Thomas Jefferson, third President of the United States, signed a bill in favour of abolition of the slave trade that had passed both the Senate and House of Representatives, and which was to come into force on 1 January 1808. But this only made the importation of slaves into the United States illegal, and a domestic trade in slaves continued, with smuggling also common.

What was particularly noteworthy about British action was that having adopted a ban on the slave trade they made considerable effort to enforce it as well as to encourage other European nations to follow suit. They tried to persuade African traders to develop trade in other traditional products including gum, beeswax, ivory, gold, rice, pepper, peanuts and palm oil. Africans naturally welcomed this trade but continued to sell slaves to other European buyers. A trade that had existed for almost 400 years, and for which a market remained, was unfortunately not going to die out overnight.

# CHAPTER TEN

# THE RECOVERY OF SAINT-LOUIS

1808-1812

Charles William Maxwell was appointed to replace Lloyd as Governor of Gorée in July 1808.[416] Having served eight years on the coast of Africa, Lloyd appears to have been happy to move on.[417] Not a lot of thought seems to have gone into Maxwell's letter of instructions.[418] It simply referred him to the instructions of his predecessor – without enclosing them – while emphasising again the importance of enlisting black troops. Surprisingly the letter included nothing specific on implementation of the abolition of the slave trade. Yet we know this was high on the Government's agenda at the time.

Maxwell arrived in Gorée on 3 September 1808 and assumed charge two days later. He was unimpressed with the state of the island's defences, as well as the condition of the hospital and barracks, consoling himself with the fact that the French forces at Saint-Louis were in no state to attack.[419] If they did, he wryly observed, the British would have no choice but to defend themselves with bayonets as the

---

416 Castlereagh to Lloyd of 7 July 1808 and Castlereagh to Maxwell of same date, CO 268/6.
417 A ceremonial sword given to Lloyd by his officers on departure is in the National Army Museum.
418 Castlereagh to Maxwell of 7 July 1808, CO 268/6.
419 Letter from Maxwell of 11 September 1808, CO 267/32.

gun carriages and platforms were too damaged to be used. He also judged his soldiers' weapons unfit for service, suitable only to be given as presents to local chiefs on the mainland.

Maxwell gave early thought, as he had been instructed, to the question of whether Africans could be enlisted as soldiers and in particular whether a regular system of recruiting and training at Gorée for the black regiments in the West Indies could be put in place. He saw no prospect of being able to enlist free Africans as soldiers in the West Indian regiments given "the inveterate idleness of the people"; the fact that wolofs, the main tribe of Senegal, were home-loving people; and because they feared – notwithstanding the abolition of slavery by the British – that they would be enslaved on the other side of the Atlantic. Two free Africans who he had enlisted to serve on Gorée had made clear to him that they would not serve anywhere else.[420]

But Maxwell thought it might be possible to man the West Indian regiments with freed slaves, reckoning that the slaves themselves would be happy to change their status and that they could be bought for 80-100 dollars from their owners. Although the British had abolished the trade in slaves the condition of slavery persisted for the many hundreds of slaves owned by free Africans, mixed-race people and Europeans on the island, and of course in the British colonies such as Barbados and Jamaica in the West Indies. Some of the African inhabitants of Gorée had benefitted so much from the slave trade they were reluctant to give it up. They sought to continue the trade clandestinely, smuggling slaves to the island from the mainland in the hope of still finding willing buyers among the ships of different nationalities visiting Gorée.[421]

One consequence of the abolition of the slave trade had been a drop in the number of ships calling at Gorée. The trade of the island now began to revolve around beeswax, hides and ivory. But much of this came from the Gambia and often ships would go straight there,

---

420 Maxwell to Castlereagh of 15 January 1809, CO 267/32.
421 Ibid.

bypassing Gorée completely.⁴²² This in turn had an impact on the garrison who were in the habit of buying articles of barter brought by the slavers – tobacco, iron, beads, gunpowder – in order to obtain poultry, corn and vegetables for themselves. The slavers had also brought other European goods at affordable prices. With fewer ships visiting prices for these items rose threefold. Flour was one commodity that was often in short supply. Regular supplies were supposed to be delivered from London along with salted meat and other provisions. But the arrival of ships from Britain was at best erratic, and the residents of Gorée often ended up buying flour from American ships instead. Maxwell focussed in early on this issue. Before he had even arrived in Gorée, he was writing from Madeira⁴²³ advising that there should be a minimum of six months' stores on the island at anytime and that supplies should arrive between the months of November and June, outside the rainy season, to avoid damage.

Maxwell reported back to London that if the garrison were forever short of food it would be harder to recruit black soldiers, for whom regular meals would be an incentive to join. Figures from 1801⁴²⁴ show the daily ration issued at Gorée included one pound of bread; one pound of beef or nine ounces of pork; half a pint of rice or oatmeal; one half of brandy (subsequently reduced to one gill) and one pound of sugar a week. Fresh fish was plentiful for most of the year and fresh meat was generally also available. Access to fresh fish was helped by the fact that relations between the garrison and the Lebuh fishermen at Dakar were good. Under the leadership of Dial Diop the Lebuh liberated themselves from the Damel of Kayoor in 1809. When he subsequently sought to blockade them, they received food supplies from Gorée and considered the garrison their allies. Maxwell noted how, from daily interaction with Europeans, the manners of the Lebuh had "assumed a character of greater mildness, and they act more in conformity to our ideas than other natives of the vicinity".

---
422  Letter from Maxwell to Castlereagh of 17 January 1809, CO 267/32.
423  Maxwell to Castlereagh of 20 August 1808, CO 267/32.
424  7 January 1801.

John Hill,[425] an Edinburgh born missionary who spent a year on Gorée on his way back from Sierra Leone recommended the island to the Missionary Societies as a promising place for a Mission. Hill worked on a Wolof-English dictionary and translated the Lord's Prayer. The first book to be published in Wolof and English as a linguistic work was by a Sheffield born Quaker by the name of Hannah Kilham who published *First Lessons in Jalof* anonymously in 1820. Kilham's knowledge of Wolof was acquired from two African sailors who she got to know in London. Three years later she was to pay her first visit to Africa, establishing a school at Bathurst in Gambia.[426]

Like his predecessors Maxwell was keen for Britain to recover Saint-Louis. He highlighted to London[427] that the French continued to use Saint-Louis as a base to export slaves and that he was powerless, for want of a naval force, to stop them. An English brig licensed to trade under American colours had also been seized by the French at the bar. He envisaged no problems from the inhabitants of Saint-Louis who were "anxious to become the subjects of Great Britain". Recovering Saint-Louis, he argued, would therefore be relatively easy:

> "If His Majesty's Government would detach, so as to arrive in the beginning of November, a frigate, two Gun Brigs, three hundred Men on board transports drawing little water, flour and wine for six months, 100 rounds of ammunition and six flints a man, some medical stores and about three hundred pieces of Blue Baft as Presents to the Kings of the Moors Senegal would be easily reduced."[428]

As luck would have it, on 24 June 1809 Captain Edward Henry Columbine arrived at Gorée with the frigate HMS *Solebay*, the sloop

---

425 *John Hill's Account of Life on Gorée Island 1807-1808* by Patricia Wilson and David P. Gamble.
426 *Sowing the World, The cultural impact of the British Foreign Bible Society 1804-2004*, edited by Stephen Batalden, Kathleen Cann and John Dean.
427 Letter from Maxwell to Castlereagh of 2 April 1809, CO 267/32.
428 Maxwell to Castlereagh of 2 April 1809, CO 267/32.

## THE RECOVERY OF SAINT-LOUIS

HMS *Derwent*, the gunbrig *Tigress*, the colonial schooner *George* and the *Agincourt* transport vessel, as well as some merchant ships.[429] Columbine[430] was heading the first anti-slavery patrol sent out to enforce the British Parliament's abolition of the slave trade. In 1809, with Britain at war with France, only a handful of ships were available. In 1818, however, after the final defeat of Napoleon, the West Africa Squadron was formally established with a base at Freetown in Sierra Leone. Its first Commander, Sir George Collier, was given the task "to use every means in [his] power to prevent a continuance of the traffic in slaves and to give full effect to the Acts of Parliament in question."[431] In the period 1808-1860 the squadron seized approximately 1600 ships and freed 150,000 slaves.

Maxwell seized his opportunity. Without waiting for instructions from London[432] he persuaded Columbine to assist him in an attack on Saint-Louis. On 4 July 1809 Columbine embarked troops from Gorée (six officers, six sergeants, four drummers and 150 rank and file),[433] and by the evening of 7 July the small British fleet was anchored off the bar at the mouth of the Senegal River. The following morning the British forces crossed the bar but, reminiscent of the first time they seized Saint-Louis in 1758, not without some difficulty. They lost a schooner in the process as well as a sloop containing provisions and ammunition. Another schooner ran aground.

Maxwell landed the troops on the left bank of the river. The next day the French attacked but were forced back to a line of defence at Babague higher up the river. HMS *Solebay* and HMS *Derwent* bombarded French positions on 11 July sailing up the river on the 12th. They were planning a night attack when the French capitulated. On the 13th British troops took possession of the battery on the small island lying south of the main island of Saint-Louis which the French

---
429 Letter from Maxwell to Castlereagh of 18 July 1809, CO 267/33.
430 Captain Columbine was briefly Governor of Sierra Leone but was to die on board HMS *Crocodile*, to the West of the Azores, from dysentery on 18 June 1811.
431 Lloyd, C p. 67.
432 Letter from Lord Liverpool to Maxwell of 2 Jan 1810 confirms this.
433 Letter from Maxwell to Castlereagh of 18 July 1809, CO 267/33.

had called Île aux Anglais.[434] The French garrison – 160 regular soldiers supported by 240 militia – laid down their arms on 14 July. According to Maxwell the operation was achieved with minimal casualties: one dead and two wounded among the French troops with the British recording one wounded and one dead "of fatigue". To this toll must be added a captain, a midshipman and six seamen who died crossing the bar.

The following day John Heddle, who had been appointed Colonial Secretary by Maxwell, signed a proclamation[435] intended both to reassure the inhabitants of Saint-Louis that they could go about their business as normal and in safety and to make clear who was now in charge. It read:

> "The Colony of Senegal having surrendered to His Britannic Majesty's Arms, The Governor takes the earliest moment to address the Merchants and Inhabitants and to assure them that he is actuated by every wish to Contribute to their prosperity, and that of the colony. Their property and privileges shall be secure; and justice shall be impartially and promptly administered. The strictest discipline shall be observed amongst the military and all Contracts and purchases made by the Government shall be regularly fulfilled – annexed to a great and commercial Nation the widest feild opens to their industry which he trusts they should profit by, and he promises that every endeavour will be used, and (if necessary) force employed to ensure respect from the Cheifs and Princes whose Dominions are Connected with the colony and its commerce."

The proclamation continued that whilst "thus desirous to protect their rights, and to contribute to their prosperity", the Governor

---

434 "English island". According to Mentelle's "Geographie Mathématique, physique et politique de toutes les parties du monde" of 1803 the Île aux Anglais measured 480' by 240'. It no longer exists.
435 Senegal Archives 9 F1

expected from them "the most perfect regularity in their conduct, and prompt obedience to the orders and police regulations, as they may from time to time receive". The Proclamation assured them that the Governor would punish any delinquency with vigour. "But he is persuaded that he will never have occasion for severity, and that the peaceable demeanour and good conduct of the inhabitants of Senegal whilst it adds to their own happiness will also tend to make his Command pleasant and agreeable to them".

Writing to Lord Castlereagh to inform him of the success Maxwell gave three reasons to justify the attack on Saint-Louis: it would be good for trade (in gum primarily, but also ivory and beeswax); its loss would be personally felt by the French; and that "by driving the enemy from their sole possessions on the coast His Majesty's settlements and the British commerce would be more secure and more easily protected".[436]

While gum exports were averaging 800 tonnes a year gold and ivory had not been exported in significant quantities for a while.[437] This was mainly because the French had been at war with local tribes on the southern bank of the Senegal River and had abandoned their forts upriver at Podor and Galam. Maxwell was confident the trade could be resumed. He kept the import duties imposed by the French (10% on "neutral" ships, 5% on domestic ones) but abolished the 5% tax on gum and corn from the river which had so incensed local traders.

Maxwell was subsequently reminded by the Privy Council for Trade[438] that under the Navigation Acts no goods or commodities could be imported into or exported from any British colony in Asia, Africa or America except in a British-built ship owned by British subjects. Nevertheless, it was agreed that a case should be made to Parliament to allow neutral ships to import lumber and other scarce provisions into Senegal and that Maxwell should be given the discretion to implement this policy in advance of Parliamentary

---

[436] Letter from Maxwell to Castlereagh of 18 July 1809, CO 267/33.
[437] Letter from Maxwell to Castlereagh of 20 July 1809, CO 267/33.
[438] Opinion of the Privy Council for Trade dated 6 September 1809, CO 267/33.

approval if the settlement seemed likely materially to suffer before then.

Prior to seizing Saint-Louis Maxwell had told London that about three hundred pieces of baft would be required as presents for the Kings of the Moors. Within a week of taking control he sent back a twenty-four page list of customs that would need to be paid to the Moorish princes of Brakna and Trarza, to their interpreters and valets, as well as to other Moorish chiefs, to the King of the Peuls, the Damel of Kayoor, and the King of Waalo. He proposed for example that the King of Waalo should receive:

> "Fifty-seven bars and a half of long iron.
> Fifteen pieces of blue baft.
> Two pieces of Platillas.[439]
> One hundred quarts of Rum.
> Thirty-five trading muskets.
> Three pairs of pistols or three touring muskets.
> Twelve pounds of gunpowder.
> Four hundred balls.
> Four hundred flints.
> One ell[440] and a quarter of scarlet.
> Thirty dollars.
> One iron bound chest.
> One padlock."[441]

The King of Waalo also received, as did the Damel, one hundred quarts of wine or rum for each of the Muslim festivals of Korite, Tabaski and the Gamou.

Maxwell listed what each prince should receive, as a daily allowance, on the occasions that they visited Saint-Louis. King Alicourie was to receive:

---

[439] A white linen fabric formerly made in Silesia.
[440] An ell was equivalent to about 1.14 metres.
[441] Letter from Maxwell to Castlereagh of 20 July 1809, CO 267/33.

"Twenty pounds fresh meat.
Eight pounds bread.
Thirty moulles[442] of corn.
Eight quarts molasses or sixteen pounds of brown sugar.
Eight quarts wine.
Five pounds loaf sugar." [443]

These gift lists were approved without discussion.

In early 1810, Maxwell received a letter from Lord Liverpool[444] informing him of the King's approbation and satisfaction at his action to recover Saint-Louis and appointing him Lieutenant Governor of the settlement of Senegal with an increase in salary to thirty shillings a day (which is what Fraser had received).

Maxwell's efforts to boost trade soon ran into difficulties. The Moors held back, hoping to force up the custom paid to them by the government, and anticipating an increase in visiting ships that would drive up the price. However, Maxwell judged that the conditions were favourable for returning to Galam and encouraged the local traders to start making preparations for the next season. Enjoying better relations than the French had done with local kings Maxwell was also able to establish a "regular, safe and constant overland communication to Gorée"[445] as London had asked him to do.[446] Others used this route too. Maxwell detained forty-one slaves sent from Saint-Louis to Dakar – then a small village on the mainland opposite Gorée – to be sold to a Spanish slave ship.

With Britain still at war with France, and Columbine and his warships having departed, Maxwell was concerned about the vulnerability of Saint-Louis, Gorée and commerce on the Gambia River. He advocated a naval force be based in the region and specifically requested a frigate, an artillery detachment and a brig for

---

442 Meaning unclear.
443 Letter from Maxwell to Castlereagh of 20 July 1809, CO 267/33.
444 Liverpool to Maxwell of 2 January 1810, CO 268/6 (copy also on CO 267/33).
445 Maxwell to Lord Liverpool of 9 March 1810, CO 267/33.
446 Lord Liverpool to Maxwell of 3 January 1810, CO 268/6.

the protection of the bar. He also asked for ordinance and engineers stores ("there is not a gun carriage which would bear six discharges without endangering the lives of the soldiers") as well as flat-bottomed, coppered gun-boats able to carry a twenty-four pound gun.[447] The list of stores he required included fifty-gun carriages, fifty wheelbarrows, six grates and fire irons for heating shot, seven thousand sand bags of various sizes, four hundred iron shovels, 9000 fuses of various sizes and 100 sheepskins.

Notwithstanding the fact that his political masters were encouraging him to enlist Africans to serve in the West Indies he also advocated the French example of bringing soldiers "of colour" from the Caribbean to West Africa "to keep in awe" the Moors and Black Africans. By this time he had enlisted forty-four Africans in the Royal African Corps.

As during the period when Senegambia was a Crown colony (1765-1783) many of the British soldiers sent to serve in the Royal African Corps at Gorée and Saint-Louis were criminals. One commander said of his men that "they were the sweepings of every parade in England; for when a man was sentenced to be flogged he was offered the alternative of volunteering for the Royal Africans."[448] The French had adopted the same approach. A contingent of soldiers from the French Antilles brought in to reinforce the garrison at Gorée at the end of the eighteenth century were described by one writer[449] as dissolute and argumentative drunks whose indiscipline was such that they burned down the church.

Maxwell lamented that soldiers who, as prisoners, had been condemned to serve their natural lives on the coast of Africa couldn't be invalided out of the Corps and became a burden to it. In September 1810, he reported to Lord Liverpool[450] that a mutiny had taken place involving a considerable number of soldiers who had recently arrived from England. Their plan had been to take possession of the island

---

447 Maxwell to Lord Liverpool of 9 March 1810, CO 267/33.
448 Lord, p. 150.
449 Maillat, p. 46.
450 Maxwell to Liverpool of 30 September 1810, CO 267/33.

and then desert to America. Maxwell had fifteen of the ringleaders tried and shot and sent a further twenty to Sierra Leone. Columbine, the Governor at Freetown, promptly sent them back claiming they represented a risk to his own settlement.[451] Later in the year, a second mutiny occurred, this time on Gorée.[452] Again it was unsuccessful and the two ring-leaders were tried and shot. Maxwell commented[453] that mutiny was a natural consequence of sending troops who were either United Irishmen[454] trained for rebellion "or vagabonds who had made a trade of desertion".

The system of duty was changed in the course of 1810 on the advice of the Lords of the Council for Trade and Plantations who proposed a tax of 2% on the invoice price of all British products and 6% on the invoice price of foreign goods. At the time the main goods imported were India blue cloth, coarse woollen cloth and cottons; iron; gunpowder; rum, sugar and molasses; wine and porter; flour, coffee and other provisions; amber, coral and beads; tin, earthenware and ironmongery; tobacco; and furniture. Gum was the only export. But Maxwell did not think the levels of commerce justified posting specialist customs officers to Saint-Louis and so advised London.

Maxwell remained hopeful that trade with the interior could be opened up and in September 1810, for the first time in several years, merchant ships departed for Galam.[455] He was to report back in February[456] that the vessels had all returned safely but having made little trade. Their prolonged absence and late start up the river had not helped. Nevertheless, he took encouragement from their safe return for the future.

In April 1811, Maxwell was appointed Governor in Sierra Leone, with supervisory responsibility for Saint-Louis and Gorée.[457] His

---

451 Maxwell to Lord Liverpool of 1 November 1810, CO 267/33
452 Maxwell to Lord Liverpool of 11 December 1810, CO 267/33.
453 Maxwell to Liverpool of 30 September 1810, CO 267/33.
454 The United Irishmen were a non-sectarian armed Irish revolutionary group that collapsed in 1804, shortly after the Union in 1800 between Great Britain and Ireland.
455 Maxwell to Liverpool of 11 December 1810, CO 267/33.
456 Maxwell to Liverpool of 23 February 1811, CO 267/33.
457 Letter from Liverpool to Maxwell of 6 April 1811, CO 268/6.

successor, Charles MacCarthy, who therefore carried the title of Lieutenant Governor[458] did not arrive in Saint-Louis until September 1812. Command in the meantime fell to Lieutenant Colonel Chisholm, Commandant at Gorée.

Standards of governance generally appear to have been far higher during Britain's occupation of Saint-Louis and Gorée in the early years of the nineteenth century than had been the case in the 1770s and 1780s. Chisholm however seems to have inspired rare loyalty among the inhabitants of Gorée. An address,[459] signed by the Mayor of Gorée and eleven other residents, mostly of French nationality or descent, is so glowing that it is worth producing in full:

> "It is with sincere regret we the undersigned being the principal inhabitants of Gorée, learn that you are about leaving this island. We cannot in justice to our feelings allow you to depart without offering our most grateful thanks for your fatherly care and constant attention to forward our welfare during the period of seven years that we have had the good fortune of being placed under your friendly protection. The great improvements you have made in this island will long bear testimony of your disinterested labour and endear you to us and our offspring. The state of defence you put the garrison in when surrounded by the Enemy's Ships of War prove you to be a man of superior talents and well worthy of the confidence reposed in you by your King and Country. The high state of discipline you have maintained in the troops under your command not only secured to us our property but also kept the most perfect harmony between the soldiers and all classes of inhabitants. The sick and distressed people of Gorée will long lament your departure and feel the want of your liberal supplies. The impartiality and moderation of your decisions

---

458 MacCarthy was only appointed in April 1812 – letter from Downing Street to MacCarthy of 3 April 1812, CO 267/34.
459 "An Address from the Inhabitants of Gorée to Lieutenant-Colonel Chisholm", dated 26 May 1816.

in the administration of justice will always be remembered by us in sentiments of the most lively sense of the obedience we owe to the happy laws of England. The Friends of the African Institution are also greatly indebted to you for your unremitted exertions in carrying their humane and liberal views into execution. As a token of our regard and gratitude we beg you to accept of few gold rings and wear them in remembrance of us. We beg leave to conclude in wishing that you may on your arrival in England meet with a reward from your King and Country which is due to your faithful services. We shall at all times be most happy to hear of your better health and prosperity and if it meets the approbation of Government to send you back to this place we shall most heartily rejoice to see you."

Chisholm was also the bearer on his return of a letter from a local king, Mactar Jall, to the Prince Regent. In his letter the king professed his opposition to slavery and his willingness to support British interests in the region. From what Chisholm reported he appears to have done everything possible to suppress the trade in slaves in his kingdom and to report instances that came to his attention in neighbouring lands. It is said that the Prince Regent instructed that the king's letter should be acknowledged, and some presents transmitted to him in return.[460]

---

[460] Report of the Directors of the African Institution read at the Institution's AGM on 26 March 1817.

## CHAPTER ELEVEN

# LOWERING THE FLAG

1812-1817

Charles MacCarthy, who succeeded Maxwell as Lieutenant Governor in Saint-Louis, was another colourful character to pass through Senegal. Born in Cork, the son of French émigré Jean Gabriel Guerault and his Irish wife Charlotte, he later took his mother's maiden name. He joined the Irish brigade of the French army in 1785, and had already served in the army of the Dutch Republic and in the French émigré army before he received his first British commission in 1799. While in Saint-Louis MacCarthy lived with a local woman, Antoinette Carpot, who was the grand-daughter of Charles O'Hara, his predecessor from the days of the Crown colony of Senegambia. From Senegal he was posted to Sierra Leone, with his responsibilities later extending to Ghana where in 1823 he declared war on the King of the Ashanti. Early the following year Ashanti forces overran his camp and MacCarthy was killed and decapitated. It is said that his gold-rimmed skull was later used as a drinking cup by Ashanti rulers.

Soon after his arrival in Saint-Louis in September 1812 MacCarthy was reporting[461] that the colony was at its lowest ebb.

---

461 MacCarthy to Maxwell of 21 September 1812, CO 267/36.

He was later to cite three main factors for the stagnation of the colony.[462] The abolition of the slave trade had led to fewer ships visiting Saint-Louis. The gum trade had still not resumed – the Moors were demanding exorbitant prices that British merchants were unwilling to pay given the large stocks of gum currently in England. Finally, wars between the Moors and black African tribes and amongst the black African tribes themselves had again caused the abandonment of the annual voyage to Galam, 700km up the Senegal River. Moreover, many of the local traders doubted that the journey to Galam could ever be made profitable again since it was no longer possible to trade in slaves.

MacCarthy made the resumption of the gum trade one of his top priorities, making clear to the Moorish princes that the customs duties they were accustomed to receive would not be increased and would only be paid once the trade resumed. By May 1813 trade with the Brakna Moors had restarted, but the new King of the Trarzas was holding out for payment of an annual present, as was given to other Moorish princes. He also complained at MacCarthy's refusal to lend him support in his wars against the King of Waalo, recalling that when Charles O'Hara had been governor he had always backed the Moors.[463] But MacCarthy knew that only by being neutral would there be any chance of the trade with Galam resuming. Gum exports were to make a good recovery in 1813 with 600 tonnes exported.[464] This was less than the 1000 tonnes regularly exported by the French at the beginning of the century but was encouraging nevertheless given there had been no exports since the British resumed control in Saint-Louis four years earlier.

By September 1813, MacCarthy was triumphantly reporting[465] back to London that over sixty ships had sailed for Galam, with $40-50,000 worth of goods, mainly bafts, baize, gun powder, coral, amber, beads and salt which they would exchange for corn, gold and ivory. In

---

462 MacCarthy to Bathurst of 20 May 1813, CO 267/36.
463 MacCarrthy to Bathurst of 9 April 1813, CO 267/36.
464 MacCarthy to Bathurst of 13 August 1813, CO 267/36.
465 Letter from MacCarthy of 22 September 1813, CO 267/36.

February of the following year, he was celebrating[466] the safe return of the fleet with about 900 tons of corn, a thousand sheep, three or four tons of ivory and nearly five thousand pounds worth of gold. This was the first visit that had taken place without major incident since 1802, evidence, he concluded, of the goodwill felt among the locals towards the British.

MacCarthy was confident of a good market for British goods in the interior, reporting that the inhabitants of Galam were eager to trade British goods to the "great markets of Sego, Timbukto and Hausa". He was also encouraged by the fact that the eldest son of the King of Karta, to whom the kings of Boundou and Bambouk were paying tribute, had met the trading party at Galam and had assured them of his father's good disposition towards the English. MacCarthy was aware that events in Europe might lead Britain to hand Saint-Louis back to France but recommended that should Saint-Louis be retained a factory should be established at Galam, protected by a fort and a garrison of about fifty men. MacCarthy was also convinced that were the French to recover Saint-Louis the slave trade would resume, lamenting that this would undermine "the benevolent intentions of His Majesty for the happiness of Africa".

British abolition of the slave trade did not remove the threat for Africans of being sold into slavery. MacCarthy reported in March 1814, that two ships under Spanish colours had taken 379 slaves from the Gambia River.[467] Less than a month later he was reporting that an American ship flying Spanish colours had taken a further 400 slaves from the same river. Following the ban on the slave trade, British warships in the area had challenging instructions both to detain any slave ships thought to be disguised as Portuguese or Spanish vessels but also not to molest any bona fide Spanish or Portuguese ships.[468] On one occasion MacCarthy sent a small detachment down to the Gambia to seize a slaver. Nine died and nine were killed in the subsequent fighting. But MacCarthy knew that it would be impossible

---
466  MacCarthy to Bathurst of 21 Feb 1814, CO 267/38.
467  MacCarthy to Bathurst of 19 March 1814, CO 267/38.
468  Maxwell to Lieutenant Moore of 16 June 1810, CO 267/30.

to enforce the abolition of the slave trade in the Gambia from Gorée and recommended that the British Government re-establish a small garrison at Fort James, both to protect British merchant vessels but also to prevent a traffic in slaves that was "chiefly carried on by Americans under Spanish or Portuguese colours."[469]

While MacCarthy's relationships with the Moors and many African kings were good he found the Damel of Kayoor, whose territory included the lands around the mouth of the Senegal River, difficult to handle. A particular problem arose in relation to salvage rights over ships that foundered on the bar entering the Senegal River. The French had entered into a treaty with the Damel, subsequently renewed and also applied during Maxwell's time, under which the garrison at Saint-Louis had twenty-four hours to recover property from any ship lost on the bar. Anything subsequently recovered was the property of the Damel. MacCarthy considered this unfair and intended to renegotiate the treaty, but the Damel thought the treaty already too generous towards the Europeans and informed MacCarthy that he wanted to revert to the earlier custom whereby anything salvaged belonged to him. Any shipwrecked seaman who fell into his hands would also be his to ransom. MacCarthy refused and as a result found his trade through the Damel's territories disrupted.[470] Later a compromise was reached[471] under which the Damel agreed to allow the captain and crew of a shipwrecked boat to salvage what they could in twenty-four hours but refused to allow them to receive any assistance from the garrison at Saint-Louis.

The West Coast of Africa was never an easy posting but MacCarthy was there at a particularly unhealthy time. Between December 1811 and July 1813 seven out of twenty-four officers and 155 out of 372 European soldiers on Saint-Louis died.[472] Similar proportions died at Gorée during the same period.

---

469 MacCarthy to Bathurst of 10 June 1814, CO 267/38.
470 Note as attachment to letter from MacCarthy to Bathurst of 18 March 1814, CO 267/38.
471 MacCarthy to Bathurst of 8 April 1814, CO 267/38.
472 Letter from MacCarthy of 20 August 1813, CO 267/36.

MacCarthy was uneasy at the absence of a court in Saint-Louis and sought guidance from London on how justice in the colony was to be administered.[473] As it was not practical to send all cases to the court in Sierra Leone he encouraged arbitration, intervening to take decisions only where the parties could not agree or where their conclusions were contrary to British law.

The Napoleonic Wars finally came to an end with the signature on 30 May 1814 of the Treaty of Paris. Article 8 stipulated that all territories under France's control at the date of 1 January 1792 were to be returned to her. This included the island of Gorée and the settlement of Saint-Louis and their respective dependent factories on the Petite Côte and the Senegal River.

In June 1814, probably as yet unaware of the terms of the Treaty of Paris, MacCarthy left Saint-Louis for Sierra Leone in order to cover for Governor Maxwell who had returned temporarily to Britain for health reasons. He returned to Saint-Louis at the end of the year to supervise the evacuation. By then a new French government had been appointed in Paris and MacCarthy had heard that a French force would sail from Brest to recover the island in January 1815. He discovered too that some of the local inhabitants, anticipating the arrival of the French "had shown some intention into slave speculation"[474] MacCarthy made very clear that any transactions of that kind would be unlawful as long as the British flag was flying over Senegal.

By mid-March 1815 there was still no sign of the French but MacCarthy reported back to Lord Bathurst[475] that "the whole of the ordnance provisions and other public property of this garrison, and most of the articles of the same description at Gorée are now on board the transports". The ordnance and stores were subsequently removed to Sierra Leone.

---

473 MacCarthy to Bathurst of 7 July 1813, CO 267/36.
474 Just two months after the return of Saint-Louis British sources were reporting that the slave trade "which was so effectively abolished during the time the British had possession of them" had resumed: "A statement of facts relating to the slave trade in the neighbourhood of the River Senegal", dated 18 March 1817, FO 95/9/2.
475 MacCarthy to Bathurst of 13 March 1815, CO 267/40.

Shortly afterwards MacCarthy heard that Britain might in fact retain the settlements – given Napoleon's escape from exile in Elba and his return to Paris – and by May 1815 he had received new instructions from Lord Bathurst, sent in March, suspending the order to deliver Gorée and Saint-Louis to the French.[476] Poor MacCarthy immediately despatched transports to Sierra Leone to bring back the ordnance, shells, gunpowder and other defensive supplies he had earlier shipped out. In June, the transports having returned, he was reassuring Bathurst[477] that the settlements were as secure as they had been before the premature evacuation.

MacCarthy returned to Sierra Leone on 12 July 1815 and, following Maxwell's resignation from the post, was later appointed Governor.[478] Thomas Brereton was in turn appointed Lieutenant Governor in Saint-Louis in succession to MacCarthy. For a while life continued much as before with no further news of when the French – following Napoleon's surrender – might now arrive to reclaim the territories restored to them in 1814. A fleet sailed to Galam during the rains, while the river was high, returning to Saint-Louis the following year after a prosperous trip.[479] On instructions from London,[480] Brereton led a group of men down to the Gambia River to re-establish a British presence there, as MacCarthy had recommended. They decided against making their main base at Fort James and instead landed on the island of Banjul, later renamed St. Mary's Island, where they cleared the land to establish a settlement.[481] This was to be named Bathurst after the then Secretary of State for War and the Colonies before becoming Banjul again in 1973, eight years after The Gambia became independent.

Following the 1814 Treaty of Paris, French battalions had been quickly despatched to recover Martinique, Guadeloupe, La Reunion

---

476 MacCarthy to Bathurst of 4 May; Bathurst to MacCarthy of 24 March, CO 267/40.
477 MacCarthy to Bathurst of 18 June 1815, CO 267/40.
478 Bathurst to MacCarthy of 7 September 1815, CO 268/19.
479 Brereton to Bathurst of 13 Feb 1816, CO 267/42.
480 Bathurst to MacCarthy of 29 July 1815, CO 268/19.
481 Brereton to Bathurst of 10 May 1816, CO 267/42.

and Guyana which had all been returned to France under the treaty. But there had been delays in finding troops to reclaim Gorée and Saint-Louis. Eventually, Julien-Désiré Schmaltz, who had been appointed commander and administrator of Saint-Louis, departed France on 17 June 1816 on the frigate *La Méduse*, accompanied by the corvette *Echo*, the brig *Argus* and the armoured transport *La Loire*.

The captain of the *Méduse* Hugues Duroy de Chaumareys had not been at sea for twenty years and had never captained a ship. Warned to steer clear of the sand bank off Arguin he somehow managed to run aground there, some thirty miles from the coast. The date was 2 July 1816. On 5 July, fearing the ship was about to break up in an increasingly rough sea Captain de Chaumareys gave the order to abandon ship. There were 400 people on board and room for only 230 on the ship's six lifeboats. The hapless Captain de Chaumareys ignoring maritime tradition made sure he was among them. Seventeen men elected to stay on the ship. The remaining 153 boarded a raft, twenty metres long by seven metres wide which sat low in the sea, weighed down with people and barrels of wine but no water. Initially the raft was pulled by one of the lifeboats but when the tow rope broke those on the lifeboat chose not to repair it fearing they would be overrun by the increasingly drunk and desparate occupants of the raft.

Violence broke out as those on board fought for safer ground at the middle of the overladen raft. Men were killed, thrown into the sea or jumped from the raft and drowned. By the time the brig *Argus* located the raft only fifteen of the original 153 remained, five of whom died within days. Two of the survivors, a surgeon called Savigny, and a geographer by the name of Corréard wrote an account of what happened. This inspired the artist Géricault to immortalise the scenes on the raft in his painting *Le Radeau de la Méduse* (1818).

Those on the lifeboats fared better but still endured a terrible time. Only two of the six lifeboats reached Saint-Louis. The others landed further up the coast, as far as 400km north of the town. During the long walk south, they were attacked by Moors and some died of hunger. One who died was the wife of Lieutenant-Colonel Guérin,

Schmaltz's second in command, who was due to take command of Gorée. It is said he cut off his wife's head to avoid it being eaten by hyenas and carried it to Saint-Louis where he died a few days later. Of the seventeen who stayed on the ship, twelve tried their luck building another raft and were never heard of again. Three of the remaining five survived and were rescued on 15 August, forty-four days after the shipwreck. All told, of the 400 on board, 151 died and 249 survived.

The first group of survivors, among them Schmaltz, arrived in Saint-Louis on 8 July. Schmaltz's immediate priority was to send the *Argus* off to search for survivors and to enlist the help of the British in looking after those who arrived exhausted in Saint-Louis in dribs and drabs until 22 July. Two days after his arrival in Saint-Louis, Schmaltz formally notified Brereton that he had come to take possession of the colony in accordance with Article 8 of the Treaty of Paris signed over two years earlier. He handed over certified copies of the Royal Warrant, dated 30 July 1814, ordering the restitution of Gorée and Senegal and a letter from Lord Bathurst dated 20 February 1816 covering this order.[482] Brereton replied that he could not return Saint-Louis to the French, because he hadn't received instructions to do so from Governor MacCarthy in Sierra Leone and he had no means in any case to transport his troops. Schmaltz immediately offered a compromise – that English troops leave Gorée for Saint-Louis – pending resolution of the matter. He even offered to lend *la Loire* to transport the English troops. Brereton stuck to his position: he must await instructions.[483]

Schmaltz was not to take charge of Gorée and Saint-Louis for several months. From the start he found Brereton ill-disposed to be helpful. Accommodation on the island of Saint-Louis was provided only for the sickest. The others were forced to remain on the French ships. *La Loire* was not even allowed to unload her stores. Frustrated by Brereton at Saint-Louis Schmaltz despatched the *Echo* to take control of Gorée on 18 July, and followed himself the following week.

---

[482] National Archives of Senegal (2B1) but also letter from Brereton to Bathurst of 25 July 1816, CO 267/42.
[483] Schmaltz to Brereton of 11 July 1816, National Archives of Senegal, 2B1.

He received a better welcome from the English commander on Gorée, Mackenzie, and he judged they were making good progress with negotiations on the handover until a British ship arrived from Sierra Leone with reinforcements and orders from MacCarthy – issued before he knew anything of Schmaltz's arrival – to hand nothing over to the French until transport had arrived. Schmaltz was forced to set up camp on the mainland opposite Gorée. Hospital facilities for the wounded from *la Méduse* initially made available by Mackenzie on Gorée were withdrawn after the intervention of Brereton.[484] This decision was later overturned but the facilities that the French were given permission to use were so crowded that Schmaltz set up his own hospital in a building elsewhere on the island. Schmaltz also sought permission for an American ship, exceptionally, because of the shipwreck, to sell supplies to the French contingent. This too was refused.

English intransigence made life hard for Schmaltz.[485] He was short of money and supplies. He was unable to settle his soldiers – or the civilians who had come to trade and farm – either at Saint-Louis or Gorée. The camp his soldiers had established at Bel-Air on the mainland opposite Gorée dissolved into drunkenness, disorder and ill-discipline. Illness was rife during the rainy season. Although he had been able to send the *Echo* back to France with some of the surviving crew from *la Méduse* he could not yet despatch *la Loire* and the *Argus* with the rest of them. Both ships were needed for accommodation and *la Loire* had still not been allowed to unload its supplies. To top it all Brereton, on McCarthy's instructions, sent Schmaltz a bill – for £569, 5s and 3 3/4d – for help rendered after the shipwreck. Schmaltz was also informed that anything salvaged from *la Méduse* belonged to the British salvager.

In fairness to MacCarthy, once he knew of Schmaltz's arrival he tried to be as helpful as he could. In early August, he sent instructions to Brereton[486] to allow the civil establishment (but not the military)

---

484 National Archives of Senegal, 2B1.
485 National Archives of Senegal, 2B1.
486 McCarthy to Brereton of 4 August 1816, CO 267/42.

to land. Sick military were however to be allowed to use the hospital. He advocated "liberality" to the French merchants to avoid retaliatory action in the future against any British traders who might remain (in the event nearly all the British traders left Gorée for the new settlement at Bathurst). But MacCarthy felt that he did not have instructions on how and to where to withdraw[487] and informed Schmaltz that he could not evacuate without them.

On 30 September, MacCarthy issued a proclamation to the effect that Gorée and Saint-Louis remained under British control but that the French were authorised to unload their stores and to trade in both settlements on the same basis as the British.[488] On 2 October, Schmaltz sent another letter to Brereton this time enclosing copies of one from the French Minister of Marine, itself covering a letter from Lord Bathurst, confirming that Gorée and Saint-Louis should be handed back to the French. He sent the original Lord Bathurst letter to MacCarthy in Freetown.

By the end of October, *la Loire* had unloaded its stores in Saint-Louis, enabling the ship to then return to France. Generously in the circumstances Schmaltz gave permission for Brereton, weakened by illness and recently widowed, to travel back on *la Loire*. Over a period of four months Schmaltz sent Brereton dozens of letters, all studiously polite and diplomatic but nevertheless betraying the intense irritation he clearly felt at what he considered Brereton's stubborn obfuscation and unhelpfulness.[489]

If he thought that after Brereton's departure things would go more smoothly with Mackenzie, temporarily in charge of both Saint-Louis and Gorée, he was wrong. The man who had earlier been disposed to be helpful now, it seemed to Schmaltz, appeared to want to outdo Brereton in making life difficult. He refused to allow two French ships, *l'Eglantine* and *la Lionne*, recently arrived with supplies and a total of 120 additional troops, to enter the Senegal River. Buoyed by the ships' arrival and in possession of yet another letter from the

---

487 MacCarthy to M. Potin of 1 August 1816 and M, Durecu of 6 August 1816, 9F1.
488 Proclamation dated 30 September 1816, CO 267/42.
489 National Archives of Senegal, 2B1.

British government ordering Saint-Louis and Gorée to be returned to the French,[490] Schmaltz wrote to Mackenzie on 12 December saying that he was ready to agree the necessary procedures for the return.[491] Mackenzie however replied that he was only temporarily in charge and that he had therefore written to MacCarthy in Freetown for instructions…

It must have been a shock for MacCarthy finally to receive on 26 December[492] Bathurst's letter of 16 September. This read:

> "His Majesty's Government have this day learnt with great regret and surprise that the Officers Commanding at Senegal have refused to surrender that settlement and Gorée to the Expedition which has been directed by His Most Christian Majesty to take possession of them. After the repeated instructions which have been transmitted to you on this subject, repeated beyond all former precedent for the express purpose of preventing any such misunderstanding, an occurrence of this nature requires more than ordinary explanation. I am therefore commanded by the Prince Regent to require from you a statement of the reasons which prevented an immediate compliance with the explicit instructions which accompanied it which appears from the statement of the French Ambassador were delivered to Colonel Brereton by the Officer Commanding His Most Christian Majesty's forces and most peremptorily to direct that those possessions on the Coast of Africa which were by the Treaty of Paris stipulated to be restored to His Most Christian Majesty may be immediately delivered over to the French Commissary without any further delay".

The letter went on to say that:

---

490  Presumably Bathurst's letter of 16 September.
491  National Archives of Senegal, 2B1.
492  MacCarthy to Bathurst of 26 January 1817, CO 267/42.

"Any difficulty as to the means of removing the garrison and stores, however important to obviate under other circumstances, is in no degree to interfere with the execution of the stipulations of the Treaty of Paris". It ended by stressing the importance of not exciting "unfounded suspicions of the good intentions of the British government".

A separate letter from Bathurst to MacCarthy of the same date instructed him to convey to Brereton the Prince Regent's displeasure that Brereton did not allow French troops to land. By the time MacCarthy received these letters Brereton was long gone.

As soon as he received Bathurst's letter MacCarthy immediately sent a couple of trusted aides from Sierra Leone to Gorée with instructions to hire boats to evacuate the troops first from Saint-Louis and then from Gorée.[493] No doubt feeling the wrath of his Regent he was furious with MacKenzie for having refused to hand over Gorée and Saint-Louis to the French, even when shown by Schmaltz a copy of Bathurst's letter of 16 September. He said it was ridiculous that MacKenzie justified his refusal on the grounds that he needed to see a copy of the original Royal Warrant when MacCarthy had had this in his possession since March 1815 and Schmaltz had previously given Brereton an authenticated copy.[494]

The preliminary arrangements for the handing over of Saint-Louis were signed by Major MacKenzie and Colonel Schmaltz on 21 January 1817 and in a formal ceremony on 25 January the French flag was raised on the battery.[495] The French and British flags flew briefly together, accompanied by a twenty-one-gun salute. The Union Jack was lowered and raised for a final time, saluted, and replaced by the French flag. French troops then took up the positions previously occupied by the British troops, who immediately embarked on their ships. Gorée was returned to the French nearly four weeks later on 15 February 1817.[496]

---

493 MacCarthy to Bathurst of 26 January 1817, CO 267/42.
494 MacCarthy to MacKenzie of 28 December 1816, CO 267/45.
495 MacCarthy to Bathurst of 4 February 187, CO 267/45.
496 Schmaltz to MacCarthy of 26 February, CO 267/45.

Having finally resumed control, Schmaltz discovered that, contrary to the provisions of the treaty all the bronze ordinance that was supposed to be at the settlements was missing as was the library the French had previously assembled which had been taken to Sierra Leone by Governor Maxwell. MacCarthy had received instructions[497] from Lord Bathurst to only remove ordinance from Saint-Louis that the British had themselves brought into the settlement since 1809. MacCarthy innocently explained to Bathurst[498] that he had removed some guns to the Gambia before receiving Bathurst's instructions. However, correspondence exists[499] which shows that MacCarthy instructed Brereton to remove the brass guns to Gambia in July 1816. As for the library he sought Bathurst's instructions on what he should do, noting that the library had been sent to Sierra Leone before the Treaty of Paris "and was in any case left to him in a wretched state and is actually of very trifling value".

After the departure of the British the slave trade returned to Senegal's shores, despite a proclamation from Schmaltz banning it.[500] One Spanish vessel departed from the coast near Gorée with 150 slaves on 3 March 1817, little more than a week after the handover. A British visitor to Saint-Louis in November 1817 reported that since the handover four French ships each with around 160 slaves had left Saint-Louis and another two schooners were waiting in the river to take on slaves.[501] Moorish tribes were again raiding black African villages to seize people to sell. Initially the loading of slaves was done in some secrecy but by March 1818 the same correspondent was reporting that the trade was taking place in full view of the French fort.[502] He listed the names and home ports of the ships that had taken on slaves and of those waiting in the river. He also observed how the

---

497 Letter from Bathurst to Brereton of 1 June 1815; also Bathurst to MacCarthy of 9 May 1816, CO 268/1.9
498 MacCarthy to Bathurst of 18 March 1817, CO 267/45.
499 MacCarthy to Brereton of 22 July 1816, CO 267/42.
500 "A Statement of fact relating to the Slave Trade in the neighbourhood of the River Senegal", dated 18 March 1817, FO 95/9/2.
501 Extract of a letter, author unclear, of 8 November 1817, FO 95/9/2.
502 Extract of a letter of 19 March 1818, FO 95/9/2.

Damel of Kayoor, on realising that the trade was resuming, had burnt and pillaged villages within his own territory, with families being dragged off and sold.

For sixty years control of Saint-Louis and Gorée had passed back and forth between Britain and France. But after 1817, Britain was never again to try to occupy either settlement. The British administered Saint-Louis for a total of twenty-nine years and Gorée for twenty-six. The British flag flew over one or other or both settlements for a total of forty-two years.

In the history of Senegal, it was but a brief sojourn. Even the most ardent admirer of British colonial history would be hard pressed to point to any significant, lasting benefit of the British presence. In terms of architecture, administration and culture we left barely a trace. It may be true, as some have argued, that the tendency of the British administration to leave trade in the hands of the private sector consolidated the wealth and influence of the métis population, notably the signares. But otherwise there is little by which to remember the British and, as a result, the British presence in Gorée and Saint-Louis has been largely forgotten.

However, the British presence did live on, long after their departure, in the names of many of the families of the two settlements. Armstrong, Patterson, Bishop all became Senegalese names. Perhaps the most famous Senegalese name of British origin was Dodds. The aide de camp of Saint-Louis's last British Lieutenant Governor, Thomas Brereton, was a man called John Dodds. In 1816, he married Sophie Feultaine, a mixed-race woman. Their son, Henry, and his wife Charlotte Billaud, had ten children, one of whom was General Alfred Amédée Dodds, a decorated military officer perhaps best known for commanding the French forces in the Second Franco-Dahomean War (1892-1894) which resulted in the Kingdom of Dahomey being incorporated in the colonial territory of French West Africa.

CHAPTER TWELVE

# THE SMILE ON THE FACE OF AFRICA

The political map of Africa is, by and large, an artificial construct of the colonial powers. Many borders were drawn without taking account of the ethno-linguistic reality on the ground. They follow lines of latitude or longitude or reflect areas of conquest or influence. As a result, villages of the same ethnic group, used to interacting as part of the same community, sometimes found themselves on opposite sides of colonial borders, subject to different jurisdictions with different laws, currencies and languages.

One of the most striking oddities of the political map of Africa is the sliver of territory that is the country of The Gambia, the smile, as the Gambians themselves would have it, on the west coast of Africa. Surrounded on all sides by Senegal, except on its short coastal seaboard, it cuts off Senegal's southern region of Casamance from the rest of the country, including the capital Dakar. Casamance's geographical isolation is just one of many factors that has contributed to the intractable if low-intensity conflict that has sapped the potential of the region now for over thirty years. And it is a factor for which Britain and France share the responsibility.

As we have seen, the Treaty of Paris, signed in 1814, provided for the return of Saint-Louis and Gorée to France and confirmed British primacy on the Gambia River, while allowing the French to retain a factory at Albreda. The British decided not to rebuild the fort on tiny James Island, 30km upriver, but instead to establish a new military and trading outpost on the larger island of Banjul at the mouth of the river. In a treaty signed on 23 April 1816, the King of Kombo ceded the island to the British in return for an annual payment. The island was renamed St. Mary's Island and the settlement that began to form was called Bathurst, after Earl Bathurst, Secretary of State for War and the Colonies at the time. By 1818, Bathurst had a population of 600, including the garrison. By 1828, the settlement had grown to have a civilian population of 1800, including thirty Europeans. Many British traders previously based on Gorée – such as Forster and Smith, Thomas Chown and William Waterman – moved to Bathurst. Around the same time the French also reoccupied Albreda, their trading post on the northern bank of the river near James Island.

Relations between the French at Gorée and Saint-Louis and the British in Gambia were strained, and not helped by the inevitable language difficulties. A wonderful letter from Captain Alexander Findlay, the Commander of the British garrison at Bathurst, to Captain Hugon, the French Commandant at Gorée, written in 1823, simply reads:

> "I have the honour to acknowledge the receipt of your letter of the 13th, but I am sorry to say that I cannot find a person at present in this place able to translate it, and as I cannot read French, I am not able to answer you on the different points it may relate to."[503]

Having abolished the slave trade in 1807, the British were determined to bring an end to it on the Gambia River, but the trade continued, with African slavers kidnapping victims from the southern bank of the river and selling them to French traders at Albreda. These traders

---

[503] Findlay to Hugon of 18 September 1823, National Archives of Senegal 1F1.

would then arrange for the slaves to be taken by land to Joal, or other points on the Senegalese coast, avoiding the mouth of the Gambia River where British warships occasionally patrolled.

However, after the French abolished the slave trade in 1818, they and the British, now no longer at war with each other, cooperated to end the trade. Subsequent correspondence between Captains Findlay and Hugon suggests there was actually good cooperation between the settlements on the Gambia River too. On one occasion Findlay wrote to inform Hugon that a local king had stolen a canoe, together with the four men who sailed it, and had sold one of the men to a resident of Gorée for a price that included 2kgs of rum, two muskets, 100 balls, 100 flints, one piece of blue cloth, three knives, two bars of iron and four snuffboxes. He asked Hugon to bring the buyer to account for "committing a crime so detestable both to your government and mine" and to return the canoeist to the Gambia.[504] Hugon must have obliged because in a subsequent letter Findlay rejoices in Hugon's shared determination "to punish those persons who commit that abominable crime of purchasing slaves, a traffick (sic) so obnoxious to our respective governments."[505]

Many French visitors to the Gambia River, however did not want to acknowledge Britain's rights on the river. French ships refused to perform the traditional gun salute when passing St. Mary's Island and, on occasion, stopped and searched British vessels in the vicinity of Albreda. They also indulged in smuggling, which had a serious impact on the tax revenue Bathurst was able to collect. The British took the view that the French had no right to trade beyond James Island, situated a short distance up the river from Albreda, but traders at Albreda would surreptitiously send canoes, laden with goods, up the river beyond James Island to trade with the local chiefs.

From the end of the Napoleonic Wars in 1815, France steadfastly sought to expand its influence in the region, including in the Casamance. Indeed, it was only at the beginning of the nineteenth

---

504 Findlay to Hugon of 25 September 1823, National Archives of Senegal 1F1.
505 Findlay to Hugon of 23 October 1823, National Archives of Senegal 1F1.

century that both the French and the British started to take a closer look at the Casamance River. Until then, if the Banun, Joola and Mandinka living along the river had come across a European he was most likely to have been Portuguese. The Portuguese considered Casamance to fall within their sphere of influence. From their base in Cacheu, in what was to become the colony of Portuguese Guinea,[506] they made occasional forays into Casamance and began to settle at Ziguinchor.

The French established trading posts in Casamance, first at Karabane in 1828 and subsequently at Seju (present day Sedhiou). Additional settlements, later abandoned, were founded at Jogue and other points on the river. The British were less interested in securing territory for themselves on the Casamance River and more concerned to ensure that their right to trade freely with the people of the Casamance was not restricted by the French.

British traders from Bathurst had been visiting the river to trade for rice, leather and wax in the years before the French established their trading posts,[507] and the locals were keen to trade with the British, not least because they preferred English guns to French ones.[508] A recommendation from the then Lieutenant Governor of the Gambia, George Rendall,[509] that Britain should occupy an island near Karabane was not approved in London to avoid upsetting the Portuguese. However, a number of British traders did establish themselves for a few years near Karabane at a place they called Lincoln.[510] The old English factory is now known as Elinkine, a small river port and point of departure by boat for tourists wishing to visit the evocative ruins of the old French settlement at Karabane. A geographical dictionary of the late nineteenth century noted, rather uncharitably, that to the "south-east of Carabane stands the old English factory of *Lincoln*,

---

506 Now Guinea-Bissau.
507 Roche, C. *Histoire de la Casamance: Conquete et resistance 1850-1920*, p. 76.
508 National Archives of Senegal 4 B 8 according to C. Roche, p. 86.
509 George Rendall, Lieutenant Governor of the Gambia, 1830-1837.
510 Saint-Martin, Yves-Jean. *Le Sénégal sous le second Empire: naissance d'un empire colonial (1850-1871)*, p. 459.

which has become the wretched village of *Elinkin*, inhabited by the riffraff of various populations, much dreaded by their neighbours".[511]

The French reluctantly accepted the competition. Governor Charmasson writing in 1839 to the French Director of Colonies noted that Casamance did not belong to the French and they would have to put up with the English traders though he also suggested they should try to keep them away from their own trading posts.[512] An English trader, by the name of Forster, set himself up in Seju under the protection of the local *Alcalde*[513] but he found it hard to make money and left within a few years. As on the Gambia River tension between British and French interests occasionally escalated. In September 1839, a British cutter, the *Highlander*, was seized by the French at Seju when it arrived to pick up a cargo of hides, rice and wax.[514] And in a later incident a French ship, *la Senegalaise*, was seized and then sold by an English court in Sierra Leone on suspicion of involvement in the slave trade.

The French trading presence at Albreda continued to be an irritation and a worry to the British. The appointment of an officer of the French Navy as Resident in Albreda prompted concern as to France's intentions and led the British Government to propose in May 1852 that the French renounce Albreda in return for Britain giving up its rights to trade for gum at Portendic.[515] The French quickly accepted this proposal although it was only on 7 March 1857 that the convention confirming this agreement was signed, with the documents of ratification exchanged a few weeks later.[516]

The presence of the British in the Gambia was a source of much frustration and irritation to the French too and successive governors begged Paris to persuade the British to exchange Gambia in return for

---

511 Reclus, Elisée. *The Universal Geography, Earth and its Inhabitants, Volume* 12 (J.S Virtue and Company Limited, 1898).
512 Charmasson to the Ministry of 12 August 1839. National Archives of Senegal 2B 18 according to Roche, p. 88.
513 A local official.
514 Ibid p. 88-89.
515 CO 879/2.
516 The exchange took place on 25 March 1857.

some French possession elsewhere. By the 1860s, the prospect was a real one. The British Parliament was becoming increasingly concerned at the cost of Britain's four West African settlements (Gambia, Sierra Leone, the Gold Coast and Lagos) and in 1865 established a cross-party Committee to consider a report and recommendations by a Colonel Ord on their future. Ord's recommendations included that the four settlements should be merged into one government, head-quartered in Freetown. But he also recommended that the British settlement at MacCarthy Island, 270km up the Gambia River, should be abandoned, and that the British presence in Gambia "should be confined as much as possible to the mouth of the river". This may have suggested to the French that the time was ripe to make an offer for the Gambia.

In 1866, the French first proposed an exchange of territories in West Africa between the two countries.[517] They suggested that Britain should cede their settlements on the Gambia River to France in exchange for French settlements at Grand Bassam, Dabou and Assinie, further east along the coast in what is today Côte d'Ivoire. A few weeks later, the French came up with an amended proposal, substituting their settlements at Gabon for those in Grand Bassam, Dabou and Assinie. The British Government declined the proposal in 1868.[518]

By 1870, the British were concerned by the advance of the French in districts to the north of Sierra Leone and the establishment by them of customs houses there. There had been an exchange of territories with the Dutch on the Gold Coast in 1867, and in 1869 the Dutch had started to think about ceding the whole of the costly Dutch Gold Coast to Britain. This encouraged the British to look again at the possibility of an exchange with the French.

On 11 February 1870, Lord Clarendon[519] wrote to Lord Lyons, the British Ambassador in Paris, to say that the government was interested

---

517 Letter from the French Ambassador, Henri-Godefroi-Bernard-Alphonse, prince de La Tour d'Auvergne, of 22 March to Lord Clarendon, CO 87/88.
518 Memorandum on proposed Exchange of Territories with France on the West Coast of Africa, 7 February 1876 (initialled A.W.L.H), CO 879/9.
519 George William Frederick Villiers, 4th Earl of Clarendon, Secretary of State for Foreign Affairs 9 December 1868 – 27 June 1870 (and previously 21 February 1853 – 26 February 1858 and 3 November 1865 – 6 July 1866).

in resurrecting the idea of ceding Gambia provided it was possible at the same time to come to an understanding on French territories on the Fouricaria and Mellacourie Rivers in Sierra Leone.[520] Lyons was therefore instructed to propose to the French Government that Britain would cede all its rights north of the River Dembia (now known as the Konkouré River, lying just west of Conakry in today's Guinea) in return for France not seeking to acquire any territory between the river Dembia and the river Shebar (now known as the Sherbro River which lies south of the island of Sherbro off the coast of Sierra Leone).

The French accepted these proposals on condition that French subjects in the territories to the south of the Dembia should enjoy the same protection and rights as British subjects and that French merchandise and ships should be subject to the same taxes as British ones. The French proposed that these same rights should be accorded on a reciprocal basis to British citizens and goods in French possessions. The British were prepared to agree this suggestion, but shortly afterwards France went to war with Prussia and the negotiations were put on ice.[521]

Sir Arthur Kennedy, Britain's Governor in Sierra Leone, under whose jurisdiction Gambia fell, was one of the most enthusiastic advocates of cession, having proposed it to the colonial authorities following a visit he made to Bathurst in 1869.[522] In Kennedy's view,[523] the Gambia was of little value, as it did not provide a sufficient financial return. He calculated the value of imports at a modest £90,000 per annum and exports only marginally higher at £91,000 per annum (though only 20% of these went to Britain). Set against that the civilian and military cost of the settlement was £40,000.

The settlement had never really prospered. There were only five English and four French trading companies in Bathurst and the European population was less than fifty. None of the British companies were doing well and some were planning to retire from a business that

---

520 Clarendon to Lord Lyons of 11 February 1870, CO 879/2.
521 Rogers, Colonial Office to Otway of 6 June 1870, CO 879/2.
522 Kennedy to Earl Granville of 29 March 1870, CO 879/2.
523 Kennedy to Granville of 29 April 1869, CO 879/2.

was no longer profitable. Kennedy reported[524] that of 188 ships that arrived at the Gambia in 1869 only thirty-four came from Britain, whereas twenty-one came from France and 90 from Senegal and Gorée. Moreover, of the thirty-four ships that had come from Britain twenty were mail steamers, which were subsidised to call at the port. In practice, he explained, only fourteen ships of a combined 3,286 tonnes called at Bathurst against 111 French ships of 11,495 tonnes.[525] Of departing ships thirty-nine went to the UK (of which nineteen were mail-steamers) but 110 went to France. Kennedy thought the transfer of the Gambia would be more unpopular with the French traders than the British, as French traders, he claimed, preferred to do business under British rather than French rule. He didn't foresee any major opposition to the transfer from the local African population provided that they received guarantees in respect of their rights and their property. Rear Admiral Patey, Administrator of the Gambia, agreed with Kennedy's downbeat assessment adding that "the settlements of the Gambia are maintained at a heavy sacrifice, morally, physically and pecunarily to the Imperial Government." [526]

There was nothing secret about these negotiations over the future of the Gambia. British troops withdrew from Bathurst and an increasing number of French officials, including the Governor of Senegal, came to visit the town.[527] The King of the Kombo wrote to Queen Victoria asking her not to give the land to strangers but to return it to him. The British merchants Forster and Smith wrote to Ministers in the Government to protest at the possibility of Gambia being ceded[528] while the Manchester Chamber of Commerce wrote to seek clarity on the Government's intentions. A question was asked in Parliament[529] as to whether negotiations were taking place with the intention of transferring Gambia to the French. The Government

---
524 Kennedy to Granville of 19 April 1870, CO 879/2.
525 Letter from Kennedy to Granville of 11 April 1870, CO 879/2.
526 CO 879/8.
527 Gray p. 437.
528 Letter to Granville of 18 June 1870, CO 879/2.
529 Question from R Fowler, reply from Monsell, Hansard HC Deb 10 June 1870 vol 201 cc1842-3

acknowledged that discussions on the limit of English and French influence on the West Coast of Africa were taking place and that a transfer was one of the steps under consideration. Both Granville[530] and Clarendon, Secretaries of State for War and the Colonies and Foreign Affairs respectively, had earlier agreed that the consent of Parliament would be needed before Gambia could be transferred to the French and assurances to this effect were given in Parliament on the same day.

On 15 July, the Duke of Manchester argued in Parliament against a transfer noting that the population was against it and that the settlement would be of very great importance in the event of war. In reply Lord Granville, now Foreign Secretary after Clarendon's death, said he could not conceive how Gambia could be useful in time of war unless "our seamen were seized with an unusual whim to run away and hide themselves from the rest of the world". He concluded by saying that "while the Colony would be of great advantage to the French in connection with their flourishing Colony of Senegal, I think it is no exaggeration to say that Gambia is to our country an absolute burden without any redeeming characteristics."[531] Views within Parliament were split with some opposing the transfer on essentially religious grounds – a Protestant community should not, they argued, be ceded to a Roman Catholic country.

Earl Kimberley,[532] Granville's successor as Secretary of State for War and the Colonies, wrote to Sir Arthur Kennedy on 23 July 1870, to inform him that as a result of the outbreak of war between France and Prussia the government thought it necessary to postpone the transfer.[533] The British Government gave the French a different

---

530 Granville George Leveson-Gower, 2nd Earl Granville. Secretary of State for War and the Colonies 9 December 1868-6 July 1870. Also three times Secretary of State for Foreign Affairs : 6 December 1851 – 27 February 1852, 6 July 1870 – 21 February 1874 and 28 April 1880 – 24 June 1885
531 HL Deb 15 July 1870 vol 203 cc339-42.
532 John Wodehouse, 1st Earl of Kimberley. Liberal Politician. Secretary of State for War and the Colonies, 6 July. 1870 – 17 February 1874. Also later Secretary of State for Foreign Affairs 10 March 1894 – 21 June 1895.
533 Kimberley to Sir A. Kennedy of 23 July 1870, CO 879/2.

explanation, initially blaming the pressure of parliamentary business for the delay in introducing a bill to give effect to the transfer before later explaining[534] that they had decided not to proceed because there was so much opposition in Parliament. However, in Parliament on 4 May 1871 the Government spokesman said that negotiations had been broken off on the outbreak of the Franco-Prussian war and there was "certainly no present probability of their being resumed".

The French returned to the charge in April 1874, the French Ambassador in London broaching to the new Foreign Secretary, Lord Derby,[535] the idea of an exchange of territories in West Africa.[536] A Foreign Office memo at the time[537] noted that objections raised in the past to the swap were of little weight and that earlier negotiations had been on the point of entering their final stages when they had been postponed because of the Franco-Prussian war. Following further discussion, endorsed by Cabinet, the British authorities decided that the price for giving up the Gambia should be that France cede to Britain all territory east of River Pongas[538] to the Benin River.[539] Judging the French possessions largely worthless the idea was also raised that the French should be asked to pay compensation for the buildings at Bathurst.

The more they thought about it the more the British decided they wanted in return for the Gambia. A map submitted to Cabinet in April 1875 showed the stretch of coast between the Benin River and Gabon being open to either Government to acquire settlements. But by May British officials were taking the view that Britain should seek to control the coast all the way to Gabon.[540]

---

534 Lyons to Duke of Gramont of 21 July 1870, CO 879/2 and FO Memorandum of 20 April 1874, CO 879/7.
535 Edward Henry Stanley, 15th Earl of Derby served as Foreign Secretary 1866 to 1868 and from 1874 to 1878.
536 Derby to Lyons of 11 April 1874, CO 879/7.
537 FO Memorandum of 20 April 1874, CO 879/7.
538 The River Pongas is located in Guinea, to the West of the River Dembia which the British had previously proposed as the border.
539 Letter from Meade (Colonial Office) to FO of 5 March 1875 (CO 879/7) and reply from Lister of 21 April 1875 (CO 879/8).
540 Lister to Colonial Office of 15 May 1875 and reply from Herbert of 17 May, CO 879/2.

The British formally conveyed their answer to the French request in a memorandum in July 1875.[541] This proposed the River Pongas as the border between the French and British zones of influence with the British undertaking not to acquire any possessions or to exercise any political influence or protection over any tribes or territories lying between the northern branch of the River Pongas "and the northern limit of the existing French possessions" and requiring that the French make a similar undertaking in respect of territories and tribes between the northern part of the River Pongas and the French settlement of Gabon. By the end of the year, the British were even considering asking the French to throw in the settlement of Gabon too, believing that this might help persuade those at home who felt that Britain was not getting a good enough deal out of the transfer.[542]

There was only limited discussion in Parliament on the question in 1875 and the Government do not appear to have shared with Parliament their detailed thinking on the matter. But in February 1876, Lord Carnarvon,[543] Secretary of State for the Colonies, made a statement in the House of Lords on the negotiations. Carnarvon set out the advantages to be had from the exchange and recalled the objections that had been raised. He denied that the colonists were unanimously opposed to the exchange, as some claimed, maintaining that British residents – who had dwindled to fewer than twenty – were at best indifferent. He rejected too the argument that Gambia was valuable to Britain noting that the trade "has passed, or is passing, from English traders into the hands of French colonists". "No doubt" he added, "it did render important service in former times: but those days are past, and the necessity for us to have that river no longer exists".

---

541 Memorandum respecting the Proposals for an Exchange between the British and French Governments of certain Territories belonging to England and France respectively on the West Coast of Africa, 23 July 1875.
542 Meade to FO of 29 December 1875, CO 879/8.
543 Henry Howard Molyneux Herbert, 4th Earl of Carnarvon, Secretary of State for the Colonies 21 February 1874 – 4 February 1878.

Carnarvon dealt with other objections too. He noted that, as often happened, "we are told that the tribes in the neighbourhood of the settlement are amiable". He pointed out that in the case of the Gambia this couldn't be further from the truth and that their neighbours were Muslim fanatics, "eminently warlike and averse to order". Carnarvon argued that the proposed exchange would enable the British to consolidate their settlements on the Gold Coast – to which Parliament attached great importance – and would more than double the Gold Coast's revenue since the French settlements in the vicinity were used to smuggle goods into the interior, which competed unfairly with British imports. Securing the Gold Coast's future, he said, required increased expenditure. This could either come from its own resources, assuming the transfer went ahead, or would have to be voted by Parliament (he knew that wouldn't be popular). Although Carnarvon's support for the exchange was clear he said the Government did not want to force the proposition but, with a view to forging a consensus, wanted Parliament to discuss the question.

Lord Granville, now Liberal leader on the opposition benches in the House of Lords, did not seek to oppose the proposition (since he had been favourable to the idea when he himself was Colonial and Foreign Secretary) but said he thought it odd that the Government were presenting ideas for debate and not bringing forward a bill to implement their chosen policy. He said the Government appeared not to have made up its mind what it wanted to do. Opinion in the House was divided. Some Lords strongly advocated the exchange. Others opposed, citing again the potential for exploiting trade with the interior of Africa and blaming the lacklustre trade that then prevailed on the uncertainty surrounding the colony's future. Earl Fortescue ventured that Britain would be "jeopardising the opportunity offered us by that great navigable river of civilizing and Christianizing the interior."[544] The Cabinet was reluctant to push the issue too hard in the face of opposition and Disraeli, the Prime Minister, announced in the House of Commons on 21 February 1876, that the Government

---
544 Hansard 17 February 1876 vol 227 cc 374-97.

had decided to appoint a Select Committee to look into the issue in greater depth.[545]

The French however had been caught by surprise by the Government's memo and by Carnarvon's speech. Their ambassador in London explained to Lord Derby that there must have been a misunderstanding.[546] France was not prepared to give up all influence on the coast south of River Pongas, (for example at Whydah and Porto Novo where it had settlements). Formal confirmation of this came in a Note Verbale on 8 March. Lord Carnarvon concluded[547] that there was a material divergence between the views of the two governments and recommended that the French Government be informed that negotiations were closed. This was done on 20 March. On the same day both Houses of Parliament were informed[548] that as the French were not willing to give up entire and exclusive control of the coast to the British negotiations had been abandoned as had plans to appoint a Select Committee in the House of Commons.

On 24 April, the French ambassador informed Lord Derby that the intention of his government had only been to inquire "what was the meaning of an expression which Her Majesty's Government had made use of with regard to influence on the coast and that far from desiring to break off the negotiation they would have been prepared to continue it on the terms of Her Majesty's Government, or to agree to all that Her Majesty's Government desired".

It seems likely that this accommodating response was a worried reaction to the apparent finality of the British decision to abandon the negotiations, which they would have liked to see continue, rather than representing a willingness to cede control of the entire coast east of present day Guinea to the British.

In May 1876, William MacArthur raised in the House of Commons his concerns that the uncertainty over the future of the Gambia was

---

545 Hansard House of Commons debate, 21 February 1876 vol 227 c561.
546 Derby to Lyons of 1 March 1876, CO 879/8.
547 Meade to FO of 15 March 1876, CO 879/8.
548 Hansard House of Lords debate 20 March 1876 vol 228 cc264-5, HC Deb 20 March 1876 vol 228 c272.

to the disadvantage of its merchants and expressed the hope that "no Government would again attempt to hand over to a foreign power some 14,000 of Her Majesty's Subjects without asking their consent and that they would not surrender for imaginary advantages one of the noblest rivers on the western coast of Africa". He spoke at length of the potential of the Gambia and appealed to the House to support the opening up of the river to legitimate commerce, including with the Upper Niger. In reply Mr Lowther said that the colony was losing money and would doubtless need a grant from Parliament to survive but confirmed "it was now determined to retain the colony."[549]

Nevertheless, the possibility of ceding Gambia was raised again in 1883, by which time not just France and Britain but all European powers were increasingly focused on the conquest of the continent in what was to become known as the Scramble for Africa. A further Memorandum[550] advocated the transfer noting in the past an "exaggerated apprehension of the unwillingness of Parliament" and that the opposition of merchants had been more about enhancing the value of their property. It conceded however that the Church remained opposed to handing the inhabitants over to Catholics. The Memorandum concluded that a transfer would be good for British settlements in the Gold Coast and Lagos (envisaging that the French would give up their territory in the vicinity of these settlements); facilitate the control of the import of arms along this section of the coast; and enable the Government to at last get rid of the Gambia, which served no useful purpose.

With Britain and France having reached an agreement the year before on their spheres of influence in the neighbourhood of Sierra Leone, Mellicourie was no longer considered an issue (even though the agreement had not yet been ratified), but the Memorandum raised the possibility of throwing some other far flung territorial disputes into the mix; including the possibility of recognising the French claim to the Pacific island of Raiatea, getting them to abolish their convict

---

549 Hansard House of Commons Debate 2 May 1876 vol 228 cc1998-2007
550 Memorandum respecting French proceedings on the West Coast of Africa dated 29 September 1883, CO 879/21/2.

settlement near Australia, and also to surrender their fishing rights off the coast of Newfoundland. This imaginative piece of brainstorming does not however appear to have gained much traction or led to a resumption of negotiations with the French.

From 1887, with the Scramble for Africa in full swing, the British became increasingly concerned about the French pushing down from their territory of Saloum, which lay to the north of the Gambia River.[551] The French had been trying to assert their authority in the district of Baddibu on the northern bank of the river. They had taken military action against Said Matti, a claimant to be chief of the district, with whom the British had recently concluded a treaty. The French supported a rival claimant Momodu N'Dare Ba, who was allied with the King of Saloum.

In February 1887, Lord Lyons, the British Ambassador to France, asked the French what they considered the southern border of French jurisdiction. The British clearly thought it should be the south bank of the Saloum River and were rather afraid the French would consider the territory of Saloum to extend to the northern bank of the Gambia River and that they would use a presence there to prevent trade from going down the river to Bathurst and instead to divert it to Gorée. By October, Lord Lyons had still not received a reply.[552]

In April 1887, Sir Samuel Rowe, Governor of Gambia, received a letter from the Colonial Office,[553] which made clear that it would be highly undesirable for the French to occupy any of the territory that currently lay between their and the British spheres of influence. Sir Henry Holland,[554] Secretary of State for Colonial Affairs since January 1887, was adamant that nothing should be done – presumably for cost reasons – to exercise a protectorate over these districts or to annex them in any way to the settlement on the Gambia. However, Rowe

---

551 CO 87/130.
552 Lord Salisbury to EH Egerton, Chargé d'Affaires in Paris, of 31 October 1887, CO 879/27 [African 348].
553 R H Meade to Rowe of 14 April 1887, CO 879/26.
554 Henry Thurstan Holland, 1st Viscount Knutsford Secretary of State for the Colonies, 14 January 1887 – 11 August 1892.

was told that steps should be taken to bring them within the British sphere of influence. He was, therefore, instructed to negotiate treaties of friendship with local chiefs that should include a promise by the chiefs that they would not cede their territories to any other power.

Rowe did not think much of these instructions. He didn't think Treaties of Friendship would work, because they did not provide the reassurance local chiefs were looking for. Any chief prepared to cede sovereignty over their territory only did so because they wanted to secure the protection of a foreign power from aggressive neighbouring tribes. Treaties of Friendship provided no guarantee that the British would intervene on their behalf should they be attacked. Rowe was in no doubt that if a local chief offered to cede, and found the British unwilling to accept, he would turn next to the French.[555]

Rowe's view[556] was that the two sides should agree on where the border between their respective territories should lie. The view of the Foreign Office's distinguished Librarian Sir Edward Hertslet, was that there was nothing in the Treaties of 1783, 1814, or 1857, on which the British could base a protest against the French acquiring influence over or possessing land in the interior of Baddibu.[557] Nonetheless there was a view that any interference by France with the chiefs whose possessions bordered the river could not fail to affect traffic on the river itself, and would therefore be incompatible with Britain's possession and full control of the river, as guaranteed by successive treaties.[558]

About this time rumours again surfaced that Britain was preparing to cede the Gambia to France, but, on this occasion, there appears to be no evidence for this. In September 1887, the Colonial Office wrote to the British and Africa Steam Navigation Company denying that cession was being considered.

In November 1887, E H Egerton, the Chargé d'Affaires in Paris, on instructions from London, sent a Note to the French

---

555 Letter from Rowe to Sir H Holland of 22 October 1887, CO 879/27.
556 Rowe to Holland of 1 July 1887, CO 879/26.
557 Note from Sir E. Hertslet of 14 June 1887, CO 879/26.
558 C0 879/27.

Government proposing "that negotiations commence between the two Governments for the exact delimitation of their spheres of influence in the Senegal and Gambia districts."[559] In a separate note, he asked the French Government to send instructions to the French civil and military authorities in the Saloum to stop their advances and to withdraw their flags from all disputed territory while negotiations between the two governments were pending.

Governor Rowe, meanwhile, was told not to hoist any flags on the north bank of the river given that negotiations with the French were underway. The British even declined an offer of cession from a local chief so as not to antagonise the French. Rowe was confined to activities on the south bank, where he made treaties with chiefs who agreed not to cede territory to any other power without the consent of the British Government.[560] Britain's self-imposed reserve effectively left the field open to the French, who had no such scruples, to extend their sphere of influence on both banks of the river.

When a reply eventually came from the French Foreign Minister, it was ambiguous and not entirely reassuring. Flourens[561] said that French authorities in the region had been instructed to observe the status quo in territories bordering British possessions dependent on Bathurst. Given that outside Bathurst Britain, strictly speaking, only controlled the Ceded Mile, a strip of land 58km long and one mile wide on the northern bank of the Gambia River, British Kombou and MacCarthy Island these instructions could be interpreted very narrowly whereas Britain was seeking to ensure that the French would not interfere anywhere along the Gambia River. Flourens's reference in his reply to British occupation of "La Basse Gambie" also strongly suggested that the French saw British claims as applying only to the lower part, and not to the whole river. Finally, Flourens said it would not be practical to take down the French flag where it had been recently raised, since it was not clear how many flags were involved or exactly where they were.

---

559 Egerton to Lord Salisbury of 7 November 1887, CO 879/27.
560 Memorandum on Affairs at the Gambia, attached to letter from John Bramston, Colonial Office, to the Foreign Office of 5 December 1887, CO 879/11.
561 Letter from Flourens of 7 December, 1877, CO 879/27.

The situation on the ground was even less reassuring. Within weeks of the instructions supposedly having been issued, the French Commandant at Foundiougne in the Sine-Saloum went with a force to Missirah, a village about 30km north of the Gambia River in an area considered by the British to be under their protection. British authorities also followed up rumours that the French were raising taxes in areas bordering the river. They found no evidence that the French had established customs houses or were directly levying taxes. However, it was patently clear they were supporting local chiefs in doing so.[562]

In November 1887, shortly after the Embassy in Paris had proposed negotiations on the border to the French, the Colonial Office wrote to the Foreign Office asking whether it was not time to propose a settlement of all outstanding West African questions, not just Gambia but also Porto Novo and Katanu in the vicinity of Lagos as well as Assinie.[563]

An internal memo identified three options for dealing with the threat posed by French advances near the Gambia River. Intervene more actively in the neighbouring districts, in order to provide local chiefs with the protection they sought; this was judged too costly. Give up Gambia; this was ruled out on the basis that it would be strongly opposed by residents, traders and MPs. The third option was to get the French to recognise Britain's influence over the Gambia in return for Britain giving up rights further east.

The Colonial Office subsequently wrote to the Foreign Office in December[564] to formally suggest that Britain relinquish its protectorate over Katanu (now Cotonou, Benin) and Appa (Apa, west of Lagos, Nigeria), that the boundary between the Protectorate of Lagos and that of Porto Novo should be drawn at a point west of the Ado (Yewa) river, and that in return for these important concessions the French should relinquish all claims to exercise authority or influence in the countries bordering the Gambia River. Furthermore, the Colonial

---

562 Griffith, Acting Administrator to Rowe (Governor), 29 May 1888, CO 879/27.
563 Bramston to FO of 16 November 1887 CO 879/27 [African 345].
564 Bramston to FO of 5 December 1887 CO 879/27.

Office insisted "that it should be distinctly understood from the outset of the negotiations that there can be no question of ceding the Gambia colony and river to France".

In January 1888, the French agreed to the British proposal for negotiations on a border between Senegal and Gambia. Bayol, the French Lieutenant Governor of Senegal, had prepared for this moment for some time. In 1886, he had written to Lieutenant Truche, Commander at Seju, encouraging him to negotiate treaties with all the independent rulers in the Casamance so that when the time came to define the borders between French and English possessions, France would be at an advantage. But Bayol has been blamed for giving too much away when the two sides eventually met to discuss the border in April 1889. It is said that the French Governor drew on a map two parallel lines[565] either side of the river as far as Yarbutenda[566] to indicate what could reasonably be claimed by Britain. This exceeded British expectations because at the time they remained confined to St. Mary's Island on which Bathurst stood, parts of Kombo on the mainland opposite St.Mary's Island and the Ceded Mile. The French controlled much of the northern bank beyond the Ceded Mile to Yarbutenda in the interior.

The talks made good progress. By June, the two sides had roughly agreed where the border should lie. An "arrangement concerning the Delimitation of the English and French Possessions on the West Coast of Africa" was formally signed at Paris on 10 August 1889 by Edwin H. Egerton, Augustus W.L. Hemming, A. Nisard and Jean Bayol. The Arrangement began as follows:

> "The Undersigned, selected by the Government of Her Majesty the Queen of Great Britain and Ireland and by the Government of the French Republic for the purpose of preparing a general understanding with a view to settle all the questions at issue between England and France with regard to their respective

---
565 CO 879/8.
566 The name of the village is also often spelt Yarbatenda, as in the formal agreement, and as Yabutenda.

possessions on the West Coast of Africa have agreed on the following provisions:

Art. 1 – In Senegambia, the frontier line between the English and French possessions shall be established as follows:

i. To the North of the Gambia (right bank) the line shall start from Jinak Creek and follow the parallel which, traversing the coast at this point (about 13 36' north), intersects the Gambia at the great bend it makes towards the north opposite a small island situated at the entrance of Sarmi Creek in the country of Niamena

From this point the frontier line shall follow the right bank as far as Yarbatenda, at a distance of 10 kilom[etres] from the river.

ii. To the south (left bank) the line, starting from the mouth of the San Pedro, shall follow the left bank as far as 13 10' of north latitude. The frontier shall thence follow the parallel which, starting from this point, goes as far as Sandeng (end of the Vintang Creek, English map).

The line shall then trend upwards in the direction of the Gambia, following the meridian which passes through Sandeng.

The frontier shall then follow the left bank of the river at the same distance of 10 kilom[etres] as far as, and including, Yarbatenda."

An Annex to the Agreement specified that "the frontier line shall be drawn round and beyond Yarbatenda" at a radius of 10km from the centre of the town. The rest of the agreement concerned arrangements for delimiting the borders of UK possessions in Sierra Leone, the Gold Coast and the colony of Lagos and the adjoining French territories.

There were plenty on the French side who, given Britain's limited presence and tenuous influence in the region, thought they had given too much away.

Delimitation and demarcation of the boundary was carried out, with only slight modifications, by a Joint Boundary Commission in 1891, 1895, 1898 and 1904.[567] It is interesting that for the Commissioners at least it was clear that the agreed border delimited not two countries, but the spheres of influence of Britain and France. So when Foday Silah, Chief of Kombo, protested that using the San Pedro River as the border cut his territory in two, and ordered the Commission to stop its work, the Commissioners felt able to reassure him that delimitation of the French and British spheres did not affect him.

> "Both the French Commissioners and I exhausted all our powers of persuasion: we said it was a matter merely between the English and French, that his authority was in no way interfered with by our work of simple delimitation of a line marking the limits beyond which the two governments mutually agreed never to attempt to extend their influence; that there was no question of any French occupation of any part of his territory".[568]

Despite the tensions that existed between the two countries, each eager to consolidate and strengthen their presence in the region, the French and British soon realised they faced common challenges, not least how to deal with local chieftains whose own territories, like those of Foday Silah, spanned both the British and French spheres of influence. One such chieftain was the Mandinka king Fode Kaba, who was causing problems for both European powers. Kaba was resisting French colonial expansion and the British were getting fed up with his repeated raids into the Gambia and his continuing involvement in slavery over eighty years after the Act of Parliament abolishing

---

567 CO 879/8.
568 *Report on the Proceedings of the Anglo-French Boundary while delimiting the Frontiers on the lower part of the River Gambia,* by Captain Kenny, 2 May 1891, CO 879/34

the slave trade. Kaba had tried to reassure the British that his actions were not directed against them and he realised it was in his interests to keep good relations with the planters and traders on the Gambia because he wanted to continue buying guns off them for his wars with the Soninke ethnic group. [569]

Despite sharing a common objective – neutralising Kaba – the French and British disagreed on how to do it. In June 1890, the British wrote to the French to request permission to enter Casamance in order to carry out an operation, jointly if the French preferred, to capture Fode Kaba.[570] The then French Governor in Saint-Louis, Clement-Thomas, clearly still needled that the British had managed to secure themselves a colony in the middle of a zone of French influence, strongly opposed the British request. A few months later his successor, Governor Lamothe, took a more pragmatic view arguing that it was in France's interests to work with the British, while being clear that any action in French territory must be led by France. However, lacking the troops to lead an operation against Kaba the operation was not carried out.

Fode Kaba continued to be an irritant to the British and, on 2 January 1892, when they knew him to be on the Gambian side of the border, at Marige, they launched an attack. Kaba escaped and retreated across the border to his stronghold at Medina. The British request to pursue him across the border was refused by the French, who nevertheless indicated a willingness to work with the British to end these cross-border raids. Correspondence between the Governor and the French Ministry suggests that the French considered the British to be exaggerating the problem, especially since an agreement reached on 26 March 1891, between Fode Kaba and Captain Forichon, Administrator at Seju. In this agreement Kaba accepted that his kingdom of Fooni came under French protection. The agreement heralded a period of collaboration between France and the ageing Fode Kaba, as they helped him

---

569 Roche, *Histoire de la Casamance*, p. 141.
570 Ibid, p. 141.

bring rebel Joola villages in his territory under control. This was followed in 7 May 1893, by a further agreement, this time signed by Governor Lamothe, in which Fode Kaba entrusted Fooni to the French in return for an annual payment of 5000 francs, paid almost entirely in millet. The French had turned Fode Kaba's hostility to the English, following their failed attack on him, to their advantage, but it was an incident on the Gambian side of the border many years later that led the French to move against Fode Kaba, by then in his 80s, leading to his death.

The village of Sankandi, on the Gambian side of the border, owed its allegiance to Fode Kaba and did not recognise the authority, imposed on them as they saw it by the British, of the chief of the neighbouring village of Batelling, Mansa Koto. The villagers of Sankandi were also feeling aggrieved that the Travelling Commissioner F.C. Sitwell had found against them in a dispute with another neighbouring village over ownership of some rice fields. Sitwell had returned to Batelling with Travelling Commissioner Silva to try to resolve the dispute and had summoned the village chief of Sankandi, Dari Bana Dabo, to meet them there. When Dabo refused the Commissioners decided that they would go to Sankandi. Arriving there on 14 June 1890, and following a further slight, Sitwell attempted to have Dabo arrested. This in turn led to some of the villagers firing on the visiting party killing both Travelling Commissioners, a British sergeant, the Batelling village Chief Mansa Koto and several others. Fearing the consequences of their actions the 135 inhabitants of Sankandi immediately fled the village and sought refuge across the border in the village of Nema in the territory of Fode Kaba. When Fode Kaba refused to hand over those responsible the British formally requested the French authorities in Saint-Louis to extradite Dari Bana Dabo, his son Lansana Dabo and a third man, Bakari Job. The French asked Fode Kaba to hand these individuals to the British but he again refused, citing the principles of hospitality. Further French efforts to persuade Dari Bana Dabo and the others to return also failed.

Lacking the necessary troops, the British did not immediately respond, but in January 1901 they assembled a force[571] comprising troops from Sierra Leone and half a battalion of the Second Central African Regiment which, returning from Somaliland, had been diverted to the cause. The force, led by a Lieutenant Colonel Blake of the Central African Regiment destroyed the village of Sankandi before moving to the north bank of the Gambia River to deal with a rebellion in some villages there. The French, having decided to end their 1893 agreement with Fode Kaba, then moved against him. A French column left Ziguinchor on 19 March 1901 and engaged Fode Kaba's troops, led by his nephew, at his base in Medina. Although his body was never recovered Fode Kaba died in the destruction of Medina that day. A few days later the French forces continued on to Nema, which they destroyed, capturing Dari Bana Dabo, Lansana Dabo and Bakari Job and handing them over to the British.[572]

With relations between the two countries better than they had ever been, and Germany seen as the common threat, Britain and France began in July 1903 to discuss a range of outstanding territorial issues. Discussion focused mainly on Egypt, Morocco and Newfoundland but also covered territory in Siam, the New Hebrides and West Africa. In West Africa, France's main concern was initially to secure a better link between their settlements in Niger and Chad by taking some of the district of Sokoto in Nigeria, which was under British control.[573] But by October that year the French were linking the abandonment of French rights in Newfoundland to the cession to France of Gambia, which they described as being primarily of sentimental value to Britain.[574] Lord Lansdowne,[575] the Foreign Secretary, replied that Britain could not possibly entertain the idea of giving up the Gambia – "Our objections to it are insuperable" – but repeated an earlier offer,

---

571 Gray, page 470.
572 Roche, p. 151.
573 CO 633/17.
574 Cambon (French Ambassador) to Lord Lansdowne of 26 October 1903.
575 Henry Charles Keith Petty-Fitzmaurice, 5th Marquess of Lansdowne, Secretary of State for Foreign Affairs 12 November 1900 – 4 December 1905.

which had been ignored by the French, to accommodate some of their concerns in Sokoto.[576]

The French were not going to give up that easily. Cambon proposed a compromise: Britain give up the Gambia but retain the island of St. Mary's with the settlement at Bathurst.[577] This idea was rejected at a meeting of the Cabinet on 11 December, but conscious of a long-standing French frustration Lansdowne[578] put to the French Ambassador in January 1904 the idea of giving them access to a navigable part of the river. The French expressed interest and suggested Deer Island located fifty kilometres to the west of MacCarthy Island and around 200km from the mouth of the river, but the British had something else in mind. On 5 February Lansdowne wrote to the French Ambassador to propose readjusting the frontier at the eastern extremity of the country so that the town of Yarbutenda, over 300km upriver, would lie on the French side of the border. The significance of Yarbutenda was that it was supposedly navigable by ocean-going ships for twelve months a year.

This is the deal that was agreed. The cession of Yarbutenda was included in the text of an Agreement, signed on 8 April 1904 by Lord Lansdowne and the French Ambassador Paul Cambon, which resolved a number of territorial disputes in Newfoundland and West and Central Africa. The agreement was one of three signed that day which together form the Entente Cordiale, generally considered to mark the end of centuries of conflict between the two countries. In arguably the most important of the three agreements France recognised Britain's control over Egypt and Britain France's pre-eminent position in Morocco.

The key paragraphs of Article 5 of the Newfoundland and Africa Agreement read:

---

576  Lansdowne to Cambon of 19 November 1903, CO 633/17.
577  Lansdowne to Sir E Monson (British Ambassador in Paris) of 9 December 1903, CO 633/17.
578  Lansdowne to Cambon of 23 January 1904, CO 663/17.

"The present frontier between Senegambia and the English Colony of the Gambia shall be modified so as to give to France Yarbutenda and the lands and landing places belonging to that locality.

In the event of the river not being open to maritime navigation up to that point, access shall be assured to the French Government at a point lower down on the River Gambia, which shall be recognized by mutual agreement as being accessible to merchant ships engaged in maritime navigation.

The conditions which shall govern transit on the River Gambia and its tributaries, as well as the method of access to the point that may be reserved to France in accordance with the preceding paragraph, shall form the subject of future agreement between the two Governments."

French parliamentarians and media were unimpressed with the agreement, commenting that only exceptionally, when the waters were particularly high was the river navigable as far as Yarbutenda by ships of over 1500 tonnes. They argued that MacCarthy Island was the furthest that could be safely navigated by maritime vessels and that the French should seek a port between Nianimaru a little to the east of Deer Island, thirty miles west of MacCarthy Island, and Kuntaur, ten miles higher up the river.[579] *The Daily Telegraph* reported that the French were likely to ask for cession of "Yannamaru" (as Nianimaru has been called on some maps) and that "it is confidently expected that His Majesty's Government will consent to this solution."[580]

In January 1905, the British Consul in Dakar reported to the Government of British Gambia that the French were still set on securing an enclave on the navigable part of the river. They wanted sovereignty over the enclave and for ships to be able to go there without

---
579 La Quinzaine Coloniale 25 April 1904, National Archives of Senegal 9F3.
580 Daily Telegraph of 27 March 1905, National Archives of Senegal 9F3.

paying duties at Bathurst. They also insisted that goods unloaded or loaded in the enclave, and transported from there to French territory should not have to pay duty when passing through Gambia.[581]

It was thought that the French still had their eyes on Nianimaru or Kuntaur.[582] Sir George Denton, Governor of British Gambia, subsequently advised that implementation of the 1904 agreement should be put on hold until the question of the leasing of a port on the lower river had been settled.[583] Privately, at least, some members of the British Government appeared to agree with the French that Yarbutenda was not accessible to ocean-going ships all year round. An Acting Governor took the view that Yarbutenda was accessible to ships drawing 10-12 feet of water – a definition at the time for ocean-going ships – only between July and October and that the rest of the year it was only accessible to ships drawing 7-8 feet of water.[584]

Sir Edward Grey, Lansdowne's successor as Secretary of State for Foreign Affairs, maintained that what the French were asking for was not justified by the terms of the Agreement.[585] The French continued pressing for an enclave until 1910, and then quietly dropped the matter. Nor, it appears, was Article 5 of the 1904 convention ever implemented. The border was not moved and if the village of Yarbutenda still exists – I have not seen it marked on any modern maps – it is still part of The Gambia.

Despite this France was still able to export directly from its territory onto the Gambia River. I visited the small Senegalese village of Guénoto which is located on the river a few kilometres from the border with Gambia and just at the point where the Barrakunda rocks make it impossible for even small boats, for much of the year, to venture further upriver. The old customs house, now with a collapsed roof, is still there. An old man I met reminisced about how Guénoto

---

581 Exact date unclear, CO 87/173.
582 Sir George Denton, Governor of Gambia (11 January 1901 – 21 December 1911) to Colonial Office, 23 May 1905, CO 87/173.
583 Denton to Colonial Office, 11 June 1905.
584 Letter from the Acting Governor to the Secretary of State for the Colonies of 21 August 1905, CO 87/173.
585 F. Villiers to Under-Secretary at Colonial Office of 12 January 1906, CO 87/176.

had been a busy port, with groundnuts sent directly from there down the river. Subsequently, however the trade had shifted to Kaolack, on the Sine-Saloum which remains the centre of Senegal's groundnut industry today.

## CHAPTER THIRTEEN

# DIPLOMATIC REPRESENTATION

There were many reasons why being British Ambassador to Senegal was so enjoyable but one most certainly was living at the Residence, as all ambassadors' houses are called. Shortly after my arrival someone told me I occupied one of the three finest houses in Dakar, the others being the residences of Nicolas Normand, the French Ambassador, and *général de brigade* Grégoire de Saint-Quentin who commanded the French forces in Senegal (les Éléments français au Sénégal). Their houses, like mine, looked across the sea to the island of Gorée. There were other impressive properties in the city, both historic and modern, but I never saw one I preferred to my own. It was the type of house I had always hoped to live in: architecturally beautiful, with pleasing shutters, high ceilings, a spacious terrace and fantastic views from the first-floor balcony looking east to Gorée and beyond.

By any standards and certainly by those of Dakar the gardens were green and lush with a huge baobab, imposing flame-trees – though sadly three of the four died of disease during my tenure – and a jacaranda planted by the then Princess Anne. A huge fig attracted large, noisy fruit-bats during the rainy season when its branches were covered with small fruit. Senegal parrots and rose-ringed parakeets would fly screeching between the trees, and the huge western grey plantain-eaters, with their striking yellow bills, would cackle outrageously from among the branches. The sky above Dakar was often full of hundreds of black kites, floating on the thermals and scavenging for fish scraps. There would always be several in the Embassy, sat high in the baobab or perched on the railings of the Residence balcony or on its roof.

The first suggestion that Britain should base a representative in the Senegambia appears to have been made in 1793, ten years after Gorée and Saint-Louis were formally restored to France under the Treaty of Paris and seven years before Britain was to seize back Gorée for the penultimate time.

In 1793, the African Association agreed to recommend to the Government "the Experimental and Temporary Appointment of a Consul to Senegambia". James Willis was formally appointed His Majesty's Consul in Senegambia on April 10, 1794.[586] His instructions, which only issued in early 1796, specified that he should establish "a permanent communication between Great Britain and the countries bordering the River Niger" and in particular to negotiate with the King of Bambouk a Treaty of Amity and Commerce "upon the most advantageous terms you can obtain."[587]

It was proposed that Willis should base himself at Fattatenda, downstream from the Barrakunda Falls on the Gambia River. However, by mid-February 1796 Sir Joseph Banks, the founder of the African Association, was recommending that the appointment of a consul to Senegambia be put on hold.[588] This change of heart followed a review of Willis's accounts and reflected the Association's concern that the Government appeared to expect the Association to cover any expenditure incurred by Willis that exceeded the grant made by Parliament for the position of Consul. The enthusiasm with which Willis had embarked upon pre-departure purchases suggested

---

586 Commission to Mr Willis, Consul-General at Senegambia, WO 1/768.
587 CO 267/10.
588 Report of the Committee of the African Association on the subject of Consul Willis's accounts..., dated 13 February 1796 and signed by Sir Joseph Banks and Andrew Stuart, CO 267/10.

to Banks and his colleagues that the grant would very rapidly be exceeded. Willis was informed of the decision to postpone his appointment indefinitely on 15 February 1796, just weeks after he had finally received his instructions.[589]

The need for a Consul soon passed. Four years later the British were back in control in Gorée, in 1809 they recovered Saint-Louis and in 1816 they established the settlement of Bathurst in Gambia. As a result, over sixty years passed before serious consideration was again given to the appointment of a British Consul in the French settlements of Senegal.

As the French consolidated their hold on their colony of Senegal, the small village on the mainland opposite Gorée began to grow in importance. Although the settlement had been known by the name of Dakar since at least the eighteenth century it was only formally founded in 1857. Soon after a commercial port was established, with a coaling station, and it became a popular stopping off point for British ships heading down the coast of Africa.

In mid-January 1869,[590] Rear Admiral Charles Patey, the British Administrator in Gambia, received a visit from Captain Cléomenes Pillot, a Frenchman based at Dakar. Captain Pillot informed Patey of the "trouble and annoyances" caused to the French authorities by the "disorderly and outrageous behaviour" of British sailors on ships calling at Dakar. Reporting the meeting back to London Patey said the French authorities desired the appointment of an "accredited agent from the English government who would be able to deal in a more summary fashion with British subjects visiting that colony". For the benefit of his readers Patey noted that Dakar "is a small place about three miles from Gorée" and that it was the coal station for the mail packet ships to South Africa. In response London said they weren't prepared to pay someone to do the job, but would have no objection if he could find someone who wanted to do it for free. They weren't at all sure however about "the propriety of appointing anyone other

---

589 Willis to [unclear but presumably Dundas] of 22 February 1796, CO 267/10.
590 Patey to Bathurst of 17 January 1869, National Archives of Senegal 9F6.

than a British subject to the post."⁵⁹¹ However according to Patey there wasn't, at that time, a single British national resident at Dakar.

It wasn't just the French colonial authorities who wanted a consul appointed. In a petition dated 7 November 1870 addressed to Earl Granville, Secretary of State for Foreign Affairs, and entitled *Procuring a Consul to Represent the English Government at Dackar* (sic), *West Coast of Africa* several masters of English vessels complained that the absence of a consul led to delays in the discharge of their cargoes causing great inconvenience and considerable loss.⁵⁹² In March the following year, G Miller,⁵⁹³ owner of a large coaling company based at Mindelo in the Cape Verde islands, wrote to Earl Granville noting that the company had sent ninety ships to Dakar since January 1867 and that the absence of a British Consular Agent had frequently caused inconvenience to the ships' masters. Part of the problem he said was that British sailors would absent themselves and get drunk for days.

The Foreign Office appears to have put aside its reservations about appointing a foreign national because on 8 April 1872 the Slave Trade Department of the Foreign Office wrote to Captain Pillot appointing him to the post of British Vice-Consul at Dakar.⁵⁹⁴ He was to receive no salary but was allowed to keep for his own use fees leviable under the Order in Council of 1 May 1858. The following year the French civilian and military administrations moved from Gorée to Dakar. Some British ships, making the regular journey from Liverpool to the Bight of Benin would still anchor at Gorée in order to avoid paying fees to the British Vice-Consul arguing that Pillot was Vice-Consul at Dakar not Gorée.⁵⁹⁵

Dakar had been part of the commune⁵⁹⁶ of Gorée but in 1887 the town became a commune in its own right. By the 1890s, Dakar was rapidly growing with merchants moving their premises from Gorée

---

591 Letter from Colonial Office of 13 February 1869, National Archives of Senegal 9F6.
592 National Archives of Senegal, 9F6.
593 Presumably linked to Millers and Nephew, the largest coal company in São Vicente, Cape Verde.
594 Letter from Slave Trade Department to Pillot of 8 April 1872, FO 84/1356.
595 FO 84/1455.
596 An administrative district.

to the mainland. The majority of foreign vessels arriving at Dakar were British. Coal was almost exclusively imported on British ships. In addition, mail ships run by the Union Steam Ship Company, the forerunner of the Union Line, later the Union Castle line, would call in at Dakar on their way down to South Africa from Southampton.[597]

The first four British Vice-Consuls at Dakar were all Frenchmen who worked for La Compagnie des Messageries Maritimes a French merchant shipping company established in 1851. Captain Pillot was followed by Ernest Simon Montoux (1879-1887), Edouard Rastoul (1887-1888) and finally Captain Pierre Gaston Faoche (1888-1894).

The first British national to be appointed as Vice-Consul in Dakar was Captain Allan Henry Maclean in October 1894. In 1896, the British representation was upgraded with Maclean appointed Consul. Soon after his arrival MacLean was writing home to point out that the cost of living in Dakar had been underestimated and seeking an increase in his salary. "I cannot think," he wrote to the Foreign Secretary, the Earl of Kimberley, "that when the salary attached to the post of Vice-Consul at Dakar was fixed, the conditions of life in Dakar were correctly known at the Foreign Office."[598] In a subsequent letter[599] he wrote "compared with posts such as Madeira and Tenerife at the same salary, Dakar has the disadvantage of being much more expensive, twice as far from England and civilisation and its climate is most trying".

MacLean eventually managed to rent a decent enough property on the high ground of Cap Manuel at £10 (250 francs) a month. "It was absolutely the only suitable building to be let in Dakar," he wrote, "and a further stay at the Hotel was, owing to the want of sanitary arrangements, unadvisable on the grounds of health and also from the impossibility of securing a proper room for the transaction of consular business".

Villa Belle Vue, as the property was called, was a two storey building, of solid construction, built in 1891 on raised ground and with a breeze on every side. MacLean recommended that the

---

597 MacLean to Secretary of State of 15 March 1895, FO 27/3246.
598 Snoxell. p. 1.
599 Snoxell, p. 1.

Government purchase it.[600] The landlord was asking the equivalent of £2000 but Maclean suggested offering £1500. The Works Department of the Foreign Office refused to agree the purchase[601] on the basis that they had insufficient evidence to assess the property's value. They also noted wearily that the purchase of new properties was almost always followed by a request from the occupant for expensive alterations. They were also very reluctant to buy something that MacLean's eventual successor might not like, recalling how "experience shows that which one consular officer approves, the other condemns".

In arguing the case for an increase in salary MacLean highlighted a long list of hardships involved in living in Dakar: "with the exception of one or two Baobab trees (Dakar was) almost devoid of vegetation"; "the white sand is most hurtful to the eyes"; "the climate is intensely hot, as hot and dry as any weather I have experienced in the plains of India"; "the scarcity of water for drinking purposes is another hardship"; "all water had to be bought and fetched from the Public Cisterns, costing two francs per barrel which comes to a considerable item per month"; "food is bad and dear, plentiful for four months of the year but almost unobtainable during the rest of the year."[602]

MacLean was presumably delighted therefore to be posted to Tenerife in January 1897, though he died there the following year. His successor as British Consul, Captain Leonard Robert Sunkersett Arthur, was appointed on 29 January 1897. It was emphasised to him[603] the very high importance the government attached to the punctual transmission of the returns and statistics required by the General Consular Instructions and of all information relating to commerce and navigation. He was to be paid £600 a year, with an additional £200 for office expenses and £135 for outfits. All fees levied in the course of performing his consular duties were to be paid to the British Government.

Like MacLean before him Arthur struggled with the conditions.

---

600 MacLean to Secretary of State for Foreign Affairs of 17 February 1896, WORK 10/318.
601 Minute from Board of Works to Foreign Office of 28 March 1896, WORK 10/318.
602 Snoxell, p 2-3.
603 FO 27/3348.

Hoping for a sympathetic hearing he complained to Lord Lansdowne,[604] the new Secretary of State for Foreign Affairs, that Dakar was hit by yellow fever epidemics every two years[605] and suggested that the Ambassador in Paris might raise this with the French Minister of Colonies and encourage them to take steps to improve the situation. Officials in London advised against raising this with the French prompting from Lansdowne the response, "I agree. Nor have we any interest in rendering Dakar less unhealthy".

While relations between Britain and France were steadily improving, and the French were supportive of a British consular presence in Dakar, suspicions of what the perfidious British were up to flourished (no doubt often with good reason). On 14 June 1901, Jules Seng, from the office of the Governor's Representative in Dakar wrote to a colleague in Saint-Louis to warn him of the imminent arrival there of Arthur's Deputy, Robert Erskine, the British Vice-Consul at Dakar.[606] Writing both in the strictest confidence but also clearly in some amusement he said he had reason to believe Erskine had been tasked by the British Government to collect information about the colony's defences. Seng said that Erskine was doing the best he could "to the point of indiscretion" and that in response to Erskine's endless questions he had "told him a pack of lies."[607]

In December 1902, the new consul, Captain Charles Cromie, was asked by the French Lieutenant Governor in Saint-Louis whether the British Government was contemplating building a more suitable consulate at Dakar given the decision to make Dakar the capital of French West Africa.[608] A new palace for the Governor-General was to be built there. The Lieutenant Governor said that not only was it a good time to buy land in Dakar but the French Government would

---

604 Henry Charles Keith Petty-Fitzmaurice, 5th Marquess of Lansdowne, Secretary of State for Foreign Affairs 1900-1905.
605 Arthur to Lord Lansdowne of 30 April 1901, FO 2/494.
606 National Archives of Senegal 9F4.
607 "Je lui ai raconté des histoires".
608 Dakar was formally to become the capital of French West Africa on 20 December 1903.

welcome a decision by the British to build a consulate and would facilitate the purchase of a suitable site.[609]

The prospect of increased social gatherings as a result of Dakar's new status, afforded Cromie a further argument for moving. While the top floor of Villa Belle Vue might have been refreshingly airy the property was wholly unsuitable for entertaining "with a dining room little better than a cellar with a naked brick floor very destructive to ladies dresses, and so small that eight persons are the utmost I can dine together, and that with inconvenience". Cromie concluded his letter with a recommendation that the Government buy land and construct a Consulate "if His Majesty's Consul is to adequately maintain his dignity, and be enabled to respond to the hospitality which will undoubtedly be offered him under the quite altered conditions of social life which will result from the removal of the seat of Government to Dakar."[610]

The Treasury 's reply to the Foreign Office[611] was that the Estimate for Diplomatic and Consular Buildings for 1903/4 was closed and it was now too late to consider the purchase of land in Dakar in that year. Nevertheless, they recommended that Cromie be instructed to find out the cost of doing so.

Cromie identified two sites, and recommended the purchase of one of these – the location of the then prison. This site had the advantage that the land could be secured immediately but payment could be deferred as it would only become available the following year.[612] The Works Department however was far from enthusiastic entertaining "very strong objections to our building responsibilities abroad at remote and isolated stations like Dakar". The Treasury, therefore, recommended that the issue of buying land for a Consulate at Dakar "remain in abeyance."[613] In an enlightened response a Foreign Office

---

609 Cromie to Lord Lansdowne of 28 December 1902, WORK 10/318.
610 Ibid.
611 Fisher (Treasury) to Under-Secretary at the Foreign Office of 18 February 1903, WORK 10/318.
612 Cromie to Lord Lansdowne of 21 March 1903, WORK 10/318.
613 Chalmers (Treasury) to Under Secretary at the Foreign Office of 9 June 1903.

official[614] said that Lord Lansdowne wanted the Lord Commissioners of the Treasury to reconsider given that there was nowhere suitable to rent and because he considered "that it is precisely at a remote and isolated station, where the absence of proper sanitary conditions renders prolonged residence injurious to health, that it is most necessary for HMG to provide the Consul with a house".

In October, Cromie, who had been given notice by his landlord to leave Villa Belle Vue by 1 January, reported that the prison site was no longer available but that a parcel of land on the plateau behind the recently built Hôpital Colonial was for sale. He noted that this was far removed from the native quarter of the town which would be advantageous as a means of avoiding malaria, as a recent visit by researchers from the Liverpool School of Tropical Medicine had demonstrated.[615] The site was being sold by the Mayor of Dakar, W. Teisseire, for 36,000 francs. Cromie estimated that the total cost of the new Dakar estate would be £8,000: £1450 for the land, £6,000 to construct the consulate and £550 to establish a shipping office in the town.[616]

The Treasury gave approval to purchase the site behind the hospital in late November 1903.[617] However, they only set aside £1500, enough to buy the land but not to build, and for the financial year 1904/05. Subsequently, the Treasury asked[618] whether it would be OK to pay for the land in April 1905, in other words at the beginning of the following financial year, as they needed to buy a new Embassy property in Madrid. Cromie stood his ground saying it was too late to delay the payment date in this way as the sale had already been approved.

With the land purchased, Cromie started to take a keen interest in the design of the house. He offered detailed recommendations back to London,[619] including that there should be a fire in the drawing room "as it is sometimes very chilly" and as a means of drying the house during

---

614 Sir Charles Hardinge to Treasury of 20 June 1903, WORK 10/318.
615 National Archives of Senegal 9F2.
616 Cromie to Lansdowne of 6 October 1903, WORK 10/318.
617 Cavendish (Treasury) to Under-Secretary at the Foreign Office of 30 November 1903, WORK 10/318.
618 In a letter dated 18 July 1904, WORK 10/318.
619 Cromie to The Secretary HM Office of Works of 12 October 1904, WORK 10/318.

## DIPLOMATIC REPRESENTATION

the damp rainy season. The fireplace remains to this day, though there was not a day in the four years I lived there when I felt it was chilly enough to light a fire. Cromie initially wanted to use the company that had built the governor's palace but they and other French companies wanted to charge too much so he recruited a British Clerk of Works, W.C. D'Harty, who estimated the costs of building the Consulate at £8500, against the original Treasury provision of £6,000.[620]

Cromie had left Dakar by the time the construction of the Residence was completed. Living up to the Works Department's adage that new arrivals were never happy with their predecessor's accommodation, the new consul, Major J Baldwin, was unimpressed.[621] "I suppose the budget necessitated it, but the bath, the fittings, as you know, are about as cheap as they could be". The landscaped garden he dismissed as "a sand heap". He had his own idea on how it might better be used. "As a matter of health and to save money in sick leave I think the Government might give me a tennis court". He noted that the consul in Monrovia had been given one. Baldwin did not have to put up with the house for long. In 1909, he moved on, to Monrovia in fact, where presumably he played lots of tennis and was never sick. Within a couple of years of his departure a tennis court was added to the Residence.

The house had been designed with an inner courtyard, open to the air. After heavy flooding the first year, with two feet of water in the basement, a decision was taken to roof over the courtyard. Successive consuls made further improvements to the property. In 1916, the then Acting Consul planted over 150 fruit trees: mango, orange, tangerine, lime and cherry. A veranda was added in 1920. And in 1923, and 1924, two further plots of land which became available were purchased at the front of the Residence.[622]

---

620 Revised estimate dated 29 May 1907 on WORK 10/318.
621 Letter from Major J. Baldwin to Sir Henry Tanner of 28 May 1908, WORK 10/318.
622 An extension to the compound of the neighbouring Hôpital Colonial had required the main road (now Rue Dr Guillet, extending into Avenue Pasteur) to be shifted westwards, leaving open land in front of the Residence which the British Government though it prudent to buy, WORK 10/318

As we will see in the next chapter, after the French surrendered to Nazi Germany in June 1940 Dakar came under the control of the Vichy Government. Following the British attacks on Vichy naval forces at Mers-El-Kébir and Dakar in July 1940, the British Consulate was vacated and the US temporarily took over the building. After the successful British-American invasion of French North Africa in late 1942, the Vichy authorities in French West Africa came over to the Allies, and early in 1943 the British returned to Dakar and repossessed the Consulate. In 1943, office buildings were built on the land that had been purchased in 1923 and 1924 and these buildings, further developed, were to become the Embassy on independence in 1960. The Embassy made its final acquisition of land in 1989, buying the adjacent property, Texaco House, leaving the Hôpital Principal (formerly the Hôpital Colonial) as the Embassy's only neighbour.

The responsibilities of the British Consul at Dakar gradually expanded. Initially, the Consulate had direct responsibility only for Dakar and Dahomey (three thousand kilometres to the east). But in 1922 Togo and Cameroun were added to their parish, shortly followed by Grand Bassam and Guinea. After Independence the Embassy's area of responsibility remained broad, if not quite so far flung. At times it has been responsible for our relationships with Guinea, Mali and Mauritania, now all served by their own embassies. Nowadays the British Embassy in Dakar has a much more manageable remit covering only Guinea-Bissau and Cabo Verde in addition to Senegal.

Two towering mangoes in the Embassy compound today may be all that remain of the 150 fruit trees planted in 1916, or they too may be more recent plantings. But with limes, bananas, coconut palms and passionfruit plants the Embassy gardens retain some feel of a tropical orchard in the heart of Dakar.

## CHAPTER FOURTEEN

# OPERATION MENACE

1940

There was a lot on Winston Churchill's plate in the summer of 1940. Britain's Prime Minister had been appointed on 10 May, shortly before the evacuation of 338,000 men, 140,000 of whom were French, by 765 British ships from the beaches of Dunkirk. Paris was to fall on 14 June, quickly followed by the French surrender. Churchill had to decide whether Britain would fight on alone against the advancing might of Nazi Germany or, as his Foreign Secretary Lord Halifax and others in the Wartime Cabinet preferred, to seek peace terms with Hitler. Churchill chose to fight, memorably telling the House of Commons on 18 June, "the Battle of France is over. I expect the battle of Britain is about to begin. Upon this battle depends the survival of Christian civilisation…".

Britain at the time was living in imminent danger of invasion. By July 1940, from their newly acquired airfields in Normandy, the German Luftwaffe had begun their bombings of Britain, sporadically at first but with increasing intensity. 258 were killed in July, 1075 in August and more than 6500 in September. Mass daylight bombing of London started on 7 September, and continued unbroken for sixty-eight consecutive nights, with just one exception. Meanwhile at sea

Britain was suffering ever greater losses of merchant shipping to German U-Boats. Churchill was in regular correspondence with US President Franklin D. Roosevelt, desperately keen to enlist more US support, but in the summer of 1940 this was slow in materialising.[623]

And yet amidst all this Churchill nevertheless found the time to get involved in a slightly chaotic episode that saw British ships and troops accompany General de Gaulle and his Free French Forces to Dakar on a mission to persuade the colonial authorities there, hitherto loyal to the Vichy Government, to declare themselves for de Gaulle.

The mission, named Operation Menace, was a failure, and led to one of the more turbulent moments in British relations with Senegal: the bombardment by British warships of the port of Dakar. Churchill was later to write that "the story of the Dakar episode deserves close study, because it illustrates in a high degree not only the unforeseeable accidents of war, but the interplay of military and political forces, and the difficulties of combined operations, especially when allies are involved".[624] The British novelist Evelyn Waugh was among the infantry embarked on transport ships in the British fleet. He used the experience – creatively as we will later see – in his comic masterpiece *Men at Arms*, the first and best book in his *Sword of Honour* trilogy.

German troops had marched into an undefended Paris on 14 June 1940, and military resistance in France had effectively come to an end two days later. France and Germany signed an armistice on 22 June, which divided France in two. Northern and Western France, including its Atlantic ports, fell under the control of Nazi Germany. The remaining third of French territory was to be governed by a French administration out of the small town of Vichy. Under the terms of the armistice the Vichy Government retained control of all France's overseas possessions as well as of the French Navy. By leaving a French government in place Hitler wanted to ensure that France would not continue to fight from its possessions in North Africa and

---

[623] The Lend-Lease Act, under which the US lent and leased arms and other wartime supplies was only adopted in March 1941.
[624] Winston Churchill, *The Second World War, Volume II* page 437.

to take the French Navy – larger and better equipped than the German Navy – out of the war. Under the terms of the armistice the Vichy France Government, and therefore its navy, were officially neutral. However, the British, and particularly Churchill, were understandably concerned that the Germans should not have access to the powerful and modern French Navy, the fourth largest in the world.

On 11 June, during his penultimate visit to France before the fall of Paris, Churchill thought he had the assurance that Admiral Darlan, Admiral of the French Fleet, would never surrender the French Navy to the enemy. He was not reassured by the eventual terms of the Armistice. Article 8 of the Treaty provided that the majority of French ships "shall be collected in ports to be specified and there demobilised and disarmed under German or Italian control". But Churchill read this to mean that the French ships would be fully armed at the point where they fell under enemy control and took no comfort from subsequent language specifying that the Germans would not use the French vessels for their own purposes. How could he trust them?

Dakar at the time was a major port in the French Empire. It had the only dry dock between Casablanca and the Cape. The US and Britain shared fears that Dakar could become a U-boat station on the Atlantic. As negotiations on the armistice took place in the French town of Compiègne a nearly completed French warship, *Richelieu*, which was ready for active service, left the port of Brest and sailed for Dakar.

In June 1940, news reaching London about the loyalties of French forces in their colonies was encouraging. On 18 June, shortly before the signing of the armistice, Commander Jermyn Rushbrooke, the British Naval Officer at Dakar had reported that the Commander in Chief of the French fleet Admiral Darlan had ordered the French Admiral at Dakar, Admiral Plançon, to continue fighting. He also reported that the French troops manning the shore batteries at Dakar had declared for the British.[625] Similarly encouraging reports had been

---

625 Naval Staff History, Second World War, Battle Summaries Nos 3 and 20. Naval Operations off Dakar July-September 1940 (1959). Much of the detail of this chapter is taken from this source.

received from Douala and Brazzaville of local French forces declaring their allegiance to the Free French forces of General de Gaulle.

The British set out to neutralise the French fleet. Fortuitously several ships including two battleships, four light cruisers, eight destroyers and several submarines were in British waters at the time of the Armistice, mainly in Portsmouth and Plymouth. British forces took control of these on 3 July, almost without incident. However, they met some resistance when seeking to take control of the submarine *Surcouf*, at the time the largest in the world. Three British and one French sailor died in the confrontation.

On the same day, Admiral James Somerville, then commander of the newly formed Force H in Gibraltar, arrived off the coast of Algeria. Two French battle-cruisers (*Dunkerque* and *Strasbourg*) together with two of its seven battleships *Provence* and *Bretagne*, were at Mers-El-Kébir near Oran. Admiral Somerville was charged by Churchill "with one of the most difficult tasks that a British admiral has ever been faced with". He was to present the French Navy there with three options: to continue to fight alongside the British against Germany and other Axis powers; to immobilise their forces completely in certain ports; or to demilitarise or sink their ships. In the event that the French did not accept any of these options Admiral Somerville was to destroy their ships.

When the French Admiral rejected all these options Admiral Somerville took the decision to open fire. The *Dunkerque* and *Strasbourg* were seriously damaged, *Provence* beached and the *Bretagne* sunk. 1299 French sailors were killed in action and 350 wounded. The same day the French Government forbid all British ships and aircraft, under penalty of being fired on without warning, to approach within twenty nautical miles of French territory. Until that date, Dakar had been regularly used by British warships and naval vessels, hence the presence in Dakar of Rushbrooke, the British Naval Liaison Officer.

British warships had been shadowing *Richelieu* on its departure from Brest on 18 June, but had allowed it to reach Dakar where it arrived on 23 June. The British authorities had reason to hope that

*Richelieu* would join the Allied cause against the Germans, fearing at the same time there was a possibility that it could be handed over to the Germans. Wary of British intentions – the aircraft carrier HMS *Hermes* was at anchor in Dakar loading British stores and HMS *Dorsetshire* was in the vicinity – *Richelieu* briefly left Dakar on 25 June only to be ordered back by the French Admiralty two days later because they feared the ship might go over to the British. On 3 July, the day the Royal Navy attacked the French Navy at Mers-El-Kébir, HMS *Dorsetshire* evaded attacks from two French submarines *L'Heros* and *Le Glorieux*.

Once it became clear that *Richelieu* was staying put at Dakar the British Government decided that the French should be given the chance to put it out of action, failing which it would be destroyed. Captain Onslow of HMS *Hermes* was given charge of the operation and temporary command of HMS *Dorsetshire*, the Australian cruiser HMAS *Australia* and the sloop HMS *Milford*.

On 7 July, Onslow presented the French Admiral at Dakar with four options: to proceed to a British port with reduced crew and without ammunition; to sail with UK forces with a reduced crew and no ammunition to a French port in the West Indies to be demilitarised; to be demilitarised in Dakar within twelve hours; or to sink *Richelieu* in Dakar within six hours. A response was demanded in four hours. The ultimatum ended with the warning that "Failing the above I have the orders of HM Government to use whatever force may be necessary to secure that your ships are unable to take further part in the war."[626]

According to British accounts the French Admiral initially declined even to accept the ultimatum but later retracted. In issuing the communication Onslow reduced the deadline to two hours. At 20:03 that day, two minutes before expiry of the ultimatum, Onslow asked for an answer. French sources suggest he received the one word reply supposedly given by the French General Pierre Cambronne, when asked to surrender at Waterloo – "Merde".[627]

---

626 Naval Staff History, Second World War, Battle Summaries Nos 3 and 20. Naval Operations off Dakar July-September 1940. 1959
627 In this context best translated as "Go to hell".

Onslow decided on a twin approach: a depth-charge attack delivered during the night by HMS *Hermes*'s fast twin-engine boats, followed by a torpedo attack by aircraft at dawn. The motorboat, with a volunteer crew of nine, commanded by Lieutenant Commander R.H. Bristowe slipped into the harbour, and past a destroyer and a sloop before being discovered. They were challenged repeatedly but the French held their fire. The motorboat dropped its depth charges at 02:10 before weaving out of the harbour with the French giving chase. The motorboat missed its rendezvous with HMS *Milford* scheduled for three o'clock and was eventually picked up, hours later, by HMS *Hermes* thirteen miles south of Cap Manuel. It was a daredevil mission but none of the four depth charges exploded due to the shallowness of the water.

In the second phase of the operation six Swordfish left HMS *Hermes* at 04:15, under the command of Lieutenant Commander Luard. The attack was only possible from one direction – the Northeast – owing to nets, shipping and the depth of the water. As they approached, anti-aircraft guns opened fire from *Richelieu*, from three destroyers and other ships in port and from the shore batteries.

With that, war returned to Gorée for the first time since 1804, then also between France and the UK. Two aircraft were hit, but suffered only minor damage and returned safely. Luard reported back that four or five of the torpedoes had hit their target and HMS *Dorsetshire* reported hearing five explosions. The Admiralty ordered a further attack but *Richelieu* moved into an inner harbour where she was protected from torpedo attack. At the time it was unclear how much damage had been done to *Richelieu* but Onslow reported back to the Admiralty that the French ship had been "definitely disabled". Later, French sources revealed that in fact only one torpedo had found its mark, blowing a hole towards the rear of the ship, flooding compartments and damaging the propeller shaft.

As the British fleet began to sail off, and when they were about 18km from the shore, the battery at Cap Manuel was ordered to fire on them. They declined to do so, claiming that the ships were at twenty-six kilometres, and therefore out of range. A subsequent inquiry led to officers at the Cap Manuel gun battery being dismissed and to the French Navy taking over command of the main coastal batteries – those on Cap Manuel and Gorée – from the colonial artillery. Initially, this role was to be performed by gunners from *Richelieu* until the arrival of reinforcements.

General de Gaulle had left France on a British plane on 17 June, and on 18 June broadcast an appeal to the French people not to give up hope, to believe in ultimate victory, and for French forces to rally to him and join the resistance. Churchill encouraged de Gaulle to secure control of French colonies and on 3 August 1940 approved an early plan of his for raising the Free French flag in West Africa. Several plans, with a variety of targets, were elaborated over the following weeks. From the outset these plans emphasised the importance of any venture being French in nature. Free French forces were to travel in ships manned by French crew. The only British involvement would be to supply some of the ships, but not the crew, and a naval escort against submarines.

By 7 August the Chiefs of Staff Committee, chaired by Churchill, had agreed that the landing should be at Dakar and that while it would remain an essentially French operation sufficient British backing would be provided to ensure it was a success. Churchill took the view that it was "extremely important to British interests that General de Gaulle should be able to take Dakar at the earliest moment."[628] By 13 August, planning had evolved to the point where it was envisaged that British forces would take the lead, landing at six beaches, including those at Yoff, Ngor, Cap Manuel, Hann and on Gorée. British forces would secure military control of the town before leaving de Gaulle's forces to occupy it. The British estimated the Dakar defences at the time to be seven companies of Senegalese infantry, five 9.4 inch guns, eight five inch and four 4.8 inch guns, *Richelieu*, two large and one small destroyer, two or three submarines

---

[628] Directive from Winston Churchill, 8 August 1940 in Naval Staff History, Second World War, Battle Summaries Nos 3 and 20. Naval Operations off Dakar July-September 1940 (1959).

and one sloop. In addition, thirty-four Glenmartin bombers and six Coastal aircraft were thought to be at Ouakam, an airfield a few kilometres to the north of Dakar.

By 17 August, the Force Commanders appointed by Churchill for the mission, Admiral John Cunningham and Major General Noel Irwin, were thinking in terms of three separate forces. The main force of 1,700 men, made up of 1,400 British and 300 French troops would capture Bel-Air fort, directly north of the port of Dakar and move on to take the airfield at Ouakam and the port itself. A second force of 200 British and 100 French troops would land at the small beach of Anse Bernard, south of the port, and take the battery at Cap Manuel. A third force of eighty British and twenty French troops would take Gorée. But these plans were quickly abandoned once the planners realised the beaches on which the troops would land were covered by heavy guns and the use of hydrophones by the Vichy French forces based at Dakar meant an undetected approach would be impossible. The objective remained a bloodless landing.

Three days later the Vice-Chiefs of Staff were discussing a new plan with de Gaulle and Churchill. This had an Anglo-French fleet arriving off Dakar in a show of force. Aircraft from a carrier would drop leaflets encouraging local French forces and residents to go over to de Gaulle. Finally, a small boat, with a French crew and emissary aboard, flying a white flag and the French tricolor would enter Dakar harbour. The emissary would carry a letter to the Governor announcing the arrival of General de Gaulle with Free French troops to deliver Dakar from possible German aggression and emphasising the French character of the force assembled off the town.

The War Cabinet gave final approval to this plan on 27 August, the same day as the Cameroons and Lake Chad Territory Administration declared its allegiance to General de Gaulle. Copies of the final Directives reached Admiral Cunningham at midnight on 28-29 August. These spelt out that the objective of the operation was to install General de Gaulle in Dakar in order that he might rally the French in West Africa to his cause. "The operation should, if at all possible, be carried out without bloodshed and in a way that will not prejudice the welcome he may receive. But in the event of encountering local opposition you will, if necessary, use all the force at your command". The Final Directives also made clear that after successfully installing General de Gaulle and making sure that he could maintain himself, the British forces should be withdrawn.

About the same time Commander Rushbrooke, until recently Naval Liaison Officer at Dakar and Captain Poulter, the Army Liaison Officer, reached London from West Africa. Interviewed by Cunningham and Irwin the next morning, Poulter stated emphatically that the mood in Dakar was against de Gaulle and that the garrison would resist. This was discouraging news given that the plan was based on the premise that there was strong support for de Gaulle in Dakar and that his arrival with Free French Forces in a show of force would be enough for the town to switch their allegiance to him. However, the news seems to have arrived too late to cause a rethink. The War Cabinet's approval had been given, preparations were well in hand and the force was being assembled.

And the force was considerable. It consisted of two battleships (HMS *Barham* and *Resolution*), the aircraft carrier HMS *Ark Royal*, two cruisers (HMS *Devonshire* and *Fiji*), no less than ten destroyers (HMS *Escapade, Echo, Eclipse, Inglefield, Faulkner, Fortune, Fury, Foresight, Forrester* and *Greyhound*), two sloops (HMS *Milford and Bridgwater*) and one boon defence vessel (HMS *Quannet*). The Free French contribution to this force was three sloops (*Savorgnan de Brazza, Commandant Duboc, Commandant Dominé*) and a patrol vessel (*President Houduce*). Among the merchant vessels four troop transports (*Sobieski, Ettrick, Kenya* and *Karanja*) were allocated to the British contingent. The *Westernland* and *Pennland* – two hired Dutch liners – were allocated to the Free French. British troops comprised the 101st and 102nd Royal Marine Brigades (1st, 2nd, 3rd and 5th battalions) and a motorcycle platoon of the 5th Loyal (Lancashire) Regiment, a General Construction Company, Royal Engineers, four Bren carriers and crews from the 8th Argyll and Sutherland Highlanders, No.10

Independent Company, and various other administrative sub-units. In total British troops numbered 4,200, the Free French 2,700.

By 1 September, the whole expedition had left the UK, with the majority of ships leaving from Scapa Flow, Liverpool or the Clyde. That same day the cruiser HMS *Fiji* was hit by a torpedo off the island of Rockall in the North Sea and had to return to base. She was replaced by HMAS *Australia*. With the force moving slower than anticipated the date for Operation Menace was pushed back to 19 September (the sixth postponement since planning had begun). As in most military operations the element of surprise was considered essential. Stories however abound of sacks of leaflets to be dropped on Dakar splitting open on station platforms as troops, equipment and supplies were rushed north and of Free French troops talking openly in Liverpool bars of their destination.[629]

As the UK force steamed south limited French naval movements were also underway in the Mediterranean. British policy in respect of Vichy warships had been set out in a telegram on 12 July. This stressed the importance of ending tension between the French and British navies (following British attacks on Vichy warships at Mers-El-Kébir and Dakar) and that no further action should be taken against Vichy ships in or travelling between French colonial or North African ports.

On 10 September, the French Admiralty requested the British Naval Attaché in Madrid to inform naval authorities at Gibraltar of the departure from Toulon of three cruisers and three destroyers. No destination was given. The French ships were allowed through Gibraltar early on the 11th but kept under surveillance. Around noon the First Sea Lord frantically ordered Admiral James Somerville based with H Force at Gibraltar to intercept the French ships. Subsequent instructions clarified that the French ships could be allowed to proceed to Casablanca but not to Dakar. Not quite believing his luck Admiral Bourrague, commander of the French fleet, decided not to linger in Casablanca and, twelve hours after arriving there, pushed on

---

629 E.g in Williams, J. The Guns of Dakar.

to Dakar arriving with the cruisers on 13 September, having sent the destroyers back to Casablanca.

Meanwhile, some of the southbound British fleet, including Admiral Cunningham on HMS *Barham* had arrived in Freetown, Britain's main naval port in West Africa, where the fleet was to assemble. At around midnight on 13 September, Cunningham was ordered to establish a patrol to prevent the French cruisers reaching Dakar. But by then they had already safely arrived.

The War Cabinet met on 16 September to review the plans for Operation Menace now that the forces at Dakar had been strengthened by the unfortunate arrival of the three cruisers. Churchill was concerned that as a result of the combination of repeated postponements and the leaking of information the Vichy Government would have got wind of the operation. He feared the French cruisers had brought troops to reinforce Dakar. He therefore recommended calling the operation off. In fact, though the War Cabinet did not know it at the time, the French had not picked up intelligence about Operation Menace and there were no troops on board the cruisers. The cruisers had been despatched to the coast of West Africa (with the permission of the Germans and Italians) in response to the declaration of the French colonial authorities in Cameroun and Chad in favour of General de Gaulle. They were bound for Pointe Noire, the railhead for the Congo-Ocean railway to Brazzaville, the capital of French Equatorial Africa. They were under instructions to attempt to regain control of Douala in Cameroun and to make sure that other territories still under Vichy control, including Libreville (Gabon) remained loyal. The ships were to refuel in Dakar, but it is likely the Vichy authorities also intended the visit to bolster support for Vichy in Dakar.

Although the French did not have any specific intelligence on Operation Menace they did know that de Gaulle was headed for West Africa. The Governor-General of Dakar was informed by telegram on 9 September that de Gaulle had left for West Africa and that General Catroux – formerly Governor-General of French Indochina – had gone over to de Gaulle. French authorities in the region were told that the two were outlaws and should be arrested, along with their accomplices, if they showed up.[630]

On 16 September, Cunningham was told of the War Cabinet's decision that Operation Menace was now impracticable and of their suggestion that General de Gaulle might land at Doula instead to consolidate his position there. Cunningham and Irwin, however, remained optimistic about the prospects, not least because their forces had been strengthened by the arrival of the heavy cruisers HMS *Cumberland* and *Cornwall*, which had been diverted to assist in intercepting the French cruisers. De Gaulle also wanted to continue and proposed that the Free French should land at Rufisque (20kms along the bay) should an unopposed landing at Dakar fail. The War Cabinet, informed of the commanders' wish to continue, sent to Cunningham[631] the kind of instructions leaders in the field want to receive: "do what you think is best".

On the evening of 18 September, the three French cruisers *Georges Leygues, Montcalm* and *la Gloire* left Dakar, under the command of Admiral Bourrague, bound for Pointe Noire and Libreville. Ahead of them sailed the *Tarn*, a French tanker, escorted by the destroyer *Primaguet*. The following day, the *Tarn* and *Primaguet* were intercepted by HMS *Cornwall* and *Delhi*, the latter a cruiser that earlier in the month had been at Pointe Noire. The captain of the *Primaguet* was told to turn round and return to Casablanca. He knew he had no choice but signalled Admiral Bourrague for instructions. The admiral gave his agreement, knowing in doing so that it was the end of his own mission. Without the *Tarn* to refuel he could not continue on to Libreville. He therefore turned round and started heading back to Dakar.

Things were to get worse for Bourrague as *la Gloire* developed mechanical problems, was intercepted by ships from Admiral Cunningham's fleet, and agreed to return to Casabalanca rather than Dakar. The *Georges Leygues* and *Montcalm* were also shadowed

---

630 Senegal Archives, 29 B 46.
631 These instructions issued on 18 September.

by HMS *Cumberland* and ordered to continue on to Casablanca. But Bourrague managed to keep ahead and the two remaining French cruisers safely reached Dakar. Bourrague was quickly relieved of his command by the Vichy Government, concerned how this failure would be seen by the German authorities, and wanting to be seen to take strong action. Stopping the French cruisers reaching Libreville was a success for the British, possibly the only good thing for them to come out of Operation Menace, but it was also accompanied by sobering news. On 17 September, another Libreville bound boat, the French cargo ship *Poitiers*, had set herself on fire rather than surrender to a British warship. That news raised further questions in the mind of de Gaulle as to the reception he would receive on arrival in Dakar.

By 20 September, the entire British and Free French forces had gathered in Freetown and planning round three scenarios (agreeably called Happy, Sticky and Nasty) was being developed. The Happy scenario involved a favourable reception for de Gaulle and an unopposed landing. Sticky would see resistance of a "formal or sporadic nature". The French sloops would move in and the British forces would be prepared to support. A Nasty scenario envisaged serious resistance in response to which British ships would move in to engage the forts and British troops would be prepared to land.

Landings were envisaged at beaches close to Dakar – including Anse Bernard, Hann and Gorée – in the event of limited resistance and at Hann and Rufisque, further down the coast, if the situation turned "Nasty". In total, three different plans were developed for a Nasty situation and a plan was also agreed for a Free French landing at Rufisque if things got Sticky. This last plan was coded CHARLES (after de Gaulle).

By now the French had some inkling something was afoot. Writing to the Minister of Colonies after the attack Governor-General Boisson said that there had been persistent rumours for a while of a possible attack on Dakar, but nothing concrete. The arrival of 2500 British troops in Freetown had confirmed something was being planned but they did not know where. Subsequently, they received intelligence suggesting Dakar would be the target with the attack said to be planned initially for 17 September and later for 22 September. The action by British ships to prevent *la Gloire* and *Primaguet* returning to Dakar confirmed Boisson in his view that the capital of French West Africa would be the target[632]. The information was timely. Following the attack on *Richelieu* on 7 July French forces in Dakar had remained on high alert but air and naval reconnaissance over the next month showed no sign of further British activity of concern. By mid-August, the French at Dakar were demobilising their reservists and mothballing secondary batteries. Now expecting an attack again, Boisson organised exercises, called up reserves once more and made sure that defensive positions were upgraded.

The French still had significant forces at Dakar, even if they were inferior to the British and Free French fleet. In addition to *Richelieu* (partly disabled but guns intact) and the cruisers *Montcalm* and *Georges-Leygues*, which had returned to port, sixteen other French vessels were present including three destroyers (*l'Audacieux*, *le Fantasque* and *le Malin*) that had rejoined the cruisers they had accompanied south, three submarines (*Persée*, *Ajax* and *Bévéziers*) and an assortment of sloops and patrol vessels. About fifty planes (notably twelve Curtis fighters and twenty-eight Glenn-Martin light bombers) were based at the airfields at Ouakam or Thiès. Five battalions were based at Dakar, a further three at Rufisque and others at Thiès, Kaolack and Saint-Louis.

Command of the sea defences had passed on 19 September from the elderly Lt. Col Chaubert, thought to be sympathetic to de Gaulle, to a naval captain called Moewus. And on the eve of the attack itself 120 additional navy gunners arrived on the liner *Banfora*. They were put to immediate work on the shore batteries relieving the *Richelieu* gunners who were able to return to their ship. The *Banfora* also brought ammunition for *Richelieu's* 15" guns.

---

632 Letter from Boisson to French Minister of Colonies of 30 September 1940, National Archives of Senegal 28 B 57.

Operation Menace was now scheduled to begin before dawn on 23 September. Earlier that night Free French agents cut phone links between Dakar and Rufisque. One, Lieutenant Hettier de Boislambert, armed with a pistol, entered the bedroom of Lt. Col Chaubert around 5 a.m. on 23 September to persuade him not to fire on the British and Free French forces. Chaubert informed him that he was no longer commander of the sea defences and, when Hettier de Boislambert had left, raised the alarm. Hettier de Boislambert was later picked up trying to make his way to the Gambia and was imprisoned in Dakar, then Bamako and finally in France from where he managed to escape, rejoining de Gaulle in London in January 1943. Claude Hettier de Boislambert was to become France's High Representative to the Federation of Mali on Independence in 1960 and, following the Federation's demise, the first French Ambassador to the Republic of Senegal.

Visibility on 23 September was unseasonably poor; only three to five miles and it decreased in the course of the day. At daybreak aircraft from HMS *Ark Royal* flew over Dakar dropping leaflets encouraging the population to welcome de Gaulle's forces. About the same time two Luciole aircraft followed by four Swordfish also departed from the deck of HMS *Ark Royal*.

In the early planning it had been decided that Free French aircraft with French markings and French crew should land at Ouakam and, once they had established that the French airforce were ready to support de Gaulle, would declare the all clear. It apparently proved difficult to find any French planes that could be used until the Lucioles, small two-seater bi-planes, were discovered at a maintenance depot. The Lucioles with two Free French flying officers as pilot and passenger landed at Ouakam at 05:54. Within ten minutes they overpowered the officer in charge[633] and had put out the prearranged ground strip – an oblong canvas strip with a circle at one end – that indicated success. Thereupon the first of the four Swordfish aircraft landed. Unfortunately, deployment of the ground strip was premature. They

---

633 Girard has it that he allowed himself to be captured and tied up

had landed successfully but they didn't have control of the airport. Rather than rallying to de Gaulle the French airmen came to the rescue of their colleague, arrested the visitors and scrambled two of their Curtis fighters. The three other Swordfish soon found themselves under a barrage of fire from these, *Richelieu* and the anti-aircraft guns on Gorée, and headed back out to sea.

At about six o'clock, an announcement by de Gaulle was broadcast on the radio. It seems doubtful that many would have been listening as the leaflets telling the population of Dakar to tune into a particular frequency were only just being dropped, but to those that were he explained that he had come to reinforce the French garrison at Dakar and that he had brought supplies. A British fleet was there in support. He announced that he would despatch some of his staff to ask the colonial authorities in Dakar to allow his troops to disembark and the supplies to be offloaded. If all went well, he said, the British forces would not be required.

The man chosen to convey the letter to the Governor announcing the arrival of de Gaulle was *Capitaine de frigate* Thierry d'Argenlieu. His speedboat, with a second in support, left the *Savorgnan de Brazza* and entered the harbour at 06:40. On arrival at the quay he was met by the harbour police and he asked to see the Governor so that he could hand over de Gaulle's letter. The officers on the quay referred for advice to Admiral Landriau, Commander of French Naval forces in West Africa. Landriau initially ordered that d'Argenlieu be sent packing but subsequently phoned through an order that he be arrested. D'Argenlieu and his colleagues managed to get away, under gunfire, and d'Argenlieu was wounded as their boat passed Gorée. The *Savorgnan de Brazza*, waiting in the wings was also fired on and withdrew. By this time, the alarm had been sounded in Dakar and reservists called up. A state of siege was proclaimed. Reinforcements were summoned from Thiès and Saint-Louis and other troops in the regions were put on standby. Orders were given for known Gaullist sympathisers to be rounded up.

Shortly after 08:00 de Gaulle broadcast again, drawing his listeners' attention to the fact that the colonial authorities had fired on a French boat and that he was waiting for an answer as to whether he would be allowed to land. Almost immediately *Richelieu* fired on the two other Free French sloops, *Commandant Duboc* and *Commandant Dominé* which had moved towards the port. At 08:41, having regained the *Savorgnan de Brazza*, d'Argenlieu formally reported to de Gaulle that their proposals had been rejected. At nine o'clock, de Gaulle broadcast for a third time that morning, again blaming the authorities in Dakar for firing on French ships and warning that the allied forces would take matters into their own hands if the Free French forces were not able to fulfil their mission.

A lull then ensued as both sides pondered their next steps. This was an unfamiliar and awkward situation. Until a few months ago, the French and British had been allies in the war against Germany. Even more delicately French forces now opposed each other: those loyal to Vichy defending the port, the Free French forces of de Gaulle embarked offshore. Shortly after ten o'clock, the silence ended when the shore batteries opened fire on the destroyer HMS *Foresight* as the British force approached. Cunningham immediately warned the French Admiral that if the fire continued, he would regretfully have to return it. General Barrau, Commander-in-chief of French land forces in French West Africa replied that if Cunningham did not want him to fire, he should withdraw more than 20km from Dakar. Soon after, a shell landed on HMS *Foresight* killing three – the first fatalities of the operation – and wounding thirteen.

By 11 o'clock the whole battle fleet was under fire from guns at Cap Manuel and the British had begun to fire back. An early British success was recorded when, shortly after an unsuccessful torpedo attack against the destroyers HMS *Foresight* and *Inglefield* the French submarine *Persée* was hit. The crew abandoned and sunk the submarine before being picked up by Vichy sloops.

Soon other ships on both sides were drawn into the action and the British were taking further hits – on HMS *Cumberland*, *Dragon* and *Ingerfield* – and more casualties. Meanwhile British ships were bombarding the port, hitting a number of merchant vessels including the Danish ship *Tacoma*, five of whose men are buried under a single plaque in Dakar's Bel-Air cemetery. Their graves are among twenty-three in Senegal, twenty-two in Dakar and one in Rufisque, tended by local people paid by the Commonwealth War Graves Commission.

A number of shells from the British ships overshot their intended targets – the port and the coastal batteries – and fell on civilian areas including the Dantec Hospital, *rues* Blanchot, Grammont and Fleurus and the Medina district. Governor Boisson, reporting to Paris at the end of the month said the first bombardment left 150 casualties, including sixty dead, mostly civilians.[634]

Shortly before midday the bombardment stopped, and Cunningham suggested to de Gaulle that the moment had perhaps come to put CHARLES into action. De Gaulle agreed. But it was far from a textbook operation. Poor visibility, deteriorating communications, wayward French transports which didn't appear where or when they were supposed to, and miscommunication between Cunningham and de Gaulle, led to complete chaos. In the end Cunningham gave the order to cancel the operation at 16:42 but it wasn't received and French troops attempted a landing from the three sloops.

Immediately the *Commandant Duboc* came under fire from guns in a blockhouse at Cap des Biches. Three men were killed. A landing boat from the *Commandant Dominé* was fired on and withdrew. All three sloops fired back destroying the lighthouse at Diokoul and causing significant casualties.[635]

Eventually, at 18:38, the signal cancelling CHARLES, issued over two hours earlier, was received and the sloops withdrew. Evelyn Waugh's version of the attempted landing in his novel *Men At Arms* is the stuff of pure fiction. Rather than a Free French force it is a plucky group of British troops who volunteer for the night-time operation. Led by the book's hero, Guy Crouchback, they successfully land before beating a retreat under fire, though not before their maverick senior officer who has slipped unseen onto the boat, had hacked off

---

634 Letter from Boisson to French Minister of Colonies of 30 September 1940, National Archives of Senegal 28 B 57.
635 According to Girard, p. 281, 30 dead and 50 wounded.

the head of a local as a trophy souvenir. French official records of the time also mistakenly (whether deliberately or not) refer to it being a British attack.

The attempted landing led indirectly to the incident with the single largest loss of life over the three days of Operation Menace. French reconnaissance aircraft having spotted a movement of ships – the Free French sloops – towards Rufisque, the *Audacieux* was sent to investigate. She in turn was spotted by aircraft from HMS *Ark Royal* and was engaged by *HMAS Australia*. She took successive hits to the bridge and caught fire. Eighty-one officers and crew members died with many more injured. The ship burnt for two days and drifted southwards with the currents beaching near the village of Popenguine. The *Audacieux* was refloated in 1941, used as a training ship, was captured by the Germans in November 1942, towed to Tunisia for repair and sunk by British planes a few days later.

The events of 23 September must have come as a huge disappointment to Churchill. Nevertheless, that evening he sent a personal message to Cunningham: "Having begun we must go on to the end. Stop at nothing". Cunningham suggested to De Gaulle, embarked on the *Westernland*, whereas Cunningham was commanding the operation from HMS *Barham*, that the situation had become "Nasty" and that the French Forces at Dakar should be issued with an ultimatum. De Gaulle agreed at 22:25.

Earlier in the evening some 511 women and children departed Dakar by train for the interior.[636] The following morning, trains in the other direction brought troop reinforcements from Thiès, Kaolack and Saint-Louis. In a message to Dakar's population broadcast at 19:15 on the evening of the 23rd Governor Boisson denounced de Gaulle for his lies.[637] De Gaulle, he said, claimed he was there to prevent the city being handed over to the Germans and to bring much needed food and other supplies. But, according to Boisson, there was not a single German in Dakar and the town had adequate

---

636 Dakar et Dépendances. Rapport Politique Annuel 1940. Senegal Archives.
637 From "L'agression de Dakar" by the Haut Commissariat de l'Afrique francaise – services d'information, Grande Imprimerie Africaine Dakar. Senegal Archives.

provisions. For maximum propaganda effect Boisson said that the British bombardment had failed to hit any military target instead destroying part of the "native hospital", civilian housing and merchant shipping. Eighty-one people had died, he said, including women and children. "Nothing justified, could justify or would ever justify such savage aggression".[638] Dakar he concluded was being attacked for its loyalty to France and Dakar would never give in.

Marshal Pétain sent Governor Boisson his own message, saying that all of France was watching with emotion, confidence and pride Dakar's courageous and faithful resistance to the betrayal of traitors and to the British aggression. Boisson assured Pétain he would defend Dakar with unshakable resolution[639] adding, "You can count on me."[640]

At 23:45 on 23 September Cunningham and Irwin issued the following ultimatum, carefully worded to imply that the Vichy commanders in Dakar were siding with the enemy against France:

> "General de Gaulle informs us, the Commanders of the British Naval and Military Force, that you have prevented him from landing his troops for the re-victualising of Dakar. Your attitude gives us every reason to believe that Dakar may at any moment be handed over by you to the common enemy. In view of the importance of this town and this Base in connection with the development of the war, and also in view of the fact that the seizing of Dakar by the enemy would cause the population to be oppressed, the Allies regard it as their duty to take such immediate steps as are necessary to prevent this eventuality. Desiring that Frenchmen should not fight against Frenchmen in a pitched battle, General de Gaulle has withdrawn his forces. Our forces are approaching. It is for us now to speak. You will not be allowed to hand over the French and Latin people who

---

638 "Rien ne justifiait, ne peut justifier, ne pourra jamais justifier une aussi sauvage agression."
639 "avec une inebranlable résolution."
640 From "L'agression de Dakar" by the Haut Commissariat de l'Afrique française – services d'information, Grande Imprimerie Africaine Dakar. Senegal Archives.

wish to remain free, to the slavery to which Germany and Italy would subject [them]. Yours is the entire responsibility for what may happen.

We have the honour to inform you that if by 06:00, 24 September, you have not given your decision to General de Gaulle the very powerful forces at our disposal will open fire. Once fire has begun it will continue until the fortifications of Dakar are entirely destroyed, and the place occupied by troops who will be ready to fulfil their duty. Only a proclamation that our conditions are accepted could interrupt the carrying out of this programme.

Our troops would not land if you decided to join your compatriots in the liberation of your country and not to remain tied to the enemy who holds France at its mercy.

There is no compromise possible. If you do not accept these terms it is your responsibility to limit the number of victims of your policy by evacuating both the civilian population and those of the military who do not intend to oppose the Free French Forces or their Allies."

The ultimatum failed. Shortly before 4 a.m. the British commanders received the Governor-General's response: "France entrusted Dakar to me, I shall defend Dakar to the end".

At dawn the next day, 24 September, six Skuas took off from HMS *Ark Royal* to launch a bombing attack on *Richelieu* and other French ships in the harbour. Swordfish aircraft also attacked *Richelieu* as well as the batteries at Cap Manuel. Four British planes were shot down. British ships also began their bombardment, more intensely than the previous day, but poor visibility hampered range-taking and few shells hit their targets. Some fell on the civilian districts of Dakar, including in the rue de Thiès and on the commercial premises of Maurel and Prom, one of France's largest shipping and trading companies.[641]

---

641 Dakar et Dépendances. Rapport Politique Annuel 1940. Senegal Archives.

In one of very few British successes that day a second French submarine, the *Ajax*, was disabled by depth charges. Its crew was taken on board by HMS *Barham*, later to be off-loaded in Freetown. The Vichy forces pounded back, using the heavy guns on *Richelieu* and the batteries at Gorée and Cap Manuel. They also deployed Glenn-Martin bombers stationed at Thiès.

By late afternoon General de Gaulle suggested – and it was agreed – that the bombardment be suspended. He also concluded that a British landing would no longer be feasible – it would be resisted at the cost of too much French loss of life – and started to contemplate landing Free French forces at Bathurst (now Banjul), the capital of the British colony of Gambia, or at Saint-Louis, and advancing on Dakar by land. The British commanders made clear to him that this would not be possible. The British fleet was needed elsewhere, and they did not have time to wait around until de Gaulle had reached Dakar.

De Gaulle went to bed that night in the belief that the operation against Dakar had ended. But embarrassed by some pointed questions from Churchill and encouraged by excellent visibility the following morning, 25 September, Cunningham and Irwin decided to continue the bombardment. The two battleships, HMS *Barham* and *Resolution* and the cruisers HMS *Devonshire* and HMAS *Australia* were particularly involved. However their accuracy was no better than the day before, despite the improved visibility. In the course of the morning, the remaining French submarine *Bévézières* hit and badly damaged HMS *Resolution* with one of four torpedoes it deployed.

Things were not going well for de Gaulle. At around 11:00 he made what was to be his final statement, read out this time on his behalf, appealing to the population of Dakar to rise up against the Vichy authorities.

At 11:52 Cunningham decided to withdraw having concluded that the chance of capturing Dakar was remote; and that it seemed improbable that the destruction of *Richelieu* and the French cruisers could be achieved without disproportionate cost to HMS *Barham* (a new ship) and the cruisers HMS *Devonshire* and HMAS *Australia*.

He was well aware that the French firing had been much more accurate than the disappointing British efforts. Moreover, one French submarine remained active (and had badly crippled HMS *Resolution*) and the scale of air opposition was increasing. Before Cunningham's signal conveying this decision could be transmitted back to London, it was anticipated from Churchill who instructed that operations against Dakar should be abandoned. This arrived at 13:19 and brought an end to what more than one author has described as the "Debacle of Dakar".

No British warship was sunk but several were damaged, most notably HMS *Resolution* which went into repair in the United States and was out of action for a year. At least six and perhaps as many as eight aircraft were shot down. There is some confusion about the exact number of British casualties, but official sources tentatively put the figures at thirty-six killed and wounded. Some French propaganda documents from the time spiritedly claim that more than a thousand British troops were killed, including a rear admiral and the captain of a ship.[642] The Vichy Government lost two submarines, the destroyer *Audacieux* received damage that put it out of action for two years and repairs to *Richelieu* took a year to complete. *Richelieu* remained at Dakar until November 1942, when she passed into Allied hands on the capture of the port. There are slight variations in the casualty figures for the defenders. One French source[643] records ninety-eight military deaths (eighty-four European, mainly the crew of the Audacieux, and fourteen African) and 143 injured (eighty-nine European and fifty-four African). Among the civilian population there were sixty-eight dead (of whom sixty were African) and 197 injured (179 African).

Later on 25 September, a message in the name of the French Minister of Colonies was read out denouncing the treacherous English and belittling the "ex-General de Gaulle and ex-Frenchmen who accompany him". Clearly influenced more by historical enmity than recent alliances he said, of the British, that those who, over

---

642 From "L'agression de Dakar" by the Haut Commissariat de l'Afrique francaise – services d'information, Grande Imprimerie Africaine Dakar. Senegal Archives.
643 Maillat. Les Garnisons de Gorée p. 222.

centuries had made a career out of dividing the French the better to conquer them were masters in the art of buying consciences (in other words, de Gaulle's). The Ministry also sent a telegram asking that a message, purportedly from Galandou Diouf, a Senegalese Deputy in the French National Assembly, be broadcast. Diouf expressed his profound indignation at the "odious British aggression" against the "imperial port of Dakar" and conveying the unbending allegiance of the Senegalese people to France and Marshal Pétain.[644]

A number of reasons have been put forward for the failure of Operation Menace. First, that the British military and political leadership and de Gaulle himself underestimated the resistance they would face. With French colonial forces elsewhere declaring for de Gaulle and rumours that the air force in Dakar in particular was sympathetic to his cause there was a strong belief that the French forces at Dakar would offer only token resistance. Captain Poulter's contrary view came at an inconvenient time – the directions had already been given to the commanders and the fleet was just days from sailing – and consequently appears not to have been given the attention it deserved. And the more optimistic view was not entirely wrong. On 20 June, a few days after the fall of Paris 2,000 Europeans had gathered in central Dakar to proclaim their will to fight on, alongside the British. Hundreds of Frenchmen went to the British Consulate seeking to enrol in British or Free French forces. However, by the time Operation Menace was launched on 23 September, the mood had changed. Gaullist sympathisers were still present and there is evidence to suggest that not only in July but also in September some of the gun batteries did not try that hard to hit British ships. But the majority view was to resist any attack on Dakar.

Why the change? Undoubtedly a key factor was the British attack on Mers-El-Kébir, which left nearly 1300 French sailors dead. This was seen as a treacherous, disloyal and – given the terms of the Armistice – unnecessary attack by France's former allies. The attack

---

644 National Archives of Senegal 29 B 46.

on Mers-El-Kébir was swiftly followed by the much less deadly but much more immediate attack on Dakar during which *Richelieu*, pride of the French Navy was disabled. The Vichy Government, and the colonial authorities in Dakar made the most of these attacks to instil patriotism in defence of France's colonial possessions.

The French Governor-General of Dakar, Boisson, also seems to have played a key role. He arrived in mid-July with the overriding goal of preserving the French Empire for France. The Armistice provided for this, but he was concerned that should the Germans consider the French colonial forces unable or unwilling to resist British or Free French forces then they would intervene. From the moment of his arrival, he attempted to calm the situation, to refocus the energies of the European population on the economy and to reassure the African population that notwithstanding events in Europe the French remained in charge and nothing had changed. Known Gaullist sympathisers were posted elsewhere, out of the way, or detained.

Second, such was the urgency given to the operation that planning was rushed and decisions were taken on insufficient intelligence. However although much was said afterwards about how the game may have been given away by leaflets to be dropped on Dakar fluttering on station platforms or by the indiscreet chatter of French forces in Liverpool bars, French war records show no evidence of prior knowledge of Operation Menace.

The operation's failure has also been put down to persistent ill-luck, not least the unseasonably poor visibility. It had been hoped that the sight of what was a reasonably impressive naval force off Dakar would encourage the local French forces to welcome de Gaulle without a fight. In the end, the visibility was such that the force could not be seen. Poor visibility also complicated execution of the operation, making it harder for gunners to take their range and complicating communication between the ships.

As Churchill indicated, the operation highlighted the difficulties of combined operations "especially where allies are involved". The four commanders were spread across three ships. Cunningham and

Irwin were on HMS *Barham*, air operations were conducted from HMS *Ark Royal* and de Gaulle, deliberately not embarked on a British naval vessel, was on the *Westernland*. A further complication, in line with Churchill's instruction, was the desire to spill as little French blood as possible given that the forces defending Dakar had, until very recently, been Britain's allies.

Whether the difficulties caused by poor visibility were the reason or not, British firepower was woefully inaccurate. Over the three days of Operation Menace about three hundred 15" shells were fired at *Richelieu* and the gun batteries at Gorée and Cap Manuel. Only one of these inflicted any damage on *Richelieu* and even that did not affect her fighting efficiency. Not a single bomb or torpedo from a British aircraft hit a military target.

It has been suggested that the Vichy forces had been on the point of running out of ammunition when Admiral Cunningham put an end to the Operation. Boisson is said to have told Cunningham when they met towards the end of the war that he had been in the act of writing out a letter of surrender on the morning of 25 September. If true, it was a detail he wisely chose to omit from the account he sent of the events of 23-25 September to the Minister of Colonies, Admiral Platon, on 30 September 1940.

The failure of Operation Menace must have been keenly felt by Churchill. He had been enthusiastically engaged in it from the start. Had the operation been successful it would have been a rare piece of good news for an increasingly beleaguered British public. He had also hoped that a plucky British/Free French victory in the face of adversity would have helped to encourage Roosevelt to bring US troops to Europe in support. In the end it was a humiliating failure, but one largely forgotten in the detail of a six-year global war and an ultimate Allied victory that ensured de Gaulle's place among France's national heroes and Churchill's status, for many, as "the Greatest Ever Briton".

# POSTSCRIPT

The history of Britain's presence in Senegal is to a large extent the story of its perpetual rivalry with France. The constant capture and return of Gorée and Saint-Louis in the period 1758 to 1817 was partly a consequence of competing French and British aspirations to control trade on that part of the coast of West Africa. But more often than not the seizure or relinquishing of one, the other or both settlements took place in the broader, global struggle between Britain and France to be the dominant imperial power.

So when in 1758 Britain seized first Gorée and then Saint-Louis they did so ostensibly to take control of the gum trade along the Senegal River, as well as to increase the opportunities for trade in slaves, beeswax and other profitable commodities. Control of Gorée was also helpful, as much in peacetime as in war, in protecting the trade, primarily in slaves, from English settlements on the Gambia River. In seizing Gorée and Saint-Louis the British sought to deprive the French of their main trading ports on the coast but also to prevent them seeking new markets in the interior and, as they were wont to do, to stop them disrupting or diverting the trade routes that supplied slaves and other goods from the interior to British settlements on the Gambia River.

But the seizure of Gorée and Saint-Louis has also to be seen in the context of the Seven Years War that started in 1756 with the French trying to block any further expansion to the west by the English colonies on the eastern seaboard of North America. In taking control of France's settlements in Senegal the British knew they could reduce the flow of slave labour to French sugar plantations in the Caribbean, thereby undermining France's wartime economy. The settlements at Gorée and Saint-Louis also became tradeable commodities in themselves. In 1763, having emerged victorious from the Seven Years War, the British returned Gorée (though not Saint-Louis) as part of an agreement that delivered the far greater, strategic prize of France giving up its territory in Canada and Louisiana, bringing an end to its presence in North America.[645]

At the dawn of the nineteenth century, when Britain again seized Gorée and was eyeing Saint-Louis, Britain and France were once more at war. Undoubtedly the potential to buy gum at a fraction of the price they had to pay when the enemy controlled the supply was a significant motivation. But wider issues were again at play. Any opportunity to inflict a defeat on France, to seize territory and to deal a blow to its economy was too good to resist. Senegal certainly offered opportunities to trade but there is little evidence to suggest that Britain by the beginning of the nineteenth century, harboured the ambition to govern either settlement in the long-term. Already Britain's priorities on the coast of West Africa lay further east, particularly on the Gold Coast and in Sierra Leone.

The conclusion of the Napoleonic Wars in 1815 brought an end to over eight centuries of on-off military conflict between France and Britain, but not to the rivalry between the two countries. This was to contribute, though other European countries were also involved, to the Scramble for Africa in the 1880s. Years before that tensions were already running high as each country sought gradually to extend its sphere of influence, including in the area around the Gambia River. Although still rivals, the nineteenth century nevertheless

---

645 Except for the islands of St. Pierre and Miquelon off the coast of Newfoundland.

saw increasing cooperation and collaboration between France and Britain. Once France had followed Britain in abolishing the slave trade, they cooperated on the ground in West Africa, including in the Senegambia region, to suppress it. And as both countries sought to bring more territory under their control they would occasionally come together to defeat any African leader, such as Fode Kabe, who presented a shared threat.

As the Franco-British rivalry played out in Senegambia in the eighteenth and early nineteenth centuries, the local African populations were not simple bystanders to events, nor were they for the most part helpless victims of European imperialism. That came later. Britain's presence in Senegal was limited to Gorée, Saint-Louis and, for a few years only, the forts at Podor and Galam on the Senegal River. Even at Gorée and Saint-Louis the English presence was precarious with the population frequently ravaged by disease. The "colony" was never much more than a couple of poorly fortified trading posts. The strength of the garrisons, and their authority, were often further undermined by alcoholism, violence and mutiny. The rest of Senegal was ruled by local kings who profited from the European presence by exacting customs and by providing supplies (wood, water, food) and services to the occupants of the islands. They sought to enlist the support of the Europeans in their wars with other kings and tribes, and sold the prisoners they took as slaves to be transported to plantations on the other side of the Atlantic. Some local Africans, including the mixed-race *signares* in Saint-Louis, became wealthy from doing business with Europeans.

The agency of local African rulers did not of course survive for long the moves by both France and Britain in the second half of the nineteenth century to expand their spheres of influence, resulting in the Scramble for Africa and the division of the continent into often arbitrarily delineated colonies. This led as we have seen to the creation of British Gambia, with communities split in two, either side of a border which determined whether their colonisers would be English-speaking Protestants or French-speaking Catholics. By the end of the nineteenth century the territory of present-day Senegal, bar parts of Casamance, had largely been brought under French control and the borders with British Gambia agreed. In 1904 the Entente Cordiale was signed, drawing a further line under nearly a thousand years of conflict and heralding a new era of greater Franco-British understanding. In 1940 when Franco-British rivalry enflamed Senegal for a final time, pitting a British fleet, and their Free French allies, against the Vichy authorities in Dakar, the African population were indeed hapless bystanders and victims to this final bizarre episode as the shells from the British fleet landed in the districts of downtown Dakar.

# REFERENCES

A Military Gentleman. An Authentic Narrative of the Life of Joseph Wall, Governor of Goree to which is annexed a faithful account of his execution, (Roach, London) 1802

Barry, Boubacar. The Kingdom of Waalo: Senegal before the Conquest (Diasporic Africa Press, 2012)

Barry, Boubacar. Senegambia and the Atlantic Slave Trade, Cambridge University Press 1998 (translation)

Beatson, Robert, Naval and Military Memoirs of Great Britain from 1727 to 1783 Volume 3 1804 (Elibron classics, 2005)

Brookes, R. The London Gazeteer; or, compendious Geographical Dictionary. Printed for Thomas Tegg, 73, Cheapside. 1831

Brooks, George. Eurafricans in Western Africa (Ohio University Press, 2003)

Carretta, Vincent and Reese, Ty M. (ed) The Life and Letters of Philip Quaque, the First African Anglican Missionary

Christopher, Emma. A Merciless Place, The Lost Story of Britain's Convict Disaster in Africa (Oxford University Press, 2010).

Corry, Joseph. Observations upon the Windward Coast of Africa (Bulmer and Co, London 1807)

Crowder, Michael. West Africa under Colonial Rule, Hutchinson University Library for Africa, 1981

Curtin, Philip D. The Image of Africa, British Ideas and Action 1780-1850 (The University of Wisconsin Press, 1964)

Dakar et Dépendances. Rapport Politique Annuel 1940. Senegal Archives.

Davidson, Basil. West Africa before the Colonial Era, Pearson Education Limited 1998

Duke, G. The Life of Major-General Worge, Colonel of the 86th Regiment of Foot and Governor of Senegal in Africa with an Account of the Settlements of Senegal and Gorée (Parker, Furnivall and Parker, 1844)

Elton, Lord. Imperial Commonwealth, (Collins, London 1945)

Gailey, Harry A. A History of the Gambia (Routledge and Kegan Paul, London, 1984)

Girard, P. De Gaulle, le mystère de Dakar (Calman-Lévy 2010)

Gray, J.M. A History of the Gambia (Cambridge University Press 1940)

Hallett, Robin. The Penetration of Africa to 1815 (Routledge and Kegan Paul, London, 1965)

Hazlewood, Nick. The Queen's Slave Trader (Harper Perennial, 2005)

Jobson, R. The Golden Trade: or a Discovery of the River Gamra, and the Golden Trade of the Aethiopians reprinted in The Mary Kingsley Travel Books and published by Speight and Walpole.

Jones, H. The Métis of Senegal (Indiana University Press, 2013)

Jordan, J and Dumas, R. French Battleships 1922-56 (Seaforth Publishing Barnsley 2009)

Journals of the Board of Trade and Plantations, Volume 14, Jan 1776-May 1782

Knight-Baylac, Marie-Helene. La vie à Gorée de 1677 à 1789

Kup, A.P. Sir Charles MacCarthy, Soldier and Administrator (John Rylands University Library, Manchester, 1978)

Laing, Alexander Gordon. Notes, Mementos and Memoranda

Law, Robin (ed). The English in West Africa 1685-1688: The Local Correspondence of the Royal African Company of England, 1681-1699, Part 2

Le Soleil, 27 September 2013 p 8-9 Babacar Dione and Aly Diouf

Lindsay, John. A Voyage to the Coast of Africa in 1758, ECCO Print Productions

Lloyd, C. The Search for the Niger. Readers Union. 1973

Lloyd, C. The Navy and the Slave Trade (Longmans, Green and co, 1949)

Lord, Walter F. Gore: A Lost Possession of England in *Transactions of the*

*Royal Historical Society*

Lippman, David H. Debacle at Dakar.

Lucas, C.P. A Historical Geography of West Africa (Clarendon Press, 1899)

McDougall, E. Ann. Quest for "Tarra": Toponymy and Geography in Exploring History in istory in Africa Vol 18 1991 p 271-289,

McLynn, Frank, *1759: The Year Britain became Master of the World,* 2004 (Vintage, 2008)

Maillat, M. Les Garnisons de Gorée (Editions du Musée Historique du Sénégal IFAN 2013)

Naval Staff History, Second World War, Battle Summaries Nos 3 and 20. Naval Operations off Dakar July-September 1940. 1959

Newbury, C.W. British policy towards West Africa. Select Documents 1875-1914 (Clarendon Press, Oxford, 1971)

Ollard, R. Man of War, Sir Robert Holmes and the Restoration Navy (Phoenix Press, London, 1969)

Olusoga, D. Black and British, A Forgotten History (Pan Books, 2016)

Park, Mungo. Travels in the Interior of Africa. Introduction and Notes by Bernard Waites. Wordsworth Editions Limited 2002

Proceedings of the Association for the Promotion of the Discovery of the Interior of Africa, 1792 (ECCO print editions)

Proceedings of the Association for the Promotion of the Discovery of the Interior of Africa, 1802, reproduced in Cambridge University Press (2011).

Ransford, Oliver. The Slave Trade, Readers Union 1972

Reclus, Elisée. The Universal Geography, Earth and its Inhabitants, Volume 12 (J.s Virtue and Company Limited, 1898)

Roche, Christian Histoire de la Casamance Conquete et Resistance : 1850-1920, Edition Karthala 1985

Saint-Martin, Yves-Jean. Le Sénégal sous le second Empire: naissance d'un empire colonial (1850-1871)

Schotte, Johann Peter. A treatise on the synochus atrabiliosa, a contagious fever, which raged at Senegal in the year 1778 (M. Scott, London, 1782)

Scott, William Robert. The Constitution and Finance of English, Scottish and Irish joint stock companies to 1720 (1951)

Searing, James F. West African slavery and Atlantic commerce, African Studies series 77 (Cambridge University Press, 1993)

Spain, Jonathan. Wall, Joseph (1737-1802) Oxford Dictionary of National

Biography, OUP, 2004 (online)

Spilsbury, Francis B. Account of a Voyage to the Western Coast of Africa, performed by His Majesty's Sloop Favourite in the Year 1805, Printed by J.G Barnard 1807

Stanhope, Philip Dormer. The Letters of Lord Chesterfield: Including His Letters to His Son, Harper and Brothers New York, 1838 [letter CCCLXIII]

Stone, Thora G. The English Historical Review, Vol 39, No 153. Jan 1924

Thomas, Hugh. The Slave Trade, Phoenix 1997

Williams, John. The Guns of Dakar (Heinemann, London 1976)

Wilson, Patricia and Gamble, David T. John Hill's Account of Life on Goree Island 1807-08 (Brisbane, CA, 2006)

Zook, George Frederik. The Company of Royal Advenurers trading into Africa. Journal of Negro History, Vol IV, Mo.2 April 1919.

Maillat – Dakar et Dependences. Raport Politique Annuel 1940

# INDEX

## A

Abercrombie, Sir George 21
accounts 54, 60, 78, 79, 89-90, 95
Adams, Captain George 104-5
African Corps *see* Royal African Corps
African Association 118-122, 125, 130, 133, 205
Albreda (Gambia) 25, 67, 78, 84, 93, 177, 180
Arguin (Mauritania) 36, 69, 77, 82-3, 85, 110, 131, 168
Ark Royal, HMS 223, 230, 235, 240
Armstrong, Sergeant Benjamin 107
Arthur, Leonard Robert Sunkersett 209-10
*Audacieux* 233

## B

Baldwin, J 213
Bambouk 121, 164, 205
Banks, Sir Joseph 117, 205
baobabs xi, 50

*Barham,* HMS xiii, 223, 225, 233, 236, 240
Barnes, John 60-6, 69, 70, 72, 146
Barrakunda Falls 23, 202
Bathurst, Lord 166-7, 169-174, 177
Bayol, Jean-Marie 194
Benin (Dahomey) 27, 30, 41, 78, 175, 188, 193, 214
Bluett, Thomas 35
Boisson, Pierre 227, 232-4, 239, 240
Booker, James 24
Boundou (Senegal) 23, 34, 121, 126, 164
Brereton, Thomas 167, 169-173
Bristowe, Lieutenant Commander Robert H. 220

## C

Canary Islands 2, 4, 27
Cap Manuel xii, 16, 208, 220-2, 231
Cape Bojador 1, 2
Cape Verde 3, 135, 207
Carey, Lieutenant Governor 53, 57, 59

Carnarvon, Lord   186

Carpot, Antoinette   162

Casamance   176, 178-9, 194

*Catherine*   8, 9

Charles I   17

Charles II   17, 19

Chisholm, Lt. Colonel   160

Christianity   53, 62-3, 75-76

Churchill, Sir Winston   xii, 215-8, 221-2, 225, 233, 236, 239-240

Clarke, John 83, 86. 95-6, 98-9, 100, 116, 120

Columbine, Edward Henry   152-3, 159

Compagnie du Senegal   22, 25, 26, 37-38, 111

Company of Merchants trading to Africa   59-70, 112

Company of Royal Adventurers into Africa (1660)   19

Company of the Royal Adventurers of England Trading into Africa (1663)   20-22

convicts   xi, 113-5, 158

Côte d'Ivoire   xii, 181

Courland, Duke of   19-20

Cromie, Charles   210-13

Cumming, Thomas   40, 43

Cunningham, Admiral John   222, 225-6, 231, 232, 234, 236-7, 239, 240

D

Dakar: 143, 151, 157; as small village 206-8; site of British consulate 208-14; becomes capital of French West Africa 2010-11; bombardment of 216-240

de Gaulle, General Charles xii, 216, 221-3, 225-5, 229-240

de Ruyter 21

Diallo, Ayuba Sulaiman   34-7

Dickson, Captain Edward   141

Dinis Dias   2

Diouf, Galandou   238

Dutch, the: as primary naval power 17; acquisition of Gorée 17; rivalry with England 18; in the Gambia 20; loss of Gorée to English and its recapture 21-22; loss of Gorée to France 24

E

Eannes, Gil   2

Elinkine   x, 179-80

Elizabeth I   7

*Entente cordiale*   200, 244

Erskine, Robert   210

Eugenius IV   2

F

Facey, Captain Morgan   21

# INDEX

Faoche, Captain Pierre Gaston 208

Fode Kaba 196-99, 243

France: seizure of Gorée for first time and loss of Gorée to English in 1693 24-25; loss of Saint-Louis and Gorée in Seven Years War 42-3, 47-8; recovery of Gorée after 1763 Treaty of Paris 55-7; recovery of Saint-Louis and Gorée in 1783 110-12; presence in the Gambia 26-27, 67, 83-84, 93-4; rivalry with English over gum 37-8, 85, 111; loss of Gorée in 1800 135; temporary recapture of Gorée 1804 140-42; loss of Saint-Louis in 1809 153-4; return of Gorée and Saint-Louis following 1814 Treaty of Paris 166-74; involvement in the slave trade 29, 30-31, 174; negotiations on the Gambia 180-196; Operation Menace 216-240.

Fraser, Colonel John 136-141, 143

Freetown (Sierra Leone) 138, 153, 159, 225, 227

Fulani (*also* Foulah, Peul) 11, 34, 36, 87, 127

# G

Gabon 181

Galam 43, 54-5, 59, 64, 67, 69, 77, 78, 110, 117, 155, 157, 159, 163-4, 167, 243

Gambia: first visits by English ships and early traders 7-13 18, 31-36 problems with the French 26-27, 67, 83-84, 93-4 ; proposals for an exchange of territory with France 180-189; competition for territory and border demarcation 190-196, 199-202 ; cooperation with the French on security 196-199

Gambia Adventurers 22

Gambia River 3, 8, 9, 18, 23, 31, 67, 68, 84, 117

George III 41, 54, 59

Ghana *see* Gold Coast

gold 2, 6 10, 14, 17, 23, 32-3, 40, 78, 128, 134, 155, 164

Gold Coast xi, 3, 17, 20, 21, 27, 30, 41, 66, 68, 78, 111, 115, 162, 181, 18, 189, 195

Gomes, Diego 3

Gorée: early European presence 16-17; first English occupation (1664) 21; second English occupation (1693) 25; links to Liverpool 30; seizure by Keppel (1758) 47-49; third occupation (1768-63) 51-54; recovery by France (1763) 55-7; fourth English occupation (1779-83) 103-111; seizure by British in 1800 135; fifth English occupation (1800-1804) 137-41; temporary recapture by France (1804) 142; sixth English occupation (1804 -17) 143-145, 149-152

*Gorée*, HMS 48

Goree Piazzas (Liverpool) 30

Goree warehouses (Liverpool) 30

*Goulden Lion* 20-21

Guénoto 202

Guinea 1, 6, 41, 182

gum  xi, 36-7, 40-1, 42, 55, 64, 5, 67, 73, 77-8, 99, 111-12, 144, 155, 159, 163, 180

gris-gris  xi, 12, 125-6, 144

*Grue*  93

## H

Hamilton, Sir Charles  135

Hanno  1

Hawkins, John  7, 14

Hawkins, William  6

Henry, Prince, The Navigator  2

Henry VII  5, 14

Henry VIII  5, 14

Hettier de Boislambert, Claude  229

Hill, John  152

Hoare, William  35

Hodges, Cornelius 23-24

Holmes, Robert  18-21

Houghton, Daniel  104, 108, 120-123

Hughes, Rear Admiral Sir Edward  104

Humphreys, Throgmorton  25

## I

Irwin, Major General Noel  222, 234

ivory  7, 19, 23, 32-33, 40, 78, 126, 128-9, 150, 155, 164

## J

James Island (Gambia) 19, 20, 23, 25-27, 30, 71, 78, 79, 103, 105, 176, 178

Joal 8, 66, 84, 93, 135, 178

Job Ben Solomon, *see* Diallo, Ayuba Sulaiman

Jobson, Richard 9-14

justice 63, 74-75, 88, 166

## K

Kayoor, Damel of  52, 62, 81-2, 156, 165, 175

Kennedy, Sir Arthur  182-3

Keppel, The Hon. Augustus x, 44, 47, 48-9

Kilham, Hannah  152

## L

Lacy, Governor  109, 110-11

Laing, Alexander Gordon  133

Latsukaabe  26

Legiboli, King of  41, 42, 51

*Lichfield*, HMS  45-7

Lindsay, John  49-51

Lisbon  3, 14, 73

Liverpool  xi, 30, 224

Lloyd, Lieutenant Colonel Richard   143, 144, 149

Lok, John   6

# M

MacCarthy, Charles   160-67, 169, 174

MacKenzie, Major Commandant at Gorée   170-173

MacLean, Allan Henry   208-9

MacLeod, Lord   103-4

MacNamara, Matthias   86-7, 92-9, 100, 122, 116

Madeira   2, 3, 5

Maison des esclaves   16, 110

Manchester 30, 54

Mandinka   11, 12, 23, 34, 35, 36, 124, 127, 138, 196

marabouts   9, 12, 99, 111

Mason, Major John Sutton 42-5, 51

Maule, Major   53

Mauritania   18, 36, 42

Maxwell, Lieutenant Colonel Charles William   132, 149-159, 166

Maxwell, Keith   145

*Méduse, la*   168

Mers-El-Kébir   214, 218, 219, 238

Montoux, Ernest Simon   208

Moore, Francis   4, 31, 49

Moors (Brakna, Trarza) 41, 46, 61, 62, 65, 69, 72-3, 80-2, 85, 87, 89, 109, 112, 152, 156-7, 163, 168

Murray, Captain William   142-3

# N

Newcastle, Duke of   40

Newton, Lieutenant Colonel   44, 48, 51-53

Nigeria   xi, 6, 189, 193, 195, 199-200

# O

O'Hara, Charles   70, 73-91, 94, 95, 106, 112, 116, 118, 162, 163

Onslow, Captain Richard   219

Operation Menace   xii, 216

# P

Park, Mungo   117, 119, 122, 123

Paton, Richard   x

Paterson, Private George   107,

pepper, malagueta,   3, 33

Peul, *see* Fulani

Pillot, Cléomenes   206-7

Pisania (Gambia)   117, 123-24

Pitt the Elder, William   40, 41-2, 43, 44, 52, 55, 58

Pitt the Younger, William   134, 147

Plançon, Admiral Jean-Baptiste

Émile 217

Podor x, 43, 55, 59, 62, 64, 67, 69, 78, 80, 81, 110, 115, 117, 155, 243

Poplette, Lieutenant Thomas 108

Portendic (Mauritania) 433, 61, 77, 82-3, 85, 110, 111, 180

Portudal 8, 18, 19, 66, 84, 93

Portugal 1-6, 8, 14, 16, 17, 29, 36, 179

Poulter, Captain 223, 238

# R

Rastoul, Edouard 208

*Resolution*, HMS xiii, 223, 236-7

*Richelieu* 217, 218, 219-21, 228, 230, 235

Rowe, Sir Samuel, 190-192

Royal African Company (1672) 22, 30, 57, 59-60

Royal African Corps 113, 137, 143, 158

Rufisque 8, 18, 84, 227, 229, 232, 233

Rupert, Prince 17

Rushbrooke, Jermyn 217, 218, 223

# S

St. *John* 9

Saint-Louis: first occupation by English (1693) 25; strategic value 41; seized by Britain in 1758 42-45; second English occupation (1758-1779) 50-51, 54-55, 59-70, 71-92, 93-103; third English occupation (1809-17) 152-159, 162-175

Sataspes 1

São Tomé and Principe 5

Schmalz, Julien-Désiré 168-174

Schotte, Dr. John Peter 102, 103, 113

Senegal Adventurers 8

Senegambia, Province of xi, 69, 71-91, 92-116

Seven Years War 39, 55, 58

Seville 4, 14

shea butter xi, 126

Shelburne, Lord 108

Sierra Leone xi, 3, 17, 21, 68, 131, 134, 138, 139, 153, 162, 166-8, 174, 180, 182, 189, 195

slavery: development of slavery in West Africa 3-5, 7, 29-31; slaves in Gorée and Saint-Louis 43, 56, 79, 80-81, 89; trade in slaves from Senegambia 23, 31-2, 36, 62, 64, 65, 66, 67, 77, 78, 97, 100, 102, 112, 145, 150, 164, 166, 174, 177-8; abolition movement 134, 145-8

Somerville, Admiral James 218, 224

Spain: 4, 14, 17

Spilsbury, Francis 142-44

# T

Tambacounda (Senegal) 125

Thevenot, Charles  80, 86, 88

Thompson, George  8-9, 10

Tidy, Captain Thomas  135, 137

Towerson, William  6

Trade in Africa Act (1697)  25

Treaty of Amiens (1802)  138

Treaty of Paris (1763)  55, 57, 58, 59, 83, 93

Treaty of Paris (1814)  166, 167, 169-71, 176

Treaty of Utrecht (1713)  29

Treaty of Versailles (1783)  110-112

## U

Upton, Captain Thomas  107

Usodimare, Antoniotto  3

## W

Waalo, King of (Naatago Alam)  61-2, 81-2, 156

Wall, Joseph  xi, 86, 92, 96, 97-8, 105-9, 112, 116, 120

Western Sahara  1, 4

*Westernland*  223, 233, 240

Wilberforce, William  146-8

Willis, James  205-6

Wilson, Captain of HMS *Racehorse*  111, 146

wolofs  34, 138, 150

women (Senegalese)  xi, 34, 37, 501, 80, 125, 128, 143, 144

Wooli, Kingdom of  121

Worge, Major-General Richard  411, 44, 48, 51-5, 59, 61, 64

Wyndham, Captain Thomas  6

wrestling, Senegalese  xi, 126

## Y

Yarbutenda (also spelt Yarbatenda)  194-5, 200-2

yellow fever  53, 64-5, 101-3, 104, 210

For exclusive discounts on Matador titles,
sign up to our occasional newsletter at
troubador.co.uk/bookshop